WEIGHT
for it

WEIGHT *for it*

A LIFE OF LIFTING

Eddie Bennett

authorHOUSE®

AuthorHouse™
1663 Liberty Drive
Bloomington, IN 47403
www.authorhouse.com
Phone: 1-800-839-8640

Some of the names have been changed to protect the guilty.

First published by AuthorHouse   12/08/2011

ISBN: 978-1-4678-7801-2 (sc)
ISBN: 978-1-4678-7802-9 (hc)
ISBN: 978-1-4678-7803-6 (ebk)

Printed in the United States of America

Any people depicted in stock imagery provided by Thinkstock are models, and such images are being used for illustrative purposes only.
Certain stock imagery © Thinkstock.

This book is printed on acid-free paper.

Dedication

Brother Bob is suffering from Alzheimers. His physiotherapist told him to write down all his memories, no matter how small just to act as an aide memoire. I started doing the same so that when I rang him up we could discuss common occurences. These scribblings gradually grew and before I knew it, a book was on its way.

Contents

Section One

In The Beginning

1

IN THE BEGINNING

My earliest memories are of being evacuated to Filey. There were four of us at the time, all brothers, although eventually we would be joined by another brother and finally a sister. My mother lived with us in a small semi whilst my dad remained behind in Hull to do his reserved job on the railways, and also doubling up as an ARP warden. The youngest of us four, Chris was still in a pram, so he would be about 1 year old. This meant that David would be 2, me 4 and older brother, Bob, 5 years old.

We were conscious of the war going on without being fully aware of its true significance. Our walks down to the beach took us along 'the Ravine' which was full of tanks sheltered from overhead attack by the overhanging trees. On a few occasions we were taken from our beds and placed in the steel shelter which doubled-up as a dining-room table. After one such evening, once the 'all clear' had sounded we ventured outside to observe the glow in the sky coming from a burning Hull 30 miles away. This in spite of the range of Yorkshire Wolds in-between. A worrying time for our mum knowing that dad was somewhere in that inferno.

Filey was a good place to be, notwithstanding the war. We usually had the beach to ourselves. The Brigg was a favourite destination and we would often bring home a bucket full of winkles for mum to boil on the gas stove. Then it was a case of spending a few hours with a pin. As a change from the beach we would walk into the countryside with woods to explore and brambles to pick in season. The full significance of war-time rationing couldn't register on our young minds but we did appreciate that it was useful to help out.

Eventually it was deemed safe to return to Hull. The war wasn't over, but the threat of being bombed had receded. There were still a couple of occasions when we were woken from our sleep and taken to the shelter in the adjoining school yard.

At last the war was over and along with the thousands of others up and down the country; our terrace had a VE party. My abiding memory of this was my first ever taste of mushy peas and vinegar. Truly the food of the gods.

Our end of terrace house shared a boundary wall with Constable Street School, which was to be our seat of learning for the next few years. More often than not the morning bell would go whilst we were still eating our breakfast, and we became very adept at scrambling over this wall on order to save a few seconds.

Our recreational patterns changed along with our changed circumstances. In the early years following the war, Hull was awash with bombed sites. Many of them got tidied up very quickly, but for some reason, our local one remained available to us for several years. Coltman Street was one street over from us and the site was a couple of hundred yards walk. The big old terraced houses were not too badly damaged and afforded us kids with many opportunities to explore from the cellars up to the roof under drawings. However, the bonus was the rear gardens. These were very long and the dividing fences quickly disappeared, whilst the various items of vegetation proliferated in their wild state. A haven for youngsters with active imaginations.

There were other more formal destinations for us kids. Beverly Westwood was one of them, particularly during the conker season. Another was the area known as 'little Switzerland' at Hessle. Many, many years later I took a French friend to this area. It is now at one end of the Humber Bridge and has been turned into a country park. My friend Jacque lives in the foothills of the Alps, and when I told him the name of the place, he had wry a smile on his face.

Food rationing continued for many years after the war ended. Although we youngsters were never conscious of being hungry, these enforced restrictions together with our active lifestyle led to our physical development. We were all growing taller, but there was not much outward growth. I was to learn many years later that this was typical for ectomorphs—those born for endurance events rather than power events.

Another close neighbour of our house in Wellsted St was 'The Boulevard'. There was two advantages to this, the first being the Carnegie library. I was an avid reader, working my way through all the 'Biggles' books and then progressing on to Dennis Wheatley. The other major resident of the Boulevard was Hull Rugby League club. Coming from a large family with only one wage earner we didn't have too much disposable income. However, the 'Airlie Birds' always used to open the gates at half time. We kids saw the 2nd half of more games than I care to remember. I can still name most of the table-topping team from that era. My love of rugby league has stayed with me all my life, and one of my happiest recent memories is working with the Bradford Bulls academy side developing their weightlifting skills.

We would play a form of touch-rugby on Wellsted Street with the local youths. The try lines were demarked with two streetlights about 75 yards apart and the 'ball' consisted of tightly rolled up newspaper, tied with string. There was no upper limit on the number of players, although the more that played the harder it became to score. Also the 'ball' precluded any kicking, so it truly became the handling game it should be. These skills were to re-emerge in the coming years.

Schooling was progressing in a serene way. Lessons reflected the nature of the school. Most pupils would leave at 14 and find work on the docks or the trawlers. However, all the teachers seemed dedicated. Lessons were of necessity restricted primarily to the three R's, but I also remember having a growing interest in geography and science. Teachers would cover more than one subject and the headmaster would often take classes himself. One day he might be explaining the relative sizes of the sun and the earth, and the following day he would be demonstrating how perspective works in art.

If I had a favourite it would be English literature. This consisted mainly of reading poems collectively. One such was 'Paul Revere's Ride!' After a few readings the teacher noticed that I was relating the poem without reference to the book. He got me out to the front of the class to repeat this feat. Shortly afterwards he told me he was putting me in for the '11 plus'.

Listen my children and you shall hear
Of the midnight ride of Paul Revere
On the eighteenth of April, in seventy-five;
Hardly a man is now alive
Who remembers that famous day and year.

Henry Wadsworth Longfellow

2

HARD LESSONS

At 10/11 years old you do not tend to think too much about what the future holds. However upon learning that I had passed my 11 plus and would be going to Kingston High School it became clear that I was at a defining point in my life. Two others from Constable Street School had passed for Kingston at the same time. One was my brother Bob and the other my great pal, Len Clark.

We spent the summer getting kitted out in the school uniform-Maroon blazer, Grey trousers, white shirts, school tie and cap. A lot of money for one student but my mum and dad had to pay for it all twice. However, in all the time that I spent at school I don't remember them once complaining. By this time there had been a couple of additions to the family, after a gap of seven years, Mike had been born. One year later Mum and Dad eventually got the girl they wanted when June arrived. However, six children living in a two bedroom house was not conducive to studying so Mum arranged for Bob and I to go and live with her Mum.Gran had a three bedroom house off Hawthorne Avenue where she lived on her own, so I assume she was glad of our company. Besides, as a former school mistress, she was invaluable to us with our homework.

Gran had lost her first husband during the 1st World War. Her second husband had been gassed in the 2nd World War. Although he survived the war, his health was affected and he died when we boys were still quite young. Gran herself was a tall, robust woman with a very placid nature. She looked indestructible to Bob and I. Imagine our great shock and despair when, after a very short illness, she died.

It was back to Wellsted Street for us boys. With the front room doubling-up as an extra bedroom, that small house remained our home for many years until our changing circumstances caused us to move on.

The first day at school was a bit of an eye-opener. Purpose built laboratories and workshops, a fully equipped gymnasium and acres of playing field. I remember rushing home that night to tell my Mum that we would be learning Latin!

The school was ostensibly mixed, but the two sexes were segregated both within the school and outside. There were two intake classes each year for both the girls and boys. In the first two years these classes were arbitrary, but in the third year these became streamed. In spite of the fact that I had done well in most subjects in the first two years, I surprisingly found myself in the 'B' stream. Even more surprising, was the fact that my pal Len, who was a genuine intellectual, was also placed in the 'B' stream. The only saving grace was that Bob made it into the 'A' stream.

In the years that followed, I have often wondered why this happened. During our first two years we had shared the same class. Bob was quiet and studious and earned the name 'The Brainy Bennett' whereas I was boisterous and continually asking questions and earned the name 'The Barmy Bennett'. If this was an attempt to separate us, it still does not explain Len's treatment. At that time of course I was not familiar with the term 'tokenism' but I've often wondered since if certain elements within the school resented the fact that we came from a lowly inner-city school. Sport at Kingston was fairly straight forward. It was a case of football in the winter and cricket in the summer. Although I loved all sports, I had no natural talent for either game, though I did eventually make it into the schools 2nd eleven at football. However, it was through football that I got my school nickname. It was a particularly cold winter's day when we took to the field for our weekly football match. I was stuck out on the wing, not seeing much action, and gradually turning blue. The French master, "Bill" Sykes, was refereeing the match and suddenly shouted out "Will somebody pass the ball to Icicle Eddie on the wing!"

From that day forth I was known as "Icicle Eddie" or more usually the shortened version of "Icy. One consequence of being in the 'B' stream was that we were given the opportunity of dropping academic subjects in favour of more practical ones. I had always struggled with French, so at the first opportunity I dropped it in favour of Surveying. This decision would have a great influence on my later life. Another unfortunate decision we had to make was between History and Geography. I loved them both and did not know which one to choose. I decided that I would leave my fate down to the outcome of the end of term exams. History was the first to be announced and I had come second, so it looked as though that would be the one. However, when the Geography results were given, it turned out that I came top, so History became a thing of the past. Another subject introduced at this time and ultimately to prove useful was Machine Drawing. One that I was forced to drop; mostly against my will was Chemistry. The teacher, Mr Stinky, had for some reason taken a great dislike to me. In one exam we had been asked to draw a 'Kipps Apparatus'. My effort wasn't too bad, but he decided to reproduce it on the black board and encouraged the rest of the class to have a good laugh at me.

I dropped Chemistry shortly after. Another decision that would have an effect on my later life. About this time I began to form my theory about school teachers. It seems to me that they fall into three categories. The first are those that generally love imparting knowledge, know their subject and can hold a class with their personality and enthusiasm. The second are those that look at the short hours and long holidays and decide that this is the life for them. They quickly become disillusioned and bitter, and teaching becomes a chore for them. Students are astute enough to know this type.

The third category is the bully. These people cannot face the prospects of working with fellow adults, preferring to indulge their nastiness on their charges. Thankfully, the days of caning and throwing board rubbers have long gone, but the mental bullying á la Mr Stinky is still alive and well. Over the years I have had many school teacher friends, and explained my theory to them, asking into which category they would place themselves. Most have claimed they are in the first one, although a few of the more honest ones have gone for number two. None have claimed to be in three, which is quite understandable- they wouldn't be my friends otherwise- but all of them know colleagues who they would place in that category.

The fifth form was to become a momentous year in many respects. It was the year for 'O' levels, and for us in the 'B' stream, it was the year we were expected to leave and seek jobs. Apparently, many 5B's in the past had become demob happy and proved very difficult, but we had no problems. In fact a lot of the older teachers said that we were the best 5B they could remember. Towards the end of the academic year, three of us went to see the headmaster, Dr Cameron Walker, and told him that we wanted to stay on into the 6th. In addition to myself and Len, there was another good friend, Clive Pickard. We eventually wanted to go on to university. He was less than pleased and put a number of obstacles in our path.

Apparently, there were three levels to the 5th form. Firstly, there were the duffers in 5B who were expected to leave. Secondly, there were the cleverer ones in 5A who had elected to leave, and thirdly the really clever clogs in the lower 6th who had decided to stay on and do 'A' levels. As we hadn't been in this preparatory class, we couldn't go into the 6th. We all agreed to drop back and go into the next year's lower 6th.

Stymied for a while, the Head then looked directly at me and told me that I couldn't go to university because I didn't have a foreign language. I replied that I was prepared to pick up French from where I left-off, and by the time I did my 'A' levels, I would make sure that I had the required language. Frustrated, Dr Walker reluctantly backed down.

At the end of term I did my 'O' levels and was pleased to start my collection, which would eventually grow to 10. At this time also, a rumour was circulating the school that summer work could be had by going to a camp in the Wolds and helping out at nearby farms. We checked out the details and the upshot was that a number of us made our way to Cottam, near Driffield to become men of the soil.

This decision led to an occurrence that shaped the rest of my life.

3

THE AWAKENING

The 'camp' was something left over from the War. Timber built communal huts, toilet blocks and dining areas, were to be our home for the next six weeks. Most of the other workers were adults, both male and female, with many of them being from overseas.

We were driven by lorry to our allocated farm and dropped off. The first job was to meet the grizzly old farm hand who was to be our mentor for the next few weeks. He told us to call him 'Shep' although I don't recall seeing any sheep in that part of Yorkshire. We were quickly put on a tractor/trailer and driven to our place of work. The farm's major crop was spring wheat and in the field a harvester was already at work. Our job was to follow on, picking up a sheaf under each arm and standing them up in a 'stook' of 10 to 12 sheaves in order to dry out. The bottom of the sheaf was cut to an angle so that they would only stand if placed correctly. Under Shep's graphic commands we very quickly learned the correct way. A welcome break came mid morning when the farmer's wife appeared with a hot drink and a bacon sandwich that resembled a door step. Another unexpected break was called when the harvester neared the centre of the field. We lads were bunched to one corner of the field and the farmer and his mates suddenly appeared bearing shotguns. A slightly worrying moment—I didn't think our stooking had been that bad! Then it all became clear. As the harvester cut the last remaining standing wheat there was a flurry of movement and rabbits ran in every direction. Shots rang out, some rabbits making it to the safety of the hedgerow but many did not.

We expected the lorry picking us up to call about 5.00 but it didn't appear. Shep then confessed that he had told them to leave us 'til 7.00. It seems that summer daylight is a precious commodity when harvesting.

Eventually we made it back to camp for a late meal, a wash and a crash-out in our beds.

The summer progressed as we gradually worked our way from field to field, until finally we, now expert stookers, placed our final sheaves. It was now time for phase two. Back to our first field where the wheat sheaves were considered to be dry enough. The next job was to load them onto flat trailers pulled by tractors, to be taken back to the farm yard and threshed. Each trailer carried a couple of farm hands expert in the art of placing sheaves in such a way that they were stable and could be stacked to a considerable height. We lads were given a pitchfork each to facilitate the loading. The job wasn't too bad when the trailers were empty, but got progressively more difficult as the height increased. The topmost layers required us to be at full stretch with a vertical pitchfork topped by a heavy bundle of spring wheat. One evening towards the end of our six week stint I was standing in front of a mirror combing my hair when I suddenly noticed a lump in my arm. As I raised and lowered my arm the lump moved. It dawned on me that this lump was a muscle. I had discovered a basic truth—that lifting heavy weights build muscles, but how was I to benefit from this new found knowledge?

4

FIRST STEPS

Back in Hull the answer was about to present itself in an unexpected way. Bob and I had got into the habit of walking into town on a Saturday to spend our paper-boy money, usually on foreign stamps which we had both started collecting. As we walked along Anlaby Road we passed the vast area of open ground that had been devastated during the War. In the centre of all this was a lone shop (I believe he sold hardware) that had somehow escaped all the destruction. The enterprising owner had printed in high letters along the side of the building 'WE STAND ALONE!' The bulldog spirit lived on among the bulldog clips.

A hundred or so yards further on the buildings started again in what could be regarded as the outer fringes of the town centre. Among these buildings was an auctioneer's saleroom and we boys always stopped to look in the window to see what weird and wonderful objects were up for sale. This particular day was no different. As our eyes roamed over the various bric-a-brac we both spotted them. A small pile of weights!

We went inside to ask the auctioneer when they would be coming up for sale. He looked at our eager faces and skinny frames and said 'Gimme a bob and they're yours'.

No stamps for us that week—something far more important to do. Bob carried home the two 5 pound discs while I managed the four 2 ½ pounders.

Back home we gazed at our purchases and wondered what to do next. We realized that we needed help and perused the pages of all our old papers and magazines avidly. Eventually we found a small ad for a bodybuilding course and sent off for it. When it arrived I realised that we had chosen well. The various exercises were well illustrated and explained, and very comprehensive. In addition, the authors must have been well aware of the post war austerity because they explained how weights could be substituted by buckets of sand and the bar replaced by a broom handle.

We had our weights but realized that we needed a bar. I considered using a broom handle but found something much better. It had started life as a sapling before being cut down and converted into a scout staff. It was about 6'00 long and 2" in diameter without its bark. In order to get the discs on I had to cut the two ends down for about 6" in and to a diameter of 1". After the initial rough chiselling I finished off with a rasp, and can immodestly claim to have done a good job.

At last I was ready to embark on a regime that would turn me into the next Mr Universe. It very quickly became clear that the two 5 pounders and the four 2 ½ pounders were woefully inadequate for most exercises, but where was I to get reinforcements?

Our terraced houses had small front gardens that had once been contained with metal railings. The railings had long since been taken to help with the war effort. All that remained was the stone plinths with a row of holes showing where the railings had once stood. One day I was sitting on one of these plinths idly watching some activity in the street. I glanced down into one of the holes and saw a dull glint. After a bit of poking about I established that it was lead that had been used to secure the bottom of the railings. Then it hit me. I could make my own weights! Armed with a hammer, a 6" nail and a bucket I began my collection. I don't recall asking anyone's permission, but similarly I don't recall being told to Bugger Off. Eventually my bucket was full and it was time for the next stage. I emptied all the bits of lead into my Mum's largest pan and placed it on the gas-stove. Whilst the lead was melting I set about phase three. This consisted of removing an area of grass from the back garden. Next I carefully dug out a circle of soil to a depth of about 2", making sure that the bottom was level and compacted. In the centre I placed an empty cotton bobbin.

By this time the lead was nicely molten. It was full of slag, as you would imagine, but after ladling it off I still had about half a pan of molten lead. I poured half of it into my mould where it solidified quickly in the cold earth. I prised it out, repaired the mould, replaced the bobbin and repeated the process. I now had two additional weights.

Cleaning them up, I weighed them on my Mum's kitchen scales. More by luck than management they turned out to be very close, weighing in the region of 10 pounds each. These additional weights enabled me to progress with my training, although the total poundage was still too low for exercises such as squat and bench press, I made up for the lack of weight by doing high repetitions, but there is a limit to the amount of repetitions one can do. Besides, the way to big muscles is low reps and heavy weights. There was nothing for it; I would have to come up with another plan. More lead was out of the question. I dare not ruin another of my Mum's best pans. As I looked at my manual again the thought of buckets filled with sand suddenly became more attractive. However, the idea of a bucket hanging from the end of a pole had always seemed to me to be very precarious. Something else was needed.

I began collecting my Mum's discarded nylon stockings. By placing one inside the other until they were five or six thick I ensured they were both strong enough and impervious enough to withstand the job in hand. With the bottom half filled with sand there was still sufficient left to tie to the end of my barbell. They also acted of collars to prevent my weights sliding about.

At last I was in business.

5

MUSIC MUSIC MUSIC

My biggest disappointment as a child was my lack of musical talent. There had always been a piano in the house with both Mum and Dad being exponents. My Mother had started going deaf during the War and by the 50's she was completely without hearing. In spite of this, her renditions of popular compositions of the day, played from sheet music was as good as the original. For example, Winifred Attwell was a huge star of the time. We boys would buy the sheet music of such classics as "Jubilee Rag" and "Black and White Rag". Just looking at all those notes, made my head spin. However, after just one cursory run through, my Mum was knocking them out in a fashion indistinguishable from the originals. Dad was different- He didn't bother with music, playing instead by ear. This feat was equally impressive to my untutored ear, and was invaluable at our family gatherings which usually evolved into a sing song. At least I could sing in tune. (Well, some of the time)

Both Bob and I asked Mum to teach us to play. Bob picked it up fairly quickly and became a musician in his own right, mastering several instruments including the piano accordion and the clarinet. I, on the other hand struggled. I practised my scales for hours and eventually could pick out a few tunes, but I was playing by memory and not by feel.

In the argument of nature verses nurture I would go for nature every time.

Radio Luxemburg was one of the only ways of listening to pop music those days, with the current top twenty being broadcast between 11.00pm and midnight on a Sunday. We boys were allowed to stay up. The range of music was quite extensive, varying from big ballads, comic songs, jazz and other instrumental music.

I was beginning to get into traditional jazz. It's simple but infectious sound appealed to my unsophisticated ear. My personal favourite was the Chris Barber jazz band.

About this time my parents bought a new piece of furniture called a radiogram. All we needed now was some records. Chris Barber's banjoist called Lonnie Donegan had just made a disc called "The Rock Island Line" and this became my first purchase. The sound was so new that Lonnie accepted a lump payment for his efforts instead of a percentage of sales. It didn't get much airplay at the time, relying instead on word of mouth. I remember it being referred to as a 'sleeper'. As the sales began to mount up it got more airplay and the circle cumulated in it getting to number 1. The age of Skiffle was born.

Some fellow jazz fans and I heard that Chris Barber was appearing at Beverley, and on the appointing night went to see him. He was as excellent as expected but unfortunately, Lonnie had left the band days previously to strike off on his own with his skiffle group. Over the subsequent years, I did manage to catch up with Lonnie several times.

Films were a big part of life in those days. We kids had gone through the entire Saturday matinee thing and were ready to move on. There were some tremendous innovations happening at that time including 3D and Cinemascope, but it was also the age of the musical.

My Gran took Bob and myself to see 'Singing in the Rain' as our first introduction to the genre. I must confess that I was less than impressed. The sight of a grown man jumping in and out of puddles was not my idea of entertainment. However, I persevered and my second musical had the complete opposite effect.

Calamity Jane' was the film that brought about this transformation. It had a good story, great action, tremendous songs and of course, Doris Day. I fell in love with her and made a point of watching everything that she made. I think she secretly reciprocated my feelings, but knowing nothing could become of it, she became a recluse.

6

EXTRA CURRICULAR ACTIVITIES

Television and its debilitating effects were still way off in the future. This was the age of make your own amusement and we boys grasped every opportunity with gusto.

First up was the local youth club. I was interested in two activities in particular, Table tennis and woodwork. I made the table tennis team and we played in a league against other youth clubs. I was number six in a six-man team! I remember one night playing the top-of-the-league side. The first five on our team all lost their matches and the game was a foregone conclusion. I was asked to concede my match so we could all go home. I refused on principle, played and won.

Some people call it Bloody Mindedness but I think it was my determination to succeed in spite of my lack of talent. This is a trait that tends to surface from time to time.

When I joined the woodwork section, the instructor told me to make an ashtray. This consisted of a block of wood with a bowl chiselled out and a pot lion stuck on the end. The instructor had a mould for making the lions and was making a few bob on the side. He asked what I wanted to do for my second project and I told him—a piano stool. He looked a bit dubious but went along with me. Between us we came up with a design. It had a container for music, with a hinge and padded seat, hidden tenon joints and shellac finish.

Several months later I proudly carried home a beautiful piano stool for my Mum.

The next institution to be graced by the Bennett clan was the local scouts' troop. It was based at a neighbourhood church hall and did all the things that boy scouts did. I can still tie a running bowline, with or without two half-hitches, but I've never been called upon to do one in anger.

We boys quickly found out that the scout master was a paedophile, although that was not the word we used at the time. Most of us made it clear that we objected to his advances but a couple seemed happy to go along with him. We always knew who these were as they would turn-up with new scout knives, or in one case, a new bike. However, things became critical at one of our weekend camps.

We had set-up with two bell-tents at North Cave. Each tent slept about six bodies. The scout master shared our tent which was illegal in itself. He had a double sleeping bag, but I was too tired that first night to take notice of which lad shared it with him.

I spent most of the second day exploring the local country side and didn't get back to camp 'til late. I looked around the tent in growing horror. There were only two sleeping bags—mine and the scout masters. It seemed that the other lads had either moved into the other tent, which was now full, or had gone home.

I packed in a state of desperation, stuffing things haphazardly into my rucksack, and ran down the track to the main road. In the distance, at the bottom of the hill I could see the last bus pulled up outside the village pub. There was a crowd of people waiting to get on. I set off running in a mad panic. As I ran, I could hear cutlery hitting the road behind me. No time to stop and pick them up. I reached the queue with several people still waiting to get on to what was now a fairly full bus. I went straight to the front and elbowed my way on. No-one objected. They probably saw the look of terror on my face.

Shortly after this, someone blew the whistle and our scout master was put away.

From the scouts I graduated to the Air Training Corps. A different uniform and different thing's to master. There was some drill, we learnt Morse code and semaphore and had aircraft recognition classes. We had weekends away at RAF camps to get a taste of the real thing. Our first one was RAF Scampton in Lincolnshire, whose claim to fame was the starting point of the dambusters raid. We were shown the grave of Guy Gibson's dog! The highlight for us though was an actual flight.

The pilots had their own flying club and we were taken-up in one of their aircraft—a Tiger Moth! With there only being enough room for one of us at a time, the flight was of necessity short, but even five minutes in the open cockpit of a classic biplane was a memorable first flight.

One day, we were told that they were putting together a small troop of ATC cadets to attend the Queen's coronation, and all interested boys could put their name forward. I thought the chances of going were fairly remote but put my name forward anyway. Some weeks later I was told that I was one of the chosen few.

At the appointed time I made my way to London and met up with the local cadet whose family had agreed to put me up in return for his place on the squad. On the Saturday morning we travelled to our rendezvous point in a street near Buckingham Palace. We formed-up into a small squad of about thirty, and then marched around to the front of the Palace. We were directed to a spot on the Victoria and Albert Memorial, directly in front of the palace gates. Eventually the coach pulled out and as she passed, the Queen gave me a wave.

We broke-up and went into the nearby park to eat our sandwiches. Then it was back to our positions in time for the return journey. The Queen gave me another wave.

Many years later, I actually met Her Majesty when she opened the new Magistrates Courts in Bradford. She said "It's nice to see you again. You haven't changed a bit." (Only kidding ma'am)

Meanwhile I persevered with my makeshift weights. It must have been a strange sight- my thick old timber bar complete with a few genuine weights, my homemade weights and nylon stockings filled with sand tied to the ends. However, it did the job and served me well for the next three years.

7

LOOSE ENDS

Those next three years of course were my time in the sixth form. Stepping back a year was no problem. The rest of the class were good lads and accepted us without question. The only minor hiccup was that in order to pick up where I left off with my French I had to go back another year. To compound my discomfort it turned out that to comply with my timetable, the only fourth form class available to me was with the girls. Actually this could have worked to my advantage, because when I did eventually sit and pass my French 'O' level, I had the bonus of passing French oral too.

Bob was now one year ahead of me. I don't ever recollect him talking about university. Instead he went straight into the RAF for four years. He then carried on working for the War Office as a civilian. I found out many years later that he had played an active role in the Cold War, taking on a number of secret missions.

Len became "Head Boy" in our final year. We learnt on the quiet that there was only one dissenting voice amongst the teachers—that of Dr Walker! After passing his 'A' levels he went on to a London university where he graduated with a good degree. He took a teaching job at a prestigious southern school, and eventually rose to the position of "Headmaster". Not bad for a 'B' stream pupil.

Clive also graduated and took a commission in the army. One day on patrol he was called upon to defuse an unexploded bomb. He found he had an aptitude for it and became a specialist whilst gaining rapid promotion.

This left me. I had written to a few universities and had actually been accepted into a couple subject to getting my grades. The trouble was, I didn't know what to do with my life, or hence, which course to study. At that time National Service was a 'threat' hanging over every 18+ male. University could delay a 'Call Up' but it couldn't override it. The thing to do therefore was to get my National Service out of the way first, and whilst I was at it, I could re-evaluate my life and decide in which direction I wanted to go. Firstly, I had to return to Kingston in order to collect my 'A' level certificates. As Dr Walker handed them too me, he grudgingly congratulated me and said "You must have worked very hard".

I felt like saying "No. I am a natural genius, but you failed to spot it". Instead, I meekly thanked him. That final summer was spent as a waiter at a cafe in Bridlington whilst I waited for my 'Call up papers'.

Bobby Eddie David Chris

Posing rather than playing—Note the pipestem arms

Section Two

For Queen and Country

8

SQUARE-BASHING AND
TRADE TRAINING

With there being an almost unlimited supply of bodies into the armed forces, some of them could afford to be very selective. Apparently, of the three branches available, the RAF got by far the largest number of applicants. It was made clear to me that what tipped the scales in my favour was the fact that I'd been in the A.T.C. at school. Fate was looking after me . . .

The first port of call for all new entrants was RAF Cardington in Bedfordshire. Its previous claim to fame was as the place where Britain's airships were based. The massive hangers were very much in evidence, and possibly still are. However, our purpose of being there was to get kitted-out and be allocated to a trade.

The uniform seemed endless- battle dress for every day wear; best blues for more formal occasions; shirts, ties, socks, vests and underpants. These last items were baggy, reached to the knees and were affectionately known as 'shreddies'. When I gave my uniform back years later, this item was still pristine, having travelled with me half-way around the world.

Some of the smaller items included a 'house wife' which was a collection of darning needles, wool, spare buttons and cotton. This actually did get used believe it or not. Another useful item was a button-hook. This consisted of a flat piece of plastic (or was it Bakelite?)

about 6" long and 2" wide with a slot half way along the centre line. The idea was to push it behind the button on our best blues so that we could clean them without getting polish on our uniform.

By far the most exciting bits of tackle were the gym equipment-shorts, vest and pumps. Looks like I would be able to carry on with my plan to conquer the bodybuilding world.

Getting allocated to a trade should have been a fairly simple matter. There were five top trades designated by the term 'fitter'. These were—air radar; ground radar; wireless; air-frame and engine. I knew that Bob was enjoying his time as a radar fitter so I put that down. The next stage was to sit an aptitude test.

A sergeant brought round an exam paper consisting primarily of basic maths problems. Having just passed two 'A' levels in both Pure and Applied Maths, they presented no problem. The sergeant came back round and collected our papers, then proceeded to mark them. After a while he began to tell the class whether or not they had qualified for their desired trade. When he came to me he said that I couldn't be a fitter but could become a technician, which was one stage lower. When I asked why he said it was because I only scored 50% on my aptitude test. I protested that I had double-checked and was certain they were all right. He agreed that everything I did was correct, but I had only done half the paper.

Apparently there was another set of questions on the back!

I asked if I could do these but he said it was more than his job was worth.

With time one becomes accustomed to encounters with 'jobsworths', and learn to cope. However, to find one so early in my fledgling career was devastating, but I felt so helpless.

One other major task was to find out where we wanted to get posted after trade training. An officer conducted this interview, and I told him that I would like to go somewhere in the Far East. He responded that National Servicemen never got posted that far away and I would need to sign-on. When I asked what was the minimum time to ensure I would go he replied "Four years". I thought it over for a moment or two. In addition to seeing an exotic part of the world, it would also double my pay from £1 per week to £2. I agreed to sign on.

After about a week at Cardington we were allocated to various square-bashing camps. I finished up at RAF Padgate, near Warrington.

Having done some drill during my time with the A.T.C, the square-bashing didn't present too big a shock to the system. Even the 'bull' was bearable if one went about it with an open mind. One of the main tasks was to get a glass-like shine on our boot toe-caps. This seemed impossible at first as the boot leather, including the toe-caps, was covered with pimples. However, our hut NCO told us how to proceed.

The first job was to remove the offending pimples. This was done by heating a table spoon over a candle and then pressing the hot metal against the leather. Eventually the toe-caps were smooth and ready for stage two. Instead of applying the polish with a brush we were advised to use a soft cloth and apply it in small circles. After five and a half weeks of this treatment the desired deep shine began to appear. On the day of our pass-out parade it rained and this deep shine disappeared, never again to reappear.

One day, early in my stay at Padgate, I was asked to go and see the station Education Officer. He had some papers in front of him which he referred to, then asked me why someone with my education was only applying for a technicians post. I explained what had happened at Cardington.

"Right" he said. "Let's get you re- assessed."

He gave me an exam paper similar to the one at Cardington and left me to it. After about 10 minutes he came back into the room and asked if I had finished. When I told him I had, he said "Well turn over and do the other side".

I told him I had finished that also. Once bitten . . .

He quickly marked them and, lo and behold I was back on course to be a fitter. I silently thanked my guardian angel.

One of the first places I sought out on my arrival at Padgate was the gymnasium. It wasn't difficult to find—a vast hanger-like structure. What was more important—it had a full set of weights, proper weights at that; bars, large and small discs, even dumb-bells. I trained whenever my bull-night duties permitted.

Days were taken up primarily with drill, but there were other calls on our time including weapons training, attending lectures and sessions in the gym. I got to know the PTI's pretty quickly, so even during these class sessions, I was allowed to carry on pumping iron. I felt slightly guilty watching the rest of my intake pummelling each other with boxing gloves and contrived to make my own training look as equally painful with grunts and groans and distorted faces. I found out much later that this was in fact an essential part of weight-training.

Early in my stay at Padgate I had found out that our hut corporal was a weight—training enthusiast, and we spent time discussing the merits of various exercises, weight versus reps, etc. One weekend I went with a friend to his hometown of Manchester. He showed me round the red-light district but I told him I was more interested in getting a few pints down. The outcome was that we were late getting back to camp and the MP on the main gate put us on a charge. I went to see our hut corporal who in turn had a word with the MP. The upshot was, the charge was dropped.

An early taste of the brotherhood of the weights.

After 6 weeks of square-bashing we were deemed to be superb specimens of fighting manhood, and sent on our way. Following a week's leave at home for much needed R and R, I found myself on my way to RAF Locking in Somerset.

The first thing I noticed about Locking was the difference in attitudes. Rank was very much played down and humanised. We still saluted officers of course, but when we met in civvies off-camp it was on first name terms.

The days consisted of classes, starting with the basic concept of radar (Radio Aids to Detection And Ranging) and gradually moving through complex circuitry, simulated faults and how to detect them. All the units were powered by valves which made them very bulky. It was not a subject that I had aptitude for, but I owed it to myself to do well and really got stuck-in.

Leave at Locking of necessity had to be organised around our classes, and I was able to get home a couple of times during the course. In addition, once a month we were given a 48 hour pass. This involved having a Friday and Saturday off, which along with the Sunday, made a long weekend. It wasn't worth while going home as the journey to Hull involved a minimum of 10 hours on the train, so I usually spent these 48's on camp, often exploring the surrounding countryside. However, I did use a couple to pay Bob a visit.

I had found out very quickly that in spite of my efforts, I was doing a different trade to Bob. He was an air radar fitter, whereas I was ground radar. He was stationed at that time at RAF Boscombe Down on Salisbury Plane, close enough for a weekend visit.

He met me at the station and we strolled back to the camp. Boscombe Down was a top-secret aerodrome where the latest fighter planes were being developed. However, both Bob and I were in our battle dress and we strolled through the main gate unchallenged. Bob informed me that he had to work that morning, so I walked with him up the hill towards the hanger. Upon entering I was struck by a sight of something straight out of a movie. Bob told me the beautiful aircraft that had me spellbound was known as a Vulcan bomber, and that was the machine he would be working on.

He climbed up into the cockpit and I followed him. As he sat in the co-pilots seat doing his stuff, I sat in the pilot's seat playing with the controls. During all the time we were inside the plane I don't recall another person coming into the hanger.

By the time of my second visit Bob had moved on to RAF North Weald where he was attached to the 'Red Arrows' display team. I had a friend from London who intended to go home this particular 48, and he offered me a lift on the back of his 500 Norton. I had no leathers or helmet, but hey, at 20 you're indestructible. We set off and I quickly learnt the biker's code. The white line down the middle of the road is there to speed along between the two lines of traffic. I idly wondered what would happen if we met another motorbike coming the other way, but dismissed the thought and spent the next four hours contemplating the back of Barry's neck.

Bob was waiting for me under the statue of Eros, and we had an interesting weekend exploring Soho and Petticoat Lane. On Sunday afternoon it was time for another four hours of speedway. I've never been on a motorbike since.

Locking is just outside Weston-Super-Mare which is a beautiful part of the world. As that first year rolled-on into summer I spent many a weekend on the beach working on my tan.

The camp had the usual hanger-like gym complete with a full set of weights, and although I spent many hours in there, I wasn't making my hoped for gains. Years later I was to learn all about somatotyping, in particular about ectomorphs or 'hard gainers' as they are popularly known. Notwithstanding my slow progress, I was enjoying my training for the adrenalin high that it gave me.

There was one other distraction during my time at Locking. There were various notices dotted about the camp advertising a dancing class that was about to start in Weston. A number of our group decided to give it a try and on the appointed day, made our way over. The class had a good turnout, although, as is the nature of these things, there were far more girls than boys. We didn't complain. There was one other familiar face we were surprised to see—the sergeant who took us for most of our instruction. We regarded him as being a bit old for dancing classes, but in truth he was probably only in his early 30's. He was happy to see us and joined our group. The dancing progressed over the following weeks with us learning both ballroom and Latin. My favourite dance was the jive as this could be done to trad jazz. I remember our dance teacher showing us a simple little move which she called the 'crush'. She explained that this was a useful manoeuvre to do when the dance floor was full. In the ensuing years I learnt that it was usually the only dance to do whether the floor was full or empty.

We didn't get far with any of the girls. They probably realised that we were transient and they were looking for something more permanent.

The thirty week course quickly passed and it was time for our final exams. I had swatted extensively for these, memorising many complicated bits of circuitry. When it was my turn to go in to see our friend, the sergeant, he asked me two very simple questions, and then had a chat with me on various subjects unrelated to work. Was this standard procedure, assuming that to make it to the end of the course was proof of ability, or was it our mutual dancing experience manifesting? I shall never know.

Passing meant instant promotion to a junior technician. One stripe stitched as an inverted V on both our battle dress and best blue. It also meant more money.

One other important duty was to be performed before we departed. We were asked to collect in our huts and an officer came in with our postings. When it came to my turn he read out "3523500 J/T Bennett—Malaya"

My whoop must have been heard in Weston.

31

9

PORT SWETTENHAM

More compulsory leave, this time fairly sad as the family and I knew we wouldn't be seeing each other again for at least two and a half years, but they were also happy for me knowing I was getting my wish to see an exotic part of the World.

After having a number or jabs for various tropical diseases and picking up my khaki uniform at RAF Insworth it was time to go. I was flying out, and because we would be passing over a number of sensitive countries I was ordered to wear civilian clothes. In addition, my passport referred to me as a 'Government Employee'. The aircraft was a Comet, the first jet liner to go into public service. In spite of this the range was fairly limited. We stopped for refuelling at Brindisi in southern Italy and Ankara in Turkey. We arrived in Baghdad in the heat of mid-day. As the hostess opened the external door a wall of hot air hit her and she fainted. Not an auspicious welcome to tropical climes.

One more stop at Bahrain then on to Karachi which was to be an overnight stay in the airport hotel. With time to kill, I decided to take a bus-ride into the city. The bus took a circuitous route calling at numerous outlying villages. There was clearly no limit on the number of passengers and no restrictions on the amount of live stock. Eventually, we reached the terminus. I stayed on the bus and returned to the airport!

The following day we resumed our stop/ start journey with refuelling at Delhi, Calcutta, Bangkok and finally Singapore. A short while after, we learnt that Comets were falling out of the sky. It seemed that the airframe was made from aluminium which, after a certain number of air miles suffered from metal fatigue and broke up.

RAF Changi had had a traumatic past but all was peaceful when I arrived at this transit camp. The 2 day stop-over gave me a chance to update my khaki drill which consisted of a couple of pair of shorts, two shirts, long socks, long pants and a jacket. The latter two items would only be used after sunset or on formal occasions, so it was important to get our rank designation on our shirts. It was suggested that while we were at the camp tailor it might be a good idea to have the uniform customized at the same time. This involved having the long sleeves of the shirts cut short; the shirt tails cut off and the body tapered to the waist. The shorts had their bagginess removed and the legs cut back so that they actually displayed the knees. This gave the old sweats the chance to air that well known phrase "Airmen! Get your bloody knees brown".

My summer on the beach at Weston thankfully saved me from such embarrassment.

I must admit that the final result was a hundred percent improvement, but did wonder a) why the RAF allowed it's uniform to be altered, and b) why it didn't issue the altered version in the first place. One other thing I noticed. There were plenty of National Servicemen out there. So much for integrity.

As it happened I was rather pleased. National Service would only have given me one year out there instead of the two and a half years that I served. Hardly enough time to visit all the places I eventually got to see.

After a couple of days at Changi it was time to move on again. A long train journey up country brought me to RAF Kuala Lumpur for another overnight stop, then a 30 mile trip in the back of a lorry to my final destination, RAF Port Swettenham.

Swettenham was a bit of a shock to the system. All the previous stations had been large, rambling places. 414 as Swettenham was known was just the opposite. It was built on what looked like the remains of an old runway in the middle if a paddy field. Down the centre was the living accommodation known as bashas. To one side were the admin blocks, the NAAFI and the mess and on the other side were the motor transport workshops. This seemed quite extensive for such a small unit, until one realised that the radar units themselves were mobile, and their traction units needed to be housed and maintained.

The structural element of all the buildings was bamboo poles and the weatherproofing was obtained with a material called attap. This was made from leaves of a banana tree folded along the spine and tied to the bamboo frame in an overlapping manner, very similar to a thatched cottage.

In spite of its crude construction it was surprisingly dry, even in the severest of monsoons. It did have one drawback though. Upon returning to the basha after my first day's work, I noticed that my bed was covered in small black specks. On enquiring I was told 'That's the shit beetles. They live in the attap and eat their way through it'. Sure enough, the roof was replaced after about 6 months.

Cleaning up was not a problem anyway. Each basha had its own 'boy' to do all the bull. Ours was a very ancient and affable Malay gentleman. His job started the moment we departed for work, making the beds, polishing the boots/shoes, cleaning brasses, sweeping the basha and rolling up and tying our mosquito nets. We paid him one Malay dollar each per week. The Malay dollar was worth about 2 shillings and 2 pence at that time. However, with there being about 30 bodies to a basha, 65 shillings a week was not a bad wage considering we erks were only on about £2 basic.

We were given a free issue of 50 cigarettes each week as a mark of appreciation from the Sultan of Selangor, the State in which we were stationed. As a non-smoker, I gave my allocation to one of the others who in turn paid my share to the basha boy. He was happy to receive so many cheap cigarettes and I was happy to get my bull done for nothing.

Every alternate Thursday was pay day, or in the colourful vernacular of the Forces 'The day the golden eagle shits'. Each hut would take turns to muster in the NAAFI and when your rank and name were called out; you would snap off a salute to the paymaster and collect your envelope. This could feel quite bulky as there were about 9 Malay dollars to the pound at that time.

In addition to the usual stoppages, there were a couple of additional ones. It was compulsory to deduct £1 every month to send to our parents. I increased this to £2—it was the least I could do. We were also advised to make a regular saving in the Post Office Savings Bank, which most of us did. It was possible to draw money out if one became desperate. A regular request was 'Lend me $10 until my POSBY comes through'.

Speaking of mossy nets, 414 was the only camp in Malaya where these were necessary, reflecting our location in the middle of a swamp. It was a bit of an art getting into bed, firstly crawling under the overhanging part, and then tucking it in from the inside. In spite of these precautions, I still managed to acquire several bites in the early days. These were as a result of me putting my arms against the mossy net in my sleep. After a while the bites stopped. I had either learnt to keep my arms under the sheet or the mossies had decided they didn't like my blood.

Malaya was counted as active service as there was a war going on with communist terrorists. 414 was in the classified red zone which meant it hadn't been designated as free of C.T.'s. In fact there was another compound next to ours which was full of communist sympathisers. We played them regularly at football.

The radar equipment was outside the compound, about 100 yards along the air strip. There were the usual two types. Firstly, the one that rotated 360 degrees and picked-up the bearing of any aircraft. Secondly was the type that could be turned towards any suspicious blip and determine its height with an up and down motion. These were known to one and all as "nodding horrors".

The business part of the operation was contained in two trucks, each having two consuls and all the other paraphernalia necessary to keep them working. The collection was completed by another large truck containing the generators essential for making the whole outfit operational. There was also a sheltered area for us fitters to hang about while we waited for something to blow-up, and the off-shift radar operators tried to get their eyeballs back to normal function. Many of us fitters made an excuse to linger in the ops rooms as these were air conditioned.

All the machines were turned on at 9 o clock in the morning and turned off again at 5 in the evening. This was a very civilised war!

After work activities were encouraged. There were film shows a couple of times a week. Although the projection room was enclosed, the audience sat on benches in the open-air. This was quite a novelty, especially if there happened to be a monsoon at the time. Camp cinema trips were augmented by visits to nearby Port Swettenham. These films were inevitably in English (or American, which is almost English) which everyone seemed to speak. This could be something to do with the population mix. There were the native Malays of course, but in the towns at least there seemed to be an equal number of Chinese. In addition, there was a fair sprinkling of Tamils. They all spoke their own language but the common tongue was English, much to our relief. In all my time out there I believe I learned about 6 words of Malay, and all of these were requests to taxi drivers.

In spite of the camp being small, it still supported a football league featuring all the various trades. It seemed that almost everyone played for one team or another. In addition, there was a camp first and second 11 who played local teams. I managed to make it into the second team.

There was also a badminton court. Badminton was the national sport in Malaya, and every Kampong, however small had its floodlit court. Ours didn't get much use. In fact the only person to use it regularly was Henry.

There was something not quite right about Henry, but as a fellow J/T radar fitter, I was prepared to give him the benefit of the doubt. I assumed that he played badminton most nights because he was a non-drinker, and that his partners were a selection of boys from the nearby Kampong because he couldn't find a partner within the camp. I had had a sheltered upbringing.

There was the inevitable NAAFI of course. Although the Malayan cost of living was much less than the U.K's, we erks were still given an overseas allowance. I often wondered if this was to keep us in a perpetual state of numbness. Malayan beer was certainly a good way of achieving this. There were two brews—Anchor Beer and Tiger Beer—both equally potent. New comers were advised to drink shandies to start with. After a while they could progress to 'tops'. This was almost a full pint but topped-up with about 1" of lemonade. Eventually you could ask for a pint of 'straight'. This was an indication that you had finally arrived.

Most evenings finished-up in the NAAFI and most sessions finished-up in a sing-song, but these songs were a bit different to the ones I had sung around the piano back home.

Another after work activity was a photography club. It was run by an airman who had been a professional photographer in Civvy Street. He taught us a lot about items such as framing, composition, use of filters etc, I joined in with enthusiasm. With Malaya being duty free I bought myself the latest twin-lens reflex Rollei.

We developed our own film in the dark room using the technique our friend had shown us. After my first session, I turned the light on to find my film lying on the floor. I had been developing the backing paper.

The biggest positive of the lot was the existence of a weights club which was in the basha next to ours. I became a very active member. After a while I went to see the Entertainment Officer for some money to buy a pair of squat stands. The sports shop in K.L. didn't have any, and not wanting to return empty handed, I bought some smaller items and some training posters for the walls. The Entertainments Officer was not pleased.

As a sop to him, and also because we needed them, I made my own stands. These consisted of two lengths of 3" x 2" timber. At the top I cut 'V' notches and the bottom end was placed in biscuit tins and filled with concrete. They did the job, but I don't know if the Officer ever forgave me. Something delayed my promotion and I often wonder if this was the incident.

I was training extensive sessions for three days a week but the results were a long time coming. Of course, the heat didn't help, nor all that running about on the football field. I was putting on weight gradually, but this probably had as much to do with all the ale I was supping as the iron I was pumping. One thing that I did learn about that time was the importance of recording all this training. It had three benefits.

Firstly, as a reminder of the exercises and poundages I was currently using.

Secondly, an indication of the repetitions I was getting and hence, the target to beat. The full name of our sport is *Progressive* weight-training, and this progression is only maintained by continually upping the poundages or repetitions. The trainee is essentially in competition with himself.

Thirdly by looking back through the training diary and seeing how much one had improved gave a strong positive feedback.

In those days I used a normal diary to record my training and I still have them to this day, going back to 1957. Although these tended to be on the small side, there was still enough room to jot down other occurrences. In most cases these confirmed my memories, but a few are at odds with what I remember. There are even some cryptic entries whose meanings are now completely lost. Nowadays I use a page a day diary. If nothing happens that day I can always jot down a few random thoughts. I use a separate book for my training diary. In fact, power lifting training is cyclical and it is very important to work backwards from a competition date in order to ensure peaking at the right time. I know athletes use a similar method as I was to find out many years later, but that is another story . . .

I occasionally get a query during my training as to why I record everything. My stock answer is 'Why don't *you* record everything?' The inevitable reply is that they can remember their poundages. I tell them if they can do that, they are training incorrectly.

If they ask why I will explain, but most just walk away with a 'silly old bugger' look on their face. The club itself was quite successful with quite a number of squaddies taking part to some degree or other. With four years of training behind me my opinion was sought quite often, and I suppose this was the beginning of my long association with coaching. I also began to notice how weight training had differing affects on different body types. Some like me were hard-gainers, whereas others seemed to grow whilst you looked at them. One other thing I noticed though. The vast majority of the drop-outs came from the 'easy gains' type.

Another lesson learnt—the harder it is to achieve something, the more one appreciates it. One of my big mates on the camp was Tank Davies. We used to talk about our mutual love of jazz which gave him an idea, and shortly after a visit to the Entertainments Officer the 414 Jazz Club opened for business. It was in the same basha as the weights club so I got the best of both worlds. Tank's preference was for modern Jazz which was far too complicated for my simple taste, but to be fair to him he did buy and equal number of trad jazz records.

I was telling him one day about my love of skiffle music, and he suggested we should start our own group. I agreed whole-heartedly, but told him of my problems with music. In spite of this we went ahead and found four other enthusiasts. Four of us were designated guitarists and ordered our instruments from the camp shop. Jai Seggie was the bassist and made himself an instrument from a tea-chest and a broom handle. Big Dave was the drummer, performing originally on a biscuit tin before graduating to a snare and brushes. Whilst we waited for our instruments to arrive it befell to me to teach the others the words of the various skiffle songs. In the previous two years, Lonnie had turned out many hits and there were quite a number of other groups about, so I had plenty to go on. My memory for learning verses was no problem, but the only way I could impart them to the others was to sing them. I must have made a decent enough job of it, because we very quickly had a repertoire sorted out.

The guitars arrived and we learnt the obligatory three chords. Tank had to tune mine up for me and I also had to learn the chord changes by heart instead of by ear. One of the other guitarists found he had an aptitude for the instrument, bought himself a more up-market model and picked out the notes instead of just strumming. Tank was the main singer with the rest of us joining in on the choruses. He even wrote a song for us called 'The 414 Blues'.

After a few rehearsals we felt ready to inflict ourselves on the world. The NAAFI became a regular venue where we received an enthusiastic welcome as you would expect from your mates, but how would a more critical audience receive us? We quickly found out.

The Corporals mess asked us to perform for them. By this time we had a good number of hours behind us and we put on quite a show. One of the corporals told me he had expected a load of rubbish but was quite pleasantly surprised. Faint praise indeed.

Our next step was a Dinner-dance in the Sergeant mess. Most of them lived off-site in the married quarters, so didn't know what to expect. I danced with one of the wives after our performance and she made it quite clear that music truly is the food of love. I didn't follow it up.

The final rung up this particular ladder was to perform in the Officers mess. Afterwards they gave us free access to the bar. There was no beer available (probably too plebeian), only spirits. Not being used to these, I was drinking much too quickly and was soon on my way to becoming Brahms. Worried about making a fool of myself in front of the Officers, I was about to leave when I took a good look at what they were up to.

They were in a far worse condition than me, in various states of undress, and playing some public schoolboy game. I expected Jack Hawkings to come in at any moment and fling himself on the top of the pile.

10

THE MOONMAN'S 21ST

There were two places to go on leave from 414—Singapore or Penang Island. A group of us decided to head up to Penang which involved a lorry ride to K.L, train to Butterworth, ferry over to the island then taxis out to the Bungah Beach Club. This was a small holiday complex for the forces and run by some well-meaning ladies from the WVS.

It had a beautiful little beach where we spent a good deal of our time. This gave us an opportunity to top up our tans. In spite of being only a few degrees north of the Equator we would lie out at all hours of the day. If protective creams were available at that time we certainly hadn't heard of them. In fact we went the other way, covering ourselves with oil to speed-up the tanning process. The preferred one was coconut oil being cheap and plentiful but lacking any refinements. After several minutes of us cooking in the sun there was a distinct aroma of a fish and chip shop.

Other attractions included site-seeing in the island capital, Georgetown, with such delights as the Snake Temple and the Thousand Buddha Pagoda. The evenings were a choice of playing bingo with the WVS ladies or going to a near-by bar and getting blotto. I never did care much for bingo.

The Moonman's claim to fame was, not only did he know all the words to Eskimo Nell, he could perform it with the appropriate actions. During our leave in Penang, he informed us that it was his 21st birthday and he would be pleased if Tank and myself could accompany him into Georgetown that evening for a meal and some libation.

After a super meal and several drinks he proposed to extend his generosity by taking us to a brothel. I told him that I did not indulge but would gladly accompany them.

At the brothel both he and Tank disappeared to their rooms with young ladies leaving me sat on the stairs. Tank reappeared in no time at all and joined me on the stairs. We heard an increasing commotion coming from the Moonman's room. Eventually the young lady rushed out followed by an animated Moonman. Between outbursts he managed to tell us what had happened. Apparently he had finished fairly quickly, but had managed to remain coupled-up and was going for seconds. The young lady had taken exception to this and managed to extract herself from under him.

It seemed to my inexperienced mind that anyone who could do that deserves seconds.

The row continued down the corridor to the front desk where the proprietor joined in. He clearly sided with the young lady which only served to make the Moonman madder. He picked up a glass ashtray and flung it at the proprietor who ducked and the ashtray broke a huge mirror behind the desk.

I was out of the door and running in a flash. The brothel was in a dark narrow alleyway and I could see Chinese men emerging from every doorway armed with huge machetes. I had heard the expression 'to run without your feet touching the ground' but had never thought it possible until that night. Eventually I reached a well-lit main street and slowed down. I saw a squad of Malay policemen standing in a side street. I rushed over and told them that my friend was being murdered and they must follow me. They obligingly began to march in the direction from which I had come.

"Double-up" I shouted and they all broke into a trot. Training has its merits.

When we reached the brothel there were no bodies. Instead, the Moonman was still arguing and Tank was looking bemused. The Officer in charge of the squad quickly sorted everything out. He told us that he would have to lock the Moonman up for the night for his own safety, but he kindly ran Tank and myself back to the Bungah. The following night I played bingo.

11

WAR IS OVER

It was during my time at Swettenham that we heard of the end of National Service. In fact my brother Dave was in the very last intake—all those who reached their 18th birthday in September 1957. It also meant that my contempories who had elected to go to university directly from school would not now have to do their National Service. Was I bitter?

Well, no actually. I was having a ball and at the same time managing to put a few bob aside. University could wait.

It is ironic that at the present time many students are electing to take a year out between finishing school and starting Uni. I would whole heartedly recommend this course of action, particularly if it involves a visit to a so-called Third-World country.

Back at Swettenham it was difficult to realise we were actually at war. In Vietnam the Americans were dropping Napalm on the villages; in Malaya the British were dropping leaflets. These leaflets served two purposes. Firstly they encouraged the communist leaders to give up peacefully on the promise they would be treated with respect. Secondly were the ones addressed to the headmen of the jungle kampongs, telling them not to cooperate with the terrorists, but to turn them in.

There was some fighting of course but this was done mainly by those magnificent little men, the Gurkhas. They had a camp near us at 414 and we often saw them setting-off on patrol. Weeks later we would see them returning looking as cheerful as ever. It was hard to imagine that they had spent days on end lying by a jungle trail waiting for an enemy patrol. They were issued with photographs of the communist leaders with instructions to target them. They were supposed to bring the bodies out for identification, but the wily Gurkhas couldn't see much point in bringing the whole body out. A quick blow from their kukri was sufficient to do the job, and they were seen emerging from the jungle swinging a bandit's head by the hair.

We often played them at football and many of them would play in their bare feet. However, if one of them happened to give you an 'accidental' kick, you would certainly know all about it.

Suddenly it was all over. The only war of insurgency to be won by the good guys. Vietnam was a dishonourable draw. The Americans had pulled out of Vietnam with their tails between their legs, yet in the perverse way that we have, the Vietnam war is remembered and the Malay war is forgotten. I don't know if the end of the war caused the next occurrence or if it was some other deep machination of Government beyond the understanding of ordinary mortals but the word came down that 414 would cease to exist. We were given a date and at the appointed time the dismantling process began. My job was disconnecting cables, pulling them into a coil and storing them. A simple enough job at face value but there was a small snag. In all the previous months that I had spent in Malaya I had only seen two snakes. Now, every pile of cables that I disturbed seemed to hide a nest of them. Fortunately they were just as surprised as me and quickly slid off into the nearby grass.

Only one thing left to do—decide on my next move. There were three choices and I submitted mine in order of preference.

1   Hong Kong
2   Singapore
3   Butterworth.

I got Butterworth.

12

RAAF BUTTERWORTH

No, that's not a misprint. It was the Royal Australian Air Force, Butterworth. So what were we Brits doing there?

Butterworth was altogether a different place to 414. It was an operational aerodrome with two runways forming a huge cross, and all the attendant trades that go with maintaining such a facility. The Aussies had only recently taken over the running and were still in the process of changing things round. They were building a permanent ground radar station at the end of one of the runway, and until this was ready we Brits were to operate the existing mobile unit at the end of the other runway.

The camp was pleasantly situated on the shore opposite Penang Island. The buildings were all brick-built and modern. Our billets resembled holiday chalets with about 6 bodies per room, and of course no black specks to brush off your bed every night.

One thing that was immediately noticeable was the quantity and choice of food available in the mess. Steaks for breakfast were an unheard of luxury.

There was no skiffle group at Butterworth. My guitar remained hanging above my bed unused until on day one of the other squaddies made me an offer I couldn't refuse, so I sold it. My short-lived days as a rock star were over.

There was a jazz club which I attended regularly. Upon leaving Swettenham the members had bought their club records for a token fee and had a meal and a few beers on the proceeds. As one of the few trad jazz fans I managed to acquire quite a lot of unusual ones with such exotic titles as 'Maggie Miles and The Kings Of Dixie' (whatever happened to her?) At Butterworth I got the chance to play these records to my fellow enthusiasts.

One day we heard that Jack Teagarden was to appear in Georgetown. On the appointed day we made our way over to the island. The hall was full including the Sultan of Penang and his entourage. Whether in deference to him or because the Orientals are naturally reticent I don't know, but it was the quietist gig I have ever attended.

The operational aircraft were American Sabres, popularly known as flying stovepipes. These were notoriously unstable. Apparently they had had the choice of the British jet but had chosen the American one instead. In fact they were known to us as U/T Yanks. The subtlety of this was lost on the Aussies. Well, they were descended from convicts.

One day I saw an old friend, the Vulcan bomber, flying overhead. It was out there doing its tropical trials. I gave it a wave and it waggled its wings back at me.

One unwelcome facet of Colonial life was that British law was followed out to the letter, even though we were many thousands of miles away. The biggest impact of this on us erks was the bar in the NAAFI closing at 10pm promptly every night. We accepted this without question. However, there was some muttering among our Australian hosts.

One evening we were sat in the NAAFI as usual and the panelled shutters slid down at 10pm as they always did. A large Australian went up to the bar and with one huge blow he punched a hole in one of the shutters. I have heard Orientals described as inscrutable without really being aware of its meaning. The Chinese barmen who carried on serving pints through the hole in the shutter demonstrated the meaning impeccably. Shortly after this the NAAFI hours were extended. I mustn't give the impression of Aussies being macho without giving the other side of the coin. They quickly decided that they didn't like either Anchor or Tiger beer and demanded that the NAAFI should also carry an Aussie beer. That was how some weeks later the NAAFI had a huge promotional event for Emu Ales. There were tables of nibbles but the main attraction was the Emu Ale itself which would be free on that first night.

We Brits were in there in numbers as you would expect and eagerly sampled this free brew. After a couple of mouthfuls it was clear that it was witches water. We went back to drinking our pints of straight, making sure that our hosts knew what we thought of their prize concoction. Possibly with thoughts of revenge, the Aussies challenged the Brits to a game of rugby union. There was well over 1000 of them to choose from, whereas there was less that 100 of we Brits. The odds seemed about right to me.

I had never played rugby union in my life, but had watched plenty of rugby league and how different could it be. Besides the Brits were short of genuine players and needed anyone who could catch and run. I agreed to play centre as that would keep me away from all those silly rucks and mauls and line outs.

There was no available pitch so we marked one out in the rough grass between the runways. The game started and it soon degenerated into the usual forward battle. I didn't see too much of the ball and when I did, it usually arrived accompanied by 15 hairy—arsed Aussies. At last I got a pass in the clear and I set off. I was back in Wellsted Street with a bundle of old newspapers under my arm, side stepping and weaving my way to that distant lamp-post. I plonked the ball down over the line. 3 nil to the Brits.

No conversions of course as we had no posts.

The game was being played in the heat of mid-day, and the Malay grass was extremely sharp on the knees. Still we played on until eventually the Aussies managed to pull a try back, and we settled for an honourable draw.

Cinema continued to be a major attraction. In addition to the camp cinema there was also a free film show every Monday in the WVS lounge. This was augmented by visits to a Georgetown cinema at the weekends, which could mean three or four films per week. This seemed a bit indulgent at the time, but in the current climate of multi-channel television one can easily watch that number every single day.

Looking back at some of the titles they are instantly forgettable, but scattered in amongst are some classics. For instance, I saw 'The Bridge on the River Kwai' about this time. It had been shot the previous year in Ceylon, and many of my former Locking companions who had been posted there were acting as extras. One of them, 'Sailor' Lupton had been chosen to play Alec Guinness's double for the distant shots. In the scene where his character had be incarcerated in the sweat-box for days and then taken in front of the Japanese Commandant, the Director decided to do a long shot over the heads of the ranked British prisoners. As Sailor emerged from the office he tripped over a lose board and stumbled down the steps.

"Brilliant!" cried the Director. "That's a wrap"

Over the road from the main camp was a large area comprising of living quarters for the married service men and their families, universally known as the "Married patch". I found what I was looking for in the married patch—the camp gymnasium. Once again this was a huge hanger-like building full of every piece of gymnastic equipment imaginable, including a full set of weights. In all the time that I trained there I don't recall seeing one other person in the gym.

Also situated within the married patch was the camp's swimming pool, beautifully located by the sea in a landscaped garden. The children from the families made great use of this facility and we got quite friendly with a number of them.

With Penang Island being only a short ferry ride away, we spent a lot of our weekends over in Georgetown. A favourite Saturday day out might include an afternoon at a cinema followed by a meal in one of the many roof top restaurants. Then it was a question of getting as much ale down our necks before departing for the last ferry. At this stage we would choose a trishaw each, put the driver into the back seat, climb into the saddle and race each other back to the ferry terminal.

13

HENRY

When I first decided to conquer the world of bodybuilding, several years before, I made myself three promises. The first one was that I wouldn't smoke. I found it very easy to stick with this one. I could never understand the attraction of paying good money to suck 200 different poisons into your lungs. Smoker friends tell me it gives them a 'high'. Well, so does lifting heavy weights but you don't get a corresponding low when the serotonins disperse.

The second promise was never to drink alcohol. This one didn't last very long. We service men had a lot of free time to kill, and in spite of my various pastimes, I usually ended up each evening in the NAAFI knocking back pints of strong ale. In fact, you could say that I went from TT to OTT in no time flat. The third promise was that I would not go with women of doubtful virtue. I can't quite remember now the rationale behind this one as jig-a-jig as it was known is a very good cardio vascular exercise. It may have been the fear of disease, although, unlike our backward country, prostitution was legal in Malaya. This had many advantages. The girls were obliged to visit the doctor at least once a week; there were no pimps and the girls paid tax on their earnings. Notwithstanding this, at that time I was still sticking to my principles.

Henry was to be the cause of my eventual downfall.

He had also been posted to Butterworth from 414. There was still this feeling about him that everything was not quite right. But nothing you could put your finger on. Then, one day it all became clear. We were sat in the cafe by the camp pool having a refreshing drink and a natter when one of the children we had got to know came over and told us that Henry had been fondling him in the dressing room. We confronted Henry and he confessed straight away. He claimed he was on the verge of going to see the camp doctor, to see if there was any cure for his problem.

The lads were very quick to talk him out of this course of action, claiming to have the perfect cure. What Henry needed was a women.

They quickly sorted out the details and on the following Saturday we made our way over to Georgetown. After a meal and drinks we proceeded to a nearby hotel/brothel. The boys had all got their special partners and had quickly pared-off. I was there merely as an observer and intended to sleep on my own as I had done in the past when missing the last ferry.

As we looked at the array of girls the proprietor had provided for Henry's approval he suddenly dropped his bombshell.

"I will only go with a woman if you do too" he said to me.

What was I to do? I couldn't let all that preparation go to waste for the sake of my principles. I picked a pleasant looking girl and we made our way to one of the bedrooms leaving Henry behind to make his choice.

We both undressed then stood looking at each other. She could obviously see my hesitancy.

"What your favourite position Johnny?" she asked.

I confessed that I didn't have a favourite. In fact this was my first time. From somewhere she produced a pack of photographs and handed them to me.

"You pick one Johnny" she said.

For a twenty year old virgin who had seen nothing more revealing than the air-brushed photos in 'Health and Efficiency', these were a real eye opener. There were eight in total, all graphically displaying different positions of coupling. If I hadn't been quite ready before, I certainly was now.

"Which one Johnny?" she asked again

"I don't know" I replied. "They all look interesting"

"All" she said picking up on that word. "You want do all?"

"Why not?" I replied with bravado.

The first position was over in a flash; the second took a little longer and the third took a little longer still. After that I dozed off. It seemed that I had just closed my eyes when she was shaking me awake.

"Number four Johnny" she said.

As the night progressed I was allowed longer and longer periods of sleep between being awoken. In the morning the house-boy brought us a cup of coffee, and afterwards we slowly completed the full set.

"You want be my boyfriend?" she asked.

I explained that I couldn't afford it. The night had cost 30 Malay dollars, equivalent to 35 shillings Sterling.

"No charge" she replied.

I agreed and we made arrangements for the following weekend.

We guys met up in one of the rooms to compare notes. They all seemed impressed by my exploits, but the main purpose was to see if their strategy had worked. Henry certainly gave that impression, telling us that he had enjoyed the company of a young lady for the night.

The following weekend I got over to the island early. I had made it clear to Ah Ling that if I was to be her boyfriend we would do it properly. We caught a bus to the far side of the island and found a deserted beach. After a while laying on the sand it became necessary to go into the sea to cool off. I learnt yet another position.

Eventually we made it back to the hotel we had used the previous week, but this time I paid $10 for a room only. I think she wanted to go for a new record, but I was learning very quickly that quality is more important than quantity. Besides, I was still a bit raw from the previous week. I stopped after seven. In the morning the house-boy came round with our coffee.

"Where your friend?" he asked me.

"Which friend is that?" I queried.

"The one who took me to his room last week" he replied

Henry confessed, went to see the doctor, and within a short time was on his way home.

14

RAF SELETAR

The Aussies finished their building work on the permanent ground radar station, and it was time to move on again. More dismantling, more cable pulling and more snakes, then time to pick my next move. We were rapidly running out of choices. I placed the two available in order of preference:-

1. Hong Kong
2. Singapore

I got Singapore.

There were three RAF camps on Singapore Island. Changi was mainly a transit camp; Tengah was an operational fighter base and Seletar was a maintenance base. It boasted one of the widest runways I had ever seen, although the only aircraft permanently on camp didn't require a runway. It was a Sunderland Flying Boat, the last one in service.

The runway served to separate the two halves of the camp, both being almost self sufficient. For instance, West Camp where I was based had its two workshops, two large 3 storey billets and a building housing a cinema, mess halls, snooker room and the inevitable NAAFI.

I don't know if the camp boasted a proper gym, but it didn't matter. I trained in the makeshift gym put together by some of the lads in a drying room attached to our billets.

East Camp was vast; resembling a small town. Our main reason for going over there was at the weekend to visit the pool. In keeping with the rest of the camp, this was the biggest I have ever seen. One of the lads had a portable gramophone which we played constantly at the side of the pool. I was still into my jazz but other things were happening in the world of music. The 60's have been described as the decade of rock and roll, but many of the groups had their beginnings in the late 50's. Two of my favourites were the Everley Brothers and Buddy Holly. The latter in fact never made it into the 60's. I was also developing a taste for Frank Sinatra and bought several of his LP's.

Immediately outside the camp's main gates was Seletar village. This consisted of a row of shops on either side of the main road. Fairly safe in the knowledge that this would be my final overseas posting, I was a frequent visitor to these shops putting together items for my "deep sea box". In addition to records, I was acquiring a collection of clothes, carved wooden artefacts and I had also started purchasing presents for the family back home.

Seletar was situated on the north coast of the island with a view of Malaya across the dividing straits. The city of Singapore was on the south east coast and represented a taxi ride for us squaddies. In the early days of my posting I travelled into town quite a lot to take in all the various attractions. Two that come to mind are the gory tableaux of the Tiger Balm Gardens and the Botanical Gardens with its giant banyan trees and the troupe of semi- tame monkeys running about. There was inevitably a cricket match taking place on the Padang in front of the Government buildings. All very colonial.

To one side of the Padang was Raffles Hotel, a place I had read about and was eager to visit. However, I was told quite firmly that Raffles was for officers only. How the officers contrived to have us banned from a civilian building I shall never know.

Recently I took my wife Irene to Singapore to show her some of my old haunts. We walked firstly into China town, now very much expanded and heaving with tourists. From there I went looking for Sago Lane but found only an area of clearance. I asked an elderly Chinese passer-by to explain to Irene what used to be there and he confirmed my memory of the 'death houses' where Chinese families took their elderly relatives to die. I never did find out why.

From here we made our way down to the water front. This is considerable further out than it used to be with the reclaimed land bursting with high rise offices. Crossing the Singapore River we eventually reached the Padang. No cricket today, although it was by now getting quite late. Crossing the green, we made our way to the Raffles hotel. At last I was going to get my wish.

At the top of the stairs stood a major domo resplendent in his Sikh uniform. I stopped to have a chat.

"When I was here nearly 50 years ago I was banned from coming in" I said.

"You're still banned" he replied.

I started to laugh until I realised he was serious. It was that old dress code thing again. I had left our hotel in mid afternoon wearing shorts and a short sleeved shirt. It was now after 7:00 pm and long pants and sleeves were the order of the day. The doorman did point out that there was an open air bar at the other end of the building and we would be welcome there. Had this always been there or was it a recent addition? The architecture certainly matched the remainder of the building.

There was an orchestra playing and a singer gave the place an air of a 30's movie.

I ordered two Singapore Gin-slings. Everything comes to those who wait.

The work at Seletar was very strange. I had been allocated an area on a work bench and given a box of tools. Units which I recognised as being from our old friend the mobile radar kept appearing on my desk. My job was to disassemble them, test the components and put them back together again. I wondered where they were all coming from and one day I found out.

I was sent over to East camp with a corporal fitter to a huge warehouse. The inside was absolutely full of old mobile units. This is probably where Swettenham and Butterworth ended up, but where had the rest come from? We were supposed to check out the immoveable units but my companion didn't seem too bothered so I took my cue from him and bought myself a book of crosswords.

Evenings were becoming a bit of a pattern. I was training on Mondays Wednesdays and Fridays before popping into the NAAFI for the last hour or so, on Tuesdays and Thursdays and usually Sundays I would go to the first house at the cinema before finishing up in the

NAAFI yet again. The films were changed every couple of days so this worked out quite well. I saw an awful lot of movies, but this was a good time for film buffs with many classics being premiered.

The cinema on West camp (or Astra as they were inevitably called) was different to others, which were usually free standing purpose built structures. This one was underneath the NAAFI which meant that the ceiling was unusually low. This had an unfortunate consequence.

In those days cinemas would always play the National Anthem at the end of a performance. However, the site of her Majesty's finest scrabbling to get out rather than stand at attention was too unedifying for the authorities, so in the Astras they always played the anthem at the beginning of the show. As we stood to attention the heads of the front row showed as shadows on the screen. It didn't take too long to realise the potential on this situation. The picture on the screen was of the Royal Standard being raised up the flag pole and then fluttering in the breeze. It was the duty of the squaddy sitting on the front row, three in from the left, to raise his arms and pull on the lanyard to help raise the flag. Points were awarded for keeping his shadow in sync with the screen.

I don't know if it was an effort to prevent this harmless pastime but after a while the picture was changed. The new one showed the queen sitting on her favourite stallion. This horse was hung . . . well, like a stallion. The new game was to "stroke" the horse. The movement in fact was very similar to the previous one, only the seat number had changed.

One night an officer from East camp was in with his wife and daughter. He complained bitterly at our deprived actions. The projectionist stuck up for us, pointing out that it was our cinema. However, I did notice he went back to using the royal standard opening.

Saturday nights would inevitably see as taxiing into town after the NAAFI closed. Curiously, there was a great shortage of bars in Singapore and we always headed for Bogis Street. I don't know how this insignificant little street came to be what it was but while I was there it was always thriving. All it consisted of was a few street stalls selling food but, more importantly they also sold bottled beer. On our recent trip to Singapore I looked on a map for Bogis Street. I managed to find it but it had mysteriously moved to the other side of the main road.

I recall two memorable nights in Bogis street both starting out in the NAAFI as things usually did. The first was Eccles's 'boat party' and he had decided to make it fancy dress. Most of us made our own from whatever we could lay our hands on. However, a few of the lads had gone the whole hog and hired the proper costumes. Two of them wore naval ratings uniform and certainly looked the part. When the NAAFI closed most of us decided to hit the town as usual and so a fleet of taxis descended on Bogis Street and spilled-out their assortment of vicars, tarts, army colonels and naval ratings. We settled at the tables for a few more drinks when there was a sudden disturbance. We saw two burly naval policemen making their way over to us. Apparently, Bogis Street was out of bounds for the Navy. They grabbed our two 'ratings' and dragged them off to spend the night in the brig. They were protesting loudly that they were in the RAF not the Navy, but their perfect uniforms said otherwise. Besides, none of us were prepared to confirm their preposterous claims. They were returned to us the following day. The second night involved one of our number called Johnny Henstock. In my eyes Johnny was always a gentle giant but he did have a reputation for being a hardcase when riled. One day he got an invite to go over to the local army camp and fight their resident psychopath. Some of the lads accompanied him to witness the event, but as a hater of violence I declined to go. He returned covered in blood and bruises but apparently the army champ was in a much worse state. They had left him comatose amid the wreckage of tables, chairs and glasses in what had once been a NAAFI.

Anyway, back to Bogis Street. A number of us had finished up there as usual and had settled down for a few quiet drinks. Suddenly a group of Chinese youths appeared from out of the shadows waving machetes. They made their way over to the stall holders who quickly produced their own machetes and a battle ensued. We were in the middle of a Tong war.

The sensible thing to do was to sit tight and wait for it to blow over. However, being sensible and being squiffy did not go together well. I stood up and wandered among the combatants imploring them to stop fighting and love each other. Johnny Henstock saw my predicament, came to my rescue and received a machete blow on his head for his trouble. It served its purpose though. The attackers melted away as quickly as they had appeared. We made our way back to our table and inspected Johnny's wound. We could clearly see his skull through the cut, and there was blood everywhere. We wanted to get him to hospital but Johnny wouldn't hear of it and insisted on carrying on with our session. Eventually as dawn was breaking we caught our taxi back to base. The first stop was the camp hospital to drop Johnny off, then over to West camp for a few hours of pit-bashing.

That night in the NAAFI we all admired Johnny's shaven head and his row of stitches.

Our other drinking spot was an all together more exclusive affair. Although named after a postal district, Larong 8 was only one house. Many a night we would be the only customers sitting at the tables in front of the house drinking our bottled beer. If you felt hungry Larong 8 had a unique solution. You walked through the house with the proprietor to the back yard where he kept a chicken run. You picked one out and half an hour later it was plucked and cooked and ready to eat. Most evenings we were entertained by the antics of the people in the house opposite. They were all transvestites.

Talking of which, I was beginning to miss my weekly love-ins. Would I be lucky again and find a young lady who required a boyfriend? The first one I tried obviously wasn't impressed with my charm. Neither was the second. However, it was a case of third time lucky and this one had her own house so there was no hotel to pay. In fact she shared the house with her family which I found very strange at first, but they were clearly at ease with the way she made her living and I got to know them quite well. I got into the habit of spending Saturday afternoons with her, then leaving her to earn the families living whilst I met up with the boys for a night on the town.

The big social event in West Camp was a darts league. Each trade put a team in and with the Corporals mess and the Sergeants mess also competing we had an entry of about ten. Each team consisted of 8 players, each player having one game of 301 against their opposite number starting and finishing on a double, followed by four games of doubles. It was up to the captain to decide the running order. At the end of the regular game the teams then played for a gallon. This consisted of one game of 1001 with every player taking it in turns until one team hit the winning double. The loosing team would then buy the opposite number a pint. 8 pints equals one gallon.

A league was in progress when I arrived, but I was invited onto our team and quickly got the hang of it. So much so that when the next league started some months later I was invited to be the league secretary. I took to the job whole-heartedly. I enjoyed playing with numbers, drawing up weekly updates on the league positions and doing the stats for the various side events. Besides, it also performed that all important task of using up some of my surplus time.

At the end of the league it was my job to organise the prize giving night. Once again I was on my way to see an Entertainments Officer for funds. However, with the league being such a well established event there was no opposition. I bought all the required trophies in the village, the camp being a great outlet for their wares. In addition to the league winners and runners up there were prizes for the most 'tons', for the highest checkout and also a booby prize. I also organised some nibbles and wine for our guests. On the chosen evening the NAAFI was full. I had invited the senior officer from West Camp to present the prizes and several other officers were present. I had dressed for the occasion and sat at the top table with the guest feeling perfectly at ease. At the appointed time I stood up, made a bit of a speech thanking the guests and invited the prize winners to collect their trophies. I was quite pleased with my performance.

Obviously someone else was too, because the following day I was invited into the senior officer's room. He told me that I was being promoted to corporal. I thanked him. He then asked if this promotion would make me consider signing-on. I told him it might have done if it had come a year earlier, but the delay hadn't endeared me to the system.

Being back on a British camp also meant that there was a strong emphasis on football again. There was an internal league of course and I represented my section, but there were also camp teams who played against locals. Once again, I made the second eleven. However, a second eleven on a large camp must be some sort of improvement over a second eleven on a small camp, but the icing on the cake came when, after a few good performances, I was promoted to the first team.

It seemed that all the training was beginning to pay-off. I was heavier, fitter and faster. Other sports were finding this basic truth about this time. I remember for instance an unfancied Rugby League team—I believe it was Leigh—suddenly begin winning everything in sight. Eventually their secret came out—they were training with weights!

Nowadays it is an essential part of all rugby training as I know from firsthand experience. All we need now is for professional football clubs to see the light.

It was during my stay at Seletar we learnt that Singapore was to be given its independence. The men at the top decided that this would lead to trouble and hence we erks were to form ourselves into riot squads. Our squad was taken to a housing estate of the outskirts of Singapore to be nearer to the action. We ate iron rations from billycans and slept on the concrete verandah of a nearby school. I was one of the riflemen with fixed bayonets stationed on the perimeter of the square. People within the square had various jobs including the officer-in-charge. He was armed with a megaphone to facilitate the reading of the riot act. To make our drills more authentic, the powers-that-be had arranged for the local Army squaddies to act as a hairy-arsed mob. Dressed in old clothes they ran round us hurling insults and grass-sods with gay abandon. I asked the OIC a pertinent question but he turned my request down.

No! We were not allowed to bayonet the buggers.

Come Independence Day and all passed off without a murmur. A perfect example of a non-event. We were stood down and returned to our previous life of debauchery.

15

HONG KONG

There was only one way I was going to make it to Hong Kong now and that was to go on leave. Singapore was the ideal starting point. There were two methods of travel and I experienced them both during that final year in the Far East. The first involved what was called an indulgence flight, and meant waiting until a transport aircraft was due to fly up there and then hitching a ride. The disadvantage was that the cargo hold was unpressurised and we sat in bucket seats slung from the walls. No windows of course, so we didn't even have a view to distract us. On the other hand the journey only took 7 hours.

The second method was to go by sea. This meant timing your leave to coincide with the movements of the troopship, HMS Oxfordshire. These movements were usually as regular as clockwork, but that hadn't been the case 18 months earlier. The squaddies that had left England to sail out about the same time I flew found themselves taking an extended cruise. They had reached the Med. at the same time that Nassar was making his bid for glory by closing the Suez Canal with scuppered vessels. The Oxfordshire did an about turn, sailed round the Cape, and what should have been a three week journey became a 5 weeker. All these troubles were far behind us when we made our trip. The only drawback in fact was the time it took to traverse the South China Seas. Four days out and another four back took a huge chunk out of our precious leave.

Both trips saw us staying at the China Fleet Club, which was ideally situated on Hong Kong Island a short tram ride from the busy down-town area. It was next door to the naval dock yards which probably gave rise to its existence, but more importantly to the existence of the many bars in the area.

We did all the tourist things of course, travelling to the top of the Peak, visiting Happy Valley, dining on a floating restaurant in Aberdeen Bay. We even took a ferry trip to the neighbouring Portuguese colony of Macau and had an overnight stay. We hired a guide to show us round and his first stop was at a live sex show. This comprised of two young ladies writhing about on a bed. However, the illusion was shattered by the presence of a baby in a cot next to the bed. Every time the baby cried one or another of the young ladies would stop what they were doing to comfort it. They asked us if we wanted to join in but we declined and departed. I was never much good with babies.

Our next port of call was more interesting to my mind. We visited one of the many gambling dens that dotted the colony. The Chinese are inveterate gamblers and the place was heaving. To make the tables more accessible they were over looked by balconies from which the punters would raise and lower their bets in wickerwork baskets. I never did find out what they were playing, which is just as well as it avoided the temptation of having a flutter.

There were no cosy travelogues in those days of course; we found our way about by word of mouth. One of the things we had been told was that Hong Kong tailors were among the best in the world. With demob on the not-too-distant horizon, I decided to find out.

I found the tailoring district and had a look round. One in particular stood out. It had a wall full of photographs of Hollywood movie stars posing in their new suits with the proprietor. He told me that many of them flew over with the sole purpose of buying a suit. If it's good enough for them it's good enough for me I thought. On our first visit I ordered a light-weight summer suit. At the beginning of my leave he took my measurements. By about the third day I was back for a fitting and by day six, just before we departed, I collected a brand new suit.

On our second leave to the colony I repeated the process, but this time I asked for a heavy weight suit to cope with the English weather. Six days later I collected it. Some months down the line, after I had returned to Blighty, I was telling this story to a friend of mine in Wellsted Street. It appeared that he had got a job at Hepworth's as a shop assistant, and was somewhat of an expert in suitings. He rubbished my assertion that I had got a top quality suit in six days so I showed it to him. He rubbed the material between his finger and thumb in a professional manor, and conceded that it was top quality English worsted. He then had a look at the inside.

"My word!" he exclaimed. "They have even piped the lining".

I didn't know what he was talking about, but after that, every time I wore my suit I opened it up to show people my piped lining.

Eventually I grew out of it as I continued to train, but there was still plenty of wear left in it so I took it down to the 'Help the Aged' shop. It intrigued me to think of some old guy walking round Bingley in a suit with my name embroidered in red cotton on the inside pocket.

As mentioned, the district around the China Fleet Club was heaving with bars. We naturally tried quite a lot, but our favourite conveniently turned out to be the one opposite our digs. With no windows the inside was illuminated with subdued lighting. In the centre was a dance floor with tables surrounding it. To one side was a dais on which played a small band. On one of our visits the American fleet were in town and a number of them would take-over the band stand and treat us to some great swing music. I got talking to one of them and said they must put in a lot of rehearsal. On the contrary, he replied. Apparently they were all based on different ships, and the only time they got together was during shore leave. There were also a number of young hostesses available. The idea was that you could dance with them or get them to sit at your table for a chat. In return you were expected to buy them drinks. Although these were charged at alcoholic prices they were obviously only soft drinks. Never mind, that was the accepted way of doing things and everybody, went along with it. Besides, the girls were paid according to the number of drinks that they had been bought. Although this gave them some degree of financial independence, it was also understood that they would offer other services if they liked the look of you. One of the girls stood out in my eyes. Mary Ann was gorgeous. I had several dances with her interspersed with long chats. After a while she stopped me buying her drinks, and shortly after that she told me I could take her home. It was late when the bar closed and we walked down the deserted street towards the sea front. Down a flight of stone steps and we stepped into a waiting sampan.

I realised that this was Mary Ann's regular route home. An outboard motor sprang into life and we made our way across the dark water to the mainland. Upon reaching Kowloon we had another short walk to Mary Ann's apartment.

After a night of getting to know each other and a leisurely morning we went for a walk round Kowloon. A meal and a visit to a cinema took care of the afternoon and it was time to catch the ferry back to the island. I dropped her off at the bar then made my way over the road to the China Fleet Club for a wash and change. I got back to the bar towards closing time to pick Mary Ann up and repeat the previous night's routine. This procedure was repeated every night except one.

On this particular night she asked me to go to her flat on my own and she would join me later. After some questioning she told me she had a client who she couldn't afford to let down. He was old, Chinese and lived near the top of the Peak. Living up there meant he must be worth a bob or two, so I could understand her wish to keep him sweet.

At her apartment I wanted to stay awake and make sure that she got home alright. However, the excesses of the previous few days caught up with me and I fell into a deep sleep. Next thing I remember was being turned onto my back and Mary Ann straddling me. After a few minutes of frantic movement she rolled off. By now I was fully awake and fully aroused. However, Mary Ann was now sleeping peacefully so I decided to leave both my frustration and curiosity until the morning. Upon awakening I tried some gentle probing. This solved one of my problems but not the other. She never did tell me the reason for her aggressiveness.

I guess I wasn't as worldly wise as I thought I was.

16

HOMEWARD BOUND

My Far East adventure was drawing to a close. The first thing to do was to sort out a "deep-sea box". I had accumulated numerous possessions over my two and a half year stay. In addition I had bought going-home presents for all the family. The only hand luggage we were allowed on board the troopship was our kitbag and one other piece. I had purchased the largest suitcase I could find, but this was still inadequate. The kitbag was virtually full with uniform, including all my blues which I had carted around Malaya for 30 months. We were advised to make sure they still fit us before setting off. Mine did. I had put on approximately 2 stone during my stay, but it was distributed over my whole body. Besides, the uniform was baggy to begin with.

Johnny Henstock hadn't fared so well when he departed a few weeks earlier. We measured the length of the 'V' insert in the back of his trousers. It was 10".

The remainder of our luggage was to travel in the hold. One of the large hangers at camp contained a number of wooden packing cases. We were allowed to select the size required and then set about painting it. The base colour was black with a blue diagonal stripe. Stencils were available so that we could print our name rank and number on one side and our home address on the other.

They didn't seem in too big a hurry to get rid of me. My 2 ½ year time came and went, although to be fair, they were tied to the sailing schedule of HMS Oxfordshire, and this was working to something like a 10 week cycle. I didn't mind waiting an extra month anyway.

My two big mates at Seletar were Pete and Geoff, and by great coincidence, they were due to return to Blighty at the same time. We arranged for our boat party on the evening before our departure and as usual it was to start in the NAAFI. However, there was a little matter of a darts league match involving our section to get out of the way first. We completed the singles and doubles in record time and made a rapid start on the 'gallon'. By the time we reached my second throw we were down to a finish. I quickly worked out the best way to go and threw for my first treble. It missed and landed in the single. Never mind, a different finish was still on. I went for my second treble, missed again and landed in the single. This left bull which I went for and plonked my arrow right in the middle. Of course I told everyone that that was the finish I had intended all the time. A good start to a great evening.

HMS Oxfordshire was a 'dry' ship. No booze at all—at least not on our decks, although I couldn't imagine the officers on the sun deck going without their G and T's. There was some 'bull' to do every morning keeping the place ship-shape, but as a corporal I was now in charge of a working party rather than having to scrub the decks myself.

Afternoons were spent sun-bathing or playing deck games. Whilst playing deck-hockey I got a stick in my face. It split the skin just under my eyebrow. I went down to sick bay where a young medical orderly put some stitches in whilst the ship was rolling about on a choppy sea. Could have been nasty!

Our first port-of-call was Colombo in Ceylon. Everyone was looking forward to getting ashore to stretch our legs and possibly sink in a couple of swift halfs. Unfortunately Ceylon is Buddhist and non-drinking. The next stop was Aden, at that time a British protectorate, so sure to have a couple of bars. 'Fraid not. This time the Muslims were the spoil sports.

As we sailed up the Red Sea the temperature began to drop. We were told that when we reached the Med. we would be changing into our blues. The Arabs knew this and were waiting for us. After negotiating the bottom end of the Suez Canal we reached the Bitter Lakes, where we moored-up in order to give the ships sailing south on the upper part time to clear. The Arabs pulled alongside us in their dhows. By shinning up the mast it put them on a level with the port-holes on our deck. Commerce then proceeded across the intervening gap.

They had a selection of gifts for sale, but also made it clear that they were prepared to trade. People were swapping their soon-to-be redundant KD's like there was no tomorrow. I made a fairly modest swap, getting a stuffed leather camel in exchange for a pair of KD socks. I did wonder why Arabs wanted long woolly socks. It also occurred that more effort went into making the camel than knitting a pair from scratch. Still, what did I know? It's probably why I'm not an international financier.

The final port of call before reaching Blighty was Gibraltar. With its British Bobbies and red letter boxes there was sure to be a bar here. Somehow I managed to be on the first tender to reach shore. There was a line of taxies waiting for us at the dock side. We didn't need to tell them where to go—they already knew. They dropped us off at a large barn-like building. Upon entering we were disappointed to find the place deserted. As we stood looking dejected, the locals began to arrive—barmen, waiters, even a band. Apparently, it was out of season and this place only opened for troopships. We had just been a bit quick off the mark, that's all.

We spent the whole of our 3 or 4 hour shore-leave at this establishment, then it was back to the waiting tenders. For some reason we were accompanied by a number of army MP's. As the tender set sail I looked across and saw an RAF lad being manhandled by one of these red caps. I went over to remonstrate with him and the next thing I knew was that my arm was twisted up my back. I was marched up the gangplank to the cheers of the squaddies hanging over the rails, and taken forward to be thrown in the brig. I remained here until the ship was well under way, then taken to a hearing conducted by the senior officer on board, who happened to be an army type.

Even if I had been slightly merry when I got on board, I was certainly sober by now. When the officer asked me why I had been arrested I went on the offensive with all guns blazing. I demanded that he find out the name of the corporal who manhandled me in order that I could redress him. He promised me that he would and dismissed me. Of course I knew that he wouldn't. The 'pongos' look after their own. Last stop Southampton, then a train ride to London. A bit of a struggle across London with a kitbag and a large suitcase. A train from Kings

Cross to Hull Paragon with a change at Doncaster, then a final taxi ride to Wellsted Street. As I walked up Salisbury Gardens I looked fondly at the row of stone plinths with their tell-tale holes.

One thing I quickly noticed was that the whole house had been almost entirely refurbished. Mum told me that she had used my money exclusively for this purpose so that I would have something to see when I got home. A very thoughtful gesture. They had even got a new piano with matching stool. I didn't ask what happened to the old one but I keep watching 'The Antique Roadshow' just in case.

I had 6 weeks leave to come. There was one week for every year that I had served abroad. In addition there was a scheme whereby you could carry forward one week per year of your annual leave to add to you disembarkation leave. I had chosen this option but in hindsight, it was not the best decision I had ever made. Both Bob and Dave were working away from home, Chris was courting and Mike and June were still at school.

A city can be a lonely place.

Pete and Geoff were going through the same withdrawal symptoms and we agreed on a series of mutual visits. First up was Pete and we other two set off for Hastings.

Pete's big hobby was fishing. Back in Singapore, I had accompanied him on several occasions to one of the local fishing ponds. Out there it had been rather pleasant sitting under a palm tree, dangling your worm in a well-stocked pond. In Hastings, Pete was planning a raid on a local pond. Because it was private we would have to go after dusk, but we were certain to strike lucky because Pete had spent the previous week preparing an area with 'ground bait'.

We made our way to the designated spot and began to assemble our tackle. Suddenly there was a flurry of movement on the water. Swimming towards us was a large flock of ducks. They were coming for their nightly supply of breadcrumbs which someone had so obligingly been providing for them.

We packed our gear and went to the "Jolly Fishermen" for a pint.

After about a week, the three of us made our way to Bolsover, near Chesterfield, to spend some time at Geoff's home. Then it was my turn to play host.

Hulls old quarters are not that extensive, but what there is had thankfully survived the worst of the blitz. I took them round the sights.

We admired King Billy sat on his golden horse guarding the public loos. If there was a prize for the strangest street name, "The Land of Green Ginger" must surely win. Whilst there, I showed them the smallest window in the World. William Wilberforce's house was conveniently situated close to Hulls oldest pub, "The Black Boy", so there was no need to get too dry from a surfeit of culture. There were several other cosy pubs all within staggering distance.

In our sober moments we taught Mike and June the intricacies of Mah Jong on a set that I had brought home. All in all they enjoyed their stay. So much so that they stayed on a couple of subsequent occasions, even though my commitments meant that I couldn't be there.

All this bonding helped to pass the time. Soon it was time to fulfil my final duty to Queen and Country.

17

RAF PATRINGTON

One of the final acts before leaving Singapore had been to nominate my next posting in Blighty. Once again I was asked for 3 possibilities in preferential order. I wrote:-

1) Patrington
2) Patrington
3) Patrington

I may be slow but I do eventually learn. I got Patrington!

So, what was the attraction of this particular spot? It was situated on the East Coast a dozen or so miles from Hull and I was "travelled-out" for the time being. It was a single purpose camp again, so quite small and compact. I even got my own room.

On my first day of work my shift drove out to a spot on the cliffs just south of Withernsea. There in a field was an updated version of the two types of ground radar. The only other structure in sight was a small hut in the centre of the field. The bus pulled up outside, we disembarked, filed in and descended a flight of stairs into a large underground control room.

This was serious stuff. We were in the middle of the Cold War. It was a 24 hour job, gazing at the screens looking for those tell-tale blips coming at us from Russia, and I was the one responsible for keeping those screens working. Fortunately, the rest of the guys on the shift were familiar with this updated equipment. If I had had more time at my disposal I would have asked to go back to Locking for a refresher course. However, with only 3 months to do it wasn't worth it. In true executive style I delegated. Those 3 months passed quickly enough and it was time for my demob party. I had chosen to hold it at the 'Spread Eagle' in Withernsea, and was very flattered at the number of mates that had come to bid farewell. After the strong ale in Malaya I couldn't get used to British beer, so had got in the habit of drinking Guinness. (bottles—no draft in those days) So many people wanted to buy me a drink that I started drinking vodka chasers between each pint.

At the end of the evening I remember climbing on a table to make a speech, but instead falling forward into a dozen pair of arms. I came round in my own bed the following day feeling fine.

At demob time one is given a chitty with a list of names on it. The idea is to visit each of these in turn and get signed-off. I had almost completed this on the previous day, and the only two names remaining were the station Warrant Officer and the station CO. I strolled into the W.O's office with my chitty in hand.

"Corporal Bennett" he said. "You had your demob party last night didn't you?"

I agreed, wondering what was coming.

"What have you done with the CO's flag?" he demanded

I protested that I didn't know what he was talking about. Apparently it had gone missing from the flag pole outside the offices. In an effort to intimidate me, he called the guardhouse and got the corporal in charge to come to his office. This guy was a mate of mine who had in fact been at the party, so we started discussing that.

Frustrated, the WO dismissed me saying that he wouldn't sign my chitty until the flag reappeared. Could he keep a civilian imprisoned on camp? I didn't know, but there was plenty to do. A nice little gym, snooker tables in the NAAFI and three meals a day. I made my way back to my room.

Out of curiosity, I looked in my locker drawer. There it was—the CO's flag! I hadn't the foggiest as to how it had got there, but one thing was sure, I wasn't prepared to give it back.

There was one thing I had to do though. Go back to the 'Spread Eagle' to apologise to my friend the landlord for any embarrassment I may have caused the night before. He told me that I had behaved impeccably, but there was just one thing. I had stacked my empty Guinness bottles under the bench seat on which I was sitting. When he cleared up the following morning, he had counted them. There were twelve!

Twelve pints of Guinness and twelve vodkas! I had done well to get to the end of the evening. The following day I got the message that the WO was prepared to sign me off. Finally there was only the CO to go. As I stood in front of him he said "So you're the bugger who's got my flag are you?" "Not me I protested.

"Never mind" he said. "I like a bit of initiative".

I was now a free man. I called a taxi, loaded all my belongings on and set off. As we drove past the guard house I flew the CO's flag out of the taxi window. My mate was on duty again and he gave me a snappy salute. 30 yards down the road I let the flag go. In the rear view mirror I saw my friend walking-on to retrieve it.

Making this sign fulfilled the secondary purpose of filling copious leisure time

Those homemade squat stands

414 Skiffle group

Lack of talent more than compensated for by our enthusiasm

On the Bungah beach

One of our many fancy dress evenings—Johnny Henstock is the totally unsuitable vicar

Pete and Geoff enjoy mums hospitality

If we didn't catch any fish at least we caught a few rays

Section Three

University

18

DARK SATANIC MILLS

In the final weeks of service, the RAF allow you time to go job-seeking. As they also issued travel warrants, **I** had taken advantage to visit a few electronic firms. I had even been offered a job at a couple. However, I had already decided on my next move.

It was clear that I was not happy with electrons. I needed something that I could see and feel. Looking at my qualifications and my love of building things, there was only one career path for me—a civil engineer.

The nearest University doing this course was Leeds, so I wrote to them with my c.v. They wrote back saying that I couldn't do a degree course in civils because I had no qualification in chemistry. Thank you very much Mr Stinky. I hope your nuts roast on the Bunsen burners of Hell! Leeds did point out however that Bradford was doing a civils course that didn't require chemistry. I wrote to them and was accepted. I managed to obtain a grant from Hull Council at very short notice, and very soon I was on my way.

It was a foggy Autumn morning when I alighted from the train at Forster Square Station. As I stood in front of the station my heart sank. There was a strange, sulphurous smell in the air and all the buildings were smoke-blackened. What had I let myself in for?

I was pondering my next move. I hadn't ruled out the possibility of returning home, when I heard an alien sound.

"Ey-up lad. Where's tha' bound?"

At least the natives were friendly. Doing a quick translation, I told him I was going to the Institute of Advanced Technology. [Bradford was still a couple of years away from getting its charter] He took my case and threw it in the back of his battered van

"Jump in" he said. "I'm going that way"

Travelling across town he pointed out various buildings such as the Wool Exchange and the City Hall. I could appreciate their magnificent architecture but what a pity they were so black. These buildings reflected the wealth that had once been generated in this industrial city. The same wealth was to be seen in the Italianate mills as their owners strove to demonstrate the principle—it is no good being powerful unless you can flaunt that power. Salt's Mill has now been declared a World Heritage Site and Lister's Mill has had a gentrified second coming, but many others have succumbed to acts of civic vandalism. We reached the College and my new friend dropped me off. Registering was relatively quick and painless, then it was a question of finding some digs. My van driving friend had written an address down for me and I took a taxi to Manningham Lane. The building that stood at the junction with Marlbourgh Road had clearly been an imposing residence at one time, but now served as the YMCA. The proprietoress was an Amazonian German lady who bore an uncanny likeness to Hattie Jacques, and I very soon found out that that was indeed her nickname.

I was allocated a bed in a large ground-floor room. Initially, I was the only occupant, but very soon there were two other arrivals. Coincidentally, they where both from Hull. Don had come with his job for Yorkshire Water, and his mate Mick had accompanied him for a change of scenery.

Another coincidence was that they were both into weight training, and we quickly set about finding somewhere to train. We found an ideal gym—The Windmill—which in those days was situated in an old mill in West Bowling. It was run by two vastly different characters. Jack was an active weight-lifter, whereas Fred was an overweight chain-smoker. I got to know them both really well over the next several years.

The gym itself was a bit of an eye-opener. After years of training by myself, I now found myself working-out with a room full of fellow enthusiasts. Many of them had attained high standards with a sprinkling of title holders including a Mr Britain. It also included a few home-made resistance machines—a foretaste of things to come.

The YMCA provided us with breakfast and an evening meal, and had a TV lounge which was normally full every evening. TV was still something of a novelty in those days and I usually joined the others on a non-training night. The fourth bed in our room was soon claimed by an Irish lad named Rod but naturally known to one and all as Paddy. He was in the same age range as us and interested in the same pursuits of getting a few beers down and chatting-up the girls

The bedrooms were bereft of furnishings apart from the beds themselves and a wardrobe each. The front door was locked every evening at 10 O'clock which wasn't a very Christian act for us young men. Being on the ground floor, I got into the habit of leaving one of the smaller sash windows slightly ajar. The trouble was, the word went round and others began availing themselves of this facility. My bed was next to this particular window, and often in the wee small hours I would be awoken by somebody crawling across my legs.

In the early days, I didn't know my way around Bradford's many drinking establishments, but I had been told that 'The Bowling Green' was a student pub, so one evening I made my way over there. There was only one other customer sitting at the bar, so I joined him and got into conversation. As the beer flowed the talk became more macho. He started bragging about his prowess at rugby union. I can't let him get away with that, I thought, so I told him I had played for the RAF in Malaya and scored the winning try against the Aussies.

"Is that so" he said. "I'm the captain of the 1st team and we're short of a good centre. You're playing on Saturday."

Too late to back out now. Too late to tell him that I didn't even know the rules. I played and I must have done alright because I got selected for the Wednesday team as well, which was at a higher level. I became quite friendly with my drinking companion and eventually confessed. By this time, I had learnt enough rules to get by, and my place in the team was secure.

B.I.T. was mainly situated in the Westfield Building on great Horton Road, but the Civil Engineering Faculty had its own salubrious spot—the remnants of the old Carlton Street School after the bulk of the building had been burnt down. I was doing the Institute of Civil Engineers course as were most of the others, although some were doing an external degree. We shared all of our classes, so they must have been doing their highly involved chemical experiments at night.

Our first year was known as a joint part one, which meant that we did hydraulics with the mechanical engineers and circuitry with the electrical engineers. I couldn't escape from those bloody electrons!

The course included structures which was mostly maths; surveying; building construction; geology and soil mechanics—all interesting stuff. Well, I thought so. The rest of the class had come straight from school which made me the eldest. As such, I was chosen to be the class representative on the Union Council, my first taste of administration.

In addition to my rugby, there was one other extra-curricular activity I was interested in—hiking. The Hiking Club had two things going for it. Firstly, Bradford was situated on the borders of the Yorkshire Dales—ideal walking country. Secondly, we shared this activity with the three teacher training colleges in the area. The coach would pick us up in Gt Horton Rd on one Sunday per month. From there, the route took in Margaret McMillans, Bingley Training College then over the tops to Ilkley Domestic Training College, known to one and all as Ilkley Pudding Club. From here, it was up the road and into one of the many Dales. The coach would drop us off at the chosen spot, and then set off to meet us at the other end. This meant that we could do linear walks as opposed to the circular ones necessary when using your own transport. Another essential when planning the route was that the walk must finish at one of the many lovely country pubs, so that we could replenish our lost energy. I got permission for Don, Mike and Paddy to accompany us on these hikes.

Paddy often managed to 'borrow' a vehicle from work most weekends and we would supplement our monthly hikes with walks of our own. I was quickly becoming familiar with the many choices on offer. Bradford may have had its own distinctive atmosphere, but one didn't have to travel far to find a green and pleasant land. Besides, there was a bonus. Once a year the mill chimneys stopped belching smoke and the other side of the valley would appear, Brigadoon-like, through the mist.

This phenomenon was known as 'Wakes Week.'

19

GOING DOWNHILL FAST

My big pal at college was Roger. He was one of the many students sponsored by British Rail. Finding out that my father was a railwayman gave us a common link. Another was that Roger lived on the outskirts of Hull. Over the next few years we found out a few more. Roger developed quite a taste for beer, and like me, he loved walking. We discovered another one by accident. The National Union of Students used to send round all sorts of interesting info. The notice that caught our eye was one promoting a skiing holiday during our Winter break. We decided to give it a go.

For the princely sum of £36 we were offered all travel from London to the resort; two weeks half-board at a pension type accommodation; ski hire; lift passes and lessons. We set off and at London we linked up with the rest of the party. Then it was a boat trip across the Channel followed by train across France, Switzerland and finally into Italy. A long journey not helped by the fact that it was done mostly in darkness. So dark that it was difficult to comprehend we were travelling through the mountains. At one point I glanced up into the darkness and saw a floodlit castle high above us. It appeared to be floating on air.

At last we disembarked the train and climbed aboard a coach to take us on our final leg. It was still dark which was just as well considering the hairpin bends and sheer drops that were revealed on our return journey. Eventually we reached Campittelo, our destination, checked-in and crashed-out.

In the morning we awoke to brilliant sunshine. I drew the curtain and gazed across at the snow-covered slope. I looked up . . . . and up . . . . and up. Finally I saw the top, the distinctive rock formation of the Dolomites. What a way to start a holiday. I have been skiing many times since, but nothing can match the thrill of that first view.

After breakfast, we got fitted out with boots and skis. In those days the method of determining your ski length was to match them to the height of your up-stretched arm. As a tall guy, this came to something like 7'6" which is a lot of ski to control when you are a beginner. Years later this method was to change and beginners were given much shorter skis.

The lessons were good. An instructor with infinite patience put us through simple drills to build our confidence then gradually introduced easy turns and stopping techniques. Lots of tumbles of course, but also lots of laughter. As we improved, we were introduced firstly to the baby lifts and finally to the main lifts. What a thrill to be stood on top of a mountain feeling lord of all you survey.

Mornings were taken up with lessons and afternoons were for free skiing. Towards the end of the holiday, we bombed down the slope to catch the last lift up again. On hindsight, not the wisest thing to do. We'd had a tiring day and it was beginning to get dark. What the Hell,—we were young and foolish. Halfway down we managed to lose the piste completely and finished up in deep snow. There is a way to ski in powder snow but we hadn't been shown how. I took off my skis with the idea of walking down. Big mistake! I immediately sunk in up to my waist. Panic was beginning to set in. Fortunately, two of the lift operators had seen our predicament and came over to help. They guided us back to the piste and then made sure we got down safely. I don't speak much Italian, but I am sure I caught the phrase 'crazy Englishmen.'

All too soon the holiday came to an end, but we were both hooked. Many years later, Roger wrote to me to let me know that he had become a part-time ski instructor.

20

THE SHAPE OF THINGS TO COME

The academic year sped by quickly and the long summer break was fast approaching. Time to think about getting a summer job. From our fire-remnant classroom we had observed the University rising Phoenix-like all around us. I went one day to the site office of the main contractor, Higgs and Hill, and after a bit of negotiation, I was offered a job as a trainee site engineer.

The site was broken down into three different areas of work, each with its own foreman. The main teaching block on Richmond Road was nearing its full 12 storey height. The link block containing the Great and Small Halls was just getting out of the ground. The workshop block was also nearing its full height but there was a quarter of the building missing where the remains of Carlton Street School stood.

I was surprised to find that there was no permanent site engineer. Instead, the foreman responsible for each block was also responsible for the basic setting out on his own patch. If they came across something they couldn't manage, they sent for an engineer from head office. Now they had me this was unnecessary. But hang on! Wasn't I supposed to be a trainee? Who was supposed to be training me? I spent the bulk of my time in the workshop block setting out the northlight roof or plumbing-up the numerous columns, but I still managed to get involved in the other blocks. For instance, I was asked to level the roof on the main block. The only way I could set-up the Dumpy level was on the two walls of an internal angle which meant that I had to stand on a scaffold plank spanning the same two walls with a 120ft drop below me. This was a predicament I would find myself in numerous times in the coming years. Good job I had a head for heights.

Another time I found myself setting-out the curved wall at the rear of the Great Hall. The University is currently going through a multi-million pound refurbishment and my wall has been enhanced with some nice timber panelling. I usually give it a bit of a polish when passing.

Every engineer requires an assistant known as a chainman. If you are levelling, the chainman holds the staff, and when setting out with a theodolite, he is usually required to bang in a peg or two. Additionally, all measuring requires someone at either end of the tape.

Ideally, the chainman should be a trainee engineer, but that was my designation so it looked like I would have to find a decent labourer and train him up. The problem was solved in an almost satisfactory manner. Another young student had been set on for the summer as a labourer. When it was discovered that he was studying civils at Leeds, he became an automatic choice. This was fine except for one small problem. Being paid as a labourer meant that he was drawing approximately double the wage I was getting as a trainee. In addition, he was being paid for overtime, whereas I, being staff, was on a flat rate and building, like farming is another industry that relies on daylight.

I went to see the site manager to protest, but there was nothing doing. I even volunteered to give-up my traineeship and be re-employed as a labourer but he reminded me that I had signed a contract, and that was binding. My first lesson that construction was a dog-eat-dog existence.

21

INVOLVMENTS

Back in the classroom for my second year, I found that my services were in great demand. My rugby-playing colleagues proposed me for the vacant position of sports secretary, and I got elected unopposed. This appointment meant a position on the Union Executive, which involved weekly meetings. Regular duties included liaising with the ground staff over pitch requirements, hiring buses for away fixtures and, most importantly, making sure that the after-match sandwiches were ordered. Not very onerous tasks. I suggested to the Exec. It would be a good idea if the Union had its own set of weights so that the rugby lads and even the footballers could get stronger. I think they must have had a few bob spare, because they agreed without question. The next job was finding somewhere to put them. The Union owned two buildings on Manville Terrace, Nos 1&5. No. 1 was the student canteen and No. 5 was the Union offices. I was offered the cellar of No. 5. It was back to the dark ages.

The ceiling was barely higher than head height, and the only way to do any overhead work was sitting down. Fortunately, this sad state of affairs didn't last too long. A building had become vacant further up Gt. Horton Rd. and the student union had temporary possession. The building was variously known as 'The old bakery' or 'The Polish Club.' No doubt it had been both in previous incarnations. Whatever, the outcome was that the weights club now had a decent-sized room. We could even take the weights outside into an enclosed courtyard if the weather was clement. In spite of this, I appeared to be the only person training there.

Another job the Sports Sec. had was responsibility for ordering club colours. The various club captains would nominate individuals for these for meritous performance. I had won mine the previous year, although I am sure it was only for turning up every week. The colours consisted of a nice blazer badge depicting the City of Bradford coat of arms. In my second year, Bradford had abandoned us as we were in the process of getting our own charter. To cover this gap, I instituted a competition to come up with our own, and the winning design was incorporated into a badge. I was awarded my club colours again for my second year. For my third year, the university had got its own insignia from the College of Heralds, and this was duly incorporated into a badge. Upon receiving my third set of colours, I was in the unique position of having three different badges.

I was asked one day if I would accompany the University Architect to Salford University to have a look at their gymnasium. It seemed that the new Richmond Road building was to include one and he was working on the layout. He explained that it was to be situated on the ground floor of the link block to the right of the Gt. Horton Rd. entrance. Having spent the previous summer roving all over this building, I was familiar with this space. The two long sides and one short side formed a rectangular shape, but the fourth side bordering Gt. Horton Rd., was at an angle. This had the effect of forming a triangular area that would normally have been difficult to fit into a gym layout. I suggested to the Architect that this might make a suitable space for a weight-training area. He was a bit dubious at first, but I had the whole journey from Bradford to Salford and back to convince him. I either did or wore him down, because he agreed, but it would be many years before I had the chance to confirm it.

Another post had become vacant. The leader of the hiking club had graduated and I was asked to take over the job. Well, I did know where all the pubs were located! This was another fairly simple task—ordering the coach, plotting the route and letting everyone know the date and location; but it still took up a bit of my time.

I was nominated for a third job. Rag Week was an important part of student life. Not only did it raise a lot of money for charity, it gave students a chance to let their hair down. The previous year, I had got involved in a number of events, and this had not gone un-noticed. I was nominated for the post of stunts coordinator. A good Rag stunt served several purposes. It brought publicity, it entertained the public and it gave the opportunity to rattle a few collection tins.

Pub crawls were a fairly standard event. The idea was to start on the perimeter of town and work your way along a main radial route into town, calling at every pub along the way for half a pint. In those days, there seemed to be a pub on every street corner. In my first year, the route had been Wakefield Rd. starting at Tong Lane. This was probably to accommodate the students living at Tong Hall, BIT's one and only hall of residence. O.K., but it was one hell of a walk. For my year I chose Manchester Road from Odsal Top. A much shorter walk, but an abundance of watering-holes

We got plenty of publicity from our local paper, The Telegraph and Argus, for one stunt which involved a bunch of us dressed in Roman togas, each throwing a discus up the side of Pen-y-Gent. The winner was supposed to be the one who took the least number of throws to reach the top. It was O.K. when we set off from Horton-in Ribblesdale with the slope being fairly gradual, but as we neared the top, the slope increased dramatically. It was not unusual to throw your discus and then duck hurriedly as it came bounding back down the slope toward you. Eventually we all managed to reach the top by fair means or foul. I don't think there was any sort of prize for the winner other than personal satisfaction, but we did get some strange looks when we called into the local dressed in our togas.

Although by definition Rag was only for one week, the process of co-ordinating it all started several weeks in advance. The event was shared by the young ladies of our three neighbouring training colleges and I found myself going to one or another of them fairly frequently to discuss one scheme or another. It was a hard job, but hey! Somebody had to do it.

Anyone of these activities would have been possible to fit in with my academic duties. However, with doing all three, I began to miss more and more lectures. It was obvious that my studying was suffering. I wrote to Hull Council to tell them I was doing a sabbatical year and would they fund me a further year. They agreed without question.

There was one other significant happening at this time. One day I was called into Hattie's office and told that I was to be ejected from the

YMCA. When I asked why, she said I was a bad influence on the other inmates. I don't remember twisting anyone's arm to force them out for a drink, but I wasn't going to argue. The YMCA was having a decidedly negative effect on my love-life. Besides, I knew of a super student flat that was shortly to have rooms available.

I told the boys about my impending departure and they became most upset, particularly Don. He stormed into Hattie's office and called her 'another Teutonic dictator.' He was also invited to leave.

Paddy came out in sympathy and the three of us began a new life at 172 Toller Lane. We had the middle and upper floors of a large end-terrace house. The middle floor had a kitchen, bathroom, study and a large lounge. The top floor contained two large single bedrooms and an even larger double bedroom. One of the existing residents was still in residence, so we had a full compliment. He was doing Pharmacy and I used to take a sneaky peek at his textbooks when he was out. Plenty of photos of naughty bits but not exactly a turn on.

This was the beginning of the 'swinging sixties' and new pop groups were appearing daily, but as a sophisticated 24 year old I was past all that nonsense. One day Roger and I walked down into town. As we passed the Gaumont I could see the posters advertising a forthcoming concert. Top of the bill was a group called 'The Beatles'. I turned to Roger and said "Fancy calling yourself Beat-less. I can't see them getting far with a name like that."

I was interested in Sinatra, Ella and other big-band singers, but my main passion was still jazz. Bradford was a good place to be if you were into Trad with there being a different venue every night of the week. I can't remember the exact sequence, but the pubs involved included The Market Tavern; The Brown Cow in Bingley; The Spotted House; Link Bob; The Bankfield was always an upmarket Sunday night venue, but the star of the show was Saturday night in the Student Club. This was a cellar with a flagged floor and vaulted ceiling, being the sole remains of a brewery that had once occupied the site. In spite of its unpretentiousness and the fact that it was unlicensed, the Student Club enjoyed most of the Country's top bands during its existence. To relieve the drabness, the management got a young lad called Hockney to come down from the Art College and paint murals on the walls. He did a nice job, but whatever happened to him?

22

HAPPY CAMPERS

As my second academic year neared its end, it was time to think about another summer job. I felt that combining a job with a holiday was more preferable than gaining more experience in the building industry. That was how, on the appointed day, I made my way to Butlins Holiday Camp at Filey to take up an executive position. I was to be chief washer-up in one of the large kitchens.

A basic job with relatively short hours with the bonus of having the run of the camp. I made use of the pool and visited a number of the shows. I saw the same wrestling match about four times. Apparently they worked on a two week cycle to correspond with the fortnight holiday periods. I got to know the script very well. As usual, there was a goody and a baddy. The baddy would use all his dirty tricks to get the audience booing. Eventually he would throw the goody out of the ring, at which point the goody lost his rag, climbed back into the ring and gave the baddy a good pasting. He was declared the winner, and everybody was satisfied.

On the fourth occasion, things went wrong. The goody was thrown out of the ring as usual, but he fell awkwardly and was unable to climb back into the ring. After much confusion, the referee had to declare the baddy the winner, to be met with thunderous booing. I didn't mind—I was the only one cheering.

After a while, the attractions of the camp began to wane. I found myself travelling into Filey to visit old stamping grounds. The staff chalets were off to one side of the main camp, and we had our own bar. Although the beer was cheaper, the place lacked atmosphere, and a number of us got into the habit of going into the nearby village of Hunmanby to do our relaxing. One free afternoon I borrowed a camp bike and rode up there for a bit of exercise. It was uphill all the way, which involved continuous pedalling. After a swift half or two, I mounted up and set off back. I came to a steepish part of the road. There was a car parked on the left and an oncoming car in the right-hand lane. I decided that there wasn't enough room to get through, so I reached for the brakes. Shock, horror! There were no brakes.

I tried to stop pedalling but the pedals refused to stop, and my feet flew off them. I realized belatedly that it was a fixed wheel bike and a crash was looming. I swerved onto the nearside footway, just managing to miss the parked car. I saw the rear door was wide open with a pair of feet showing below. There was no corresponding head at the top and I just about had time to realize that he was bending forward as my foot slammed into the door. There was a loud cry of shock and pain as the owner was projected into the back of his vehicle. Unable to stop, I careered on my way. Eventually, the bike slowed sufficiently for me to get it under control, but by then I was a long way from the scene. I sometimes wonder if the owner extracted himself in time to see my disappearing back, or if he is still wondering what hit him.

In order to fill the time and make some extra cash, I took an evening job as a waiter in one of the bars. I was doing alright, making a few tips and enjoying listening to the band playing all the latest hits. The closing number, as I recall was an excellent rendition of Billy Fury's 'Halfway to Paradise.'

Don, Mike and Paddy had decided to come and visit me. They pitched their tent close by and came in through the main gate. They shouted 'Hi-di-hi' to the security man and he duly shouted 'Ho-di-ho' back. They found a seat in my section, ordered a round, and invited me to join them. I told them I wasn't supposed to drink on duty but they were insistent, so we came to a compromise. I got a pint and left it on their table, having a crafty sip each time I passed. I thought I had got away with it, but no such luck. Someone on the bar had seen what was happening and had shopped me. I had to go and see the Bar Manager. He asked if there was a good reason why he shouldn't sack me. "Yes." I replied. "Because I am a bloody good waiter."

He considered this for a moment, and then said "OK, you are reinstated."

I thanked him, but told him I was leaving anyway as I couldn't work with sneaks.

Was I being bloody-minded again, or just making a point?

I was prepared to give my weight-training a miss for this particular summer, but I struck lucky. I quickly found that one of the other workers had brought a set of weights with him, and was in the habit of rolling them onto the grass outside his chalet in the evening to train. I learnt that his name was Eric and he worked in the ladies hairdressing shop. He was happy for me to join him.

All the other hairdressers were young women and they used to sit outside the chalets in the evening sunlight watching us perform. As Eric was a colleague of theirs, he came in for a lot of stick, but with me being a stranger, I got off lightly. One girl was being particularly cheeky, and Eric picked her up and threatened to drop her in a patch of nettles. However, she was laughing so much, she wet herself. Eric got most of it on his hand.

23

COINCIDENCE OR FATE

Back at the Uni. for my third and final year and things were happening. The remnants of Carlton St. School needed to be demolished in order that the workshop block could be completed. In spite of the main building not being finished, the Civil Engineering Faculty moved into the lower floors.

Social life revolved around the Windsor Hall complex. A nice dance floor, a big bar and a bandstand that hosted many of the top bands of the day. Humphrey Littleton was a frequent visitor. There was a dance every Saturday night and they were always well attended, being open to students and non-students alike.

On the first Saturday of term, Paddy and I went down as usual, and also as usual, we remained in the bar until closing time. Sufficiently lubricated, we made our way onto the dance floor to split two girls who were dancing together. My partner looked vaguely familiar.

"Didn't I see you a couple of weeks ago peeing on Eric's hand?" I said.

Not the World's greatest chat-up line.

"That wasn't me "she protested. "It was my friend."

She told me her name was Irene and she lived in Bradford, but as that was the last dance, we had no time for further conversation. The following Saturday, the same thing happened. In the bar 'til the death, staggering onto the dance floor, splitting a pair of young ladies, and finding I was dancing with Irene again. A few more hurried words, then cheerio.

On the following Friday, Paddy and I decided to go to the Mecca for a change. Different location, same routine, but this time the dancing continued after last orders had been called. We did our usual trick of separating two young ladies and once again I found myself dancing with Irene. After a couple of dances, we went upstairs for a coffee. She told me that she hardly ever went out on a Friday as the following day she had to go to work. I found out that she lived very close to our flat and we arranged a date for the following night.

Our Pharmacy friend had departed, and there was just the three of us living in the flat. I must admit to feeling a slight twinge of regret as the boys set off for the usual Saturday night shenanigans. I had been down to the off-licence to buy a container-full of wine from the wood. The last job to do before I set off to the meeting place was to light all the candles I had placed around the room.

We had agreed to meet at the telephone boxes at the Toller Lane roundabout, a spot roughly half way between where we both lived. I got to the appointed place early and waited . . . . and waited . . . . and waited. I had been stood-up. Naturally, I was disappointed, but at least I could catch up with the boys and drown my sorrows. The bus-stop was just round the corner, but wait a minute. What about all those bloody candles! I went back to the flat to blow them out, and then set off to join the boys. The quickest way to the Toller Lane bus stop was straight down Little Lane, but I decided to take the longer route via Toller Lane roundabout. As I passed the telephone box, I glanced inside and there was Irene looking all sweet and demure. Of course, it befell me to explain that I was not the one who was late. Anyway, it didn't really matter as we made our way back to the flat. I had got Irene there on the pretext of listening to my collection of jazz records, which we did, but we also did a lot of talking.

On reflection, I had led a very male oriented life. Four brothers, boys' schools, the RAF and now an all-male engineering course. I usually found it hard work talking to girls, but not with Irene. The conversation just flowed, and when there was a lull, I was happy with the silence too. By the end of the evening we had decided to become an item. After that we saw each other constantly. On a lunchtime I would walk across town to where Irene worked and we would stroll over to have a bite at Pie Tom's in Kirkgate Market.

I had arranged to go home in October to visit Hull Fair, something I loved as a child but had not seen for several years. Irene came with me and stayed the weekend with my parents. I had never taken a girl home before, let alone one I had only known for a few weeks. The hands of fate were at work. I don't ever remember proposing, we just started discussing a wedding date. Neither of us believed in long courtships. If you are sure, why wait. Early Spring should give us enough time to make all the arrangements.

I had booked to go skiing again and I couldn't fit in another holiday, so we decided to make that our honeymoon. I pulled a few strings and got Irene on the NUS compliment. It was back to the Dolomites again, although a different resort. It snowed persistently which wasn't conducive to skiing, so we stayed indoors a lot. The guy I was rooming with and the girl in with Irene were also a courting couple, so it didn't take much to organize a room swap. Well you can't fight your destiny.

Upon returning to Bradford, we went to see the vicar and set the date. I organized a couple of venues for post nuptial celebrations, bought a ring and sent out the invitations. I also set about finding somewhere for us to live. I spent days travelling around Bradford looking for something suitable, but didn't have much success. I remember looking at one in Great Horton where all the walls were hung with pink chiffon. As the two guys that showed me round where similarly attired, I didn't spend too much time at that one.

There was no doubt that 172 Toller Lane had spoiled us for choices. Eventually, Irene suggested that she could move in there as a temporary measure. It would be a cheap solution, and she certainly hit it off with the boys. I told our landlady what we had in mind and she allowed me to personalize one of the rooms for our own use.

For my stag party, we did a tour of our favourite pubs, finishing up in the upstairs room of the "Alex." We decided to give them our repertoire of rugby songs. The manager invited us to leave and never darken his doors again.

March 2nd 1963 is a date I shall never forget. It was the last time I ever visited a barber. Oh, and it was also our wedding day.

In spite of all my best intentions, they had persuaded me to be the Rag stunts chairman again. With Rag Week fast approaching, many of my fellow students thought that my wedding was a stunt. Some of them still do.

My classmates formed a guard of honour with survey poles. Our niece and nephew, David and Diana were our pageboy and bridesmaid and Roger was my best man. It was a chilly day with flurries of snow about and little David was freezing in his thin sailor's suit. He came out with that well known phrase "I'm never going to be a bloody bridesmaid again" and, as far as I know, he hasn't. Irene's sister, Mary, was plastered and had to be carried into church. She had broken her leg a couple of weeks earlier. The first reception was for relatives and close friends only and was in the upstairs room of the "Alex". I don't think the manager recognized me.

The second reception was held at the University clubhouse at Woodhall and was for everyone else. It seemed that most of the University was there, including classmates, rugby club and hiking club members. Irene had brought many of her hairdressing friends, and there was a good sprinkling of young ladies from the various Training Colleges. Many of these were dressed in black and weeping for some reason. Music was supplied via a record player, but this was supplemented to a great extent by my Mum on the piano. For our parties back in Hull, we had always bought a beer barrel. With Woodhall having no bar, we had elected to do the same. Of course, the barrel was much larger. I had checked the law and we didn't need a licence if the beer was being given away. It took some emptying and the party went on into the small hours of the morning. My family was supposed to go back to Hull that evening, but had missed their last train. Dave and his future wife Diana risked the journey on his scooter, a friend put Mum and Dad up for the night and Irene and I found ourselves bedding down Chris, Mick and June in our lounge at 3.00AM. It was a good job we had already had the honeymoon.

Posing again

Pen-y-Gent became considerably steeper

The forbidden pint

David not enjoying being a bloody bridesmaid

The blushing bride

Skiing continued to be an attraction for many years, its benefits are many—the fitness factor, the exotic locations and the fact that it's a family sport.

Section Four

Building a Better Britain

24

NEW BEGINNINGS

The academic year rolled on. I did my finals and started looking for a job. The early 60's were boom years for the building trade, and one of my first letters elicited a positive reply. After a successful interview, I found myself working for George Wimpey.

I started work in early August and Irene finished work a few weeks later. It seemed that her 'lump' was kicking her customers in the back of their heads.

My first job was setting out flats and maisonettes on a site at Gaisby Lane. This wasn't too far from the flat as the crow flies, but much further when undertaken on two buses. Also, the usual early start and late finish associated with the building industry made for long days. Management always used to say that we would get the time back during the dark nights of winter. However, I have never seen a programme of works that allowed for short hours, and can remember many an occasion when I have levelled a floor, for instance, by torchlight. Notwithstanding any of this, the work was varied and interesting, and I concluded that I had made the right choice.

Irene's pregnancy was progressing smoothly, although it worried me that she was still doing some of her regular customers at home. It might be flattering to know that 'nobody does it like you' but that doesn't excuse making a person stand on her feet for long periods in her condition.

The work was fairly straightforward. Being a greenfield site, the first job was to strip-off all the topsoil and stack it for re-use. The various blocks were then roughly set out and the ground reduced to give a level platform. The corners of the blocks were then accurately set out and projected onto hurdle-like profiles clear of the working area. Strip footings were dug down to load-bearing strata and concreted. Brickwork would bring the building up to ground floor level, which could then be concreted.

Wimpey had their own unique way of constructing walls above ground—'no-fines' concrete. Concrete is usually a mixture of cement, sand and aggregate, and when mixed properly, is a strong load-bearing material. By eliminating the sand, the strength was reduced, but other qualities were gained. No-fines had the appearance of cinder toffee with the voids giving it the thermal properties of a cavity wall. Strangely enough, it was also water-proof. Rain could penetrate of course, but gravity took over before it got too far, and the voids were too big for capillary action. Anyway, external walls were always rendered for appearance and all internal walls would be plastered. Construction was very quick with the no-fines being poured between two shutters. It was load bearing to a height of about five storeys.

Low rise blocks did not need too much engineering input once they had got out of the ground, so I often found myself going out to other sites for the day. I visited a number of speculative housing sites around the district, sometimes to set a few houses out, or, if it was a new site, to survey and level it.

Irene was getting near her time, and I had agreed with the site agent that when she telephoned, I would get a lift in the site van back to the flat. On the day it all kicked off, Sod's Law was in full operation. I had been sent to Hoyle Court, on the far side of Baildon to survey a field for some future spec. housing.

The van driver eventually found me and drove me back to Gaisby Lane to drop the theodolite off and get changed. He then drove me over to the flat where I arrived almost three hours after Irene had rung. I ran down to our telephone box at the roundabout and 'phoned for an ambulance.

At St Luke's, Irene asked if I could stay with her for the birth. In those days this was unheard off, but Irene can be very persuasive. They dressed me up in a gown, cap and mask and gave me a leg to hang on to. I remember there being a lot of screaming until a nurse told me to shut-up, then it was all quiet.

Anne Louise arrived shortly after weighing-in at 8lb 1oz.

25

A MOVING TIME

At the flat things were happening. Paddy had decided to change jobs but he was late for work on his first morning and was sacked. He returned to Ireland.

Don was busy courting and it wouldn't be long before he was moving on. Two new students moved in. Dave and Mont were potholers and had a battered old van which was to prove useful. They organized parties at the flat just as we had done, but most of their guests were strangers to us. Anne slept through all the racket, but it was clearly time to move on.

I began looking at houses once again. We did look at other parts of the City but our main search area was Heaton. It was close to Irene's parents, was close to the shops and had good bus connections. We quickly found what we were looking for although I am sure we both had different reasons for our choice.

Irene had lived all her life in a back-to-back in the shadow of Lister's Mill and had always considered the large semis on Duchy Drive to be the epitome of high-class living. Although my upbringing had been similarly cramped, my reasons were far more practical.

The house had stood empty for about a year, and the previous owner had not attempted to modernise it. This probably conspired to keep the price down to within our budget. Also, I could see the potential. On our first visit, we stood in the breakfast room at the side of the house. This was separated from the rather small kitchen by a rather large range extending up to the ceiling. I picked up a poker which was lying nearby and gave the range an almighty crack.

"This will have to go for a start" I said.

"Yes dear," said Irene. "But don't you think we ought to buy it first?"

We put in an offer and after a bit of haggling, we settled on a price of £2250. This was approximately two and a half times my salary, which was the maximum available in those financially prudent times.

Upon receiving the keys, I took a week off work to be at home on the range. The metalwork was easy and soon succumbed to a large hammer. The remaining brickwork was a different matter. With the kitchen being a lean-to, this brickwork was actually supporting an outside wall above first floor level. I had of course realized this, and had already discussed the procedure with various tradesmen on site.

The first job was to obtain a steel joist. With my usual luck, I found one at the very first scrap yard that I visited. Eight feet long was spot-on; 6" deep equated to two courses of brickwork and 4" wide was just right for supporting a brick wall. Mont gave me a lift in his van and I was ready.

I made a hole in the inside wall large enough to take one end of the joist. This end was placed on a piece of slate to act as a fulcrum and the other end which projected into the kitchen was supported on an acrow prop which I had 'borrowed' from Uncle George. I removed a couple of bricks along the line of the joist and the whole assembly was swung over to occupy this space. This procedure was slowly repeated and the joist was gradually eased into position. The final job was to remove a few bricks from the outer wall so that the final inch or so of easing could be achieved. As I removed the plaster, I was surprised to find timber. It was the end of the lintel spanning the back door. I took out a few bricks from above it and swung my joist in. It was a perfect fit. I must have been good in a previous life.

Over the coming years I would knock a few other walls down, but the current priority was to make the place habitable. The first mortgage payment would soon be due and it was not a good idea to be paying rent at the same time.

From living in one room to living in seven was quite a change. We didn't need a removals van—Mont's small vehicle was enough to move our few belongings. With donated bits and pieces from friends and family, we had enough to keep us going. Far from feeling like paupers, we felt like royalty. Besides, with all the work still to do in the house, it was to our advantages to keep it uncluttered. The dining room, for example remained unfurnished for quite some time. It became a storeroom for all the building materials I was accumulating.

It also became a temporary gymnasium.

26

SPREADING THE WORD

My training had become somewhat restricted of late with the long hours of work and the responsibilities of fatherhood. Shortly after moving into the house, I got a message from the Student Union. It seemed that the new gym was up and running and the 'Old Bakery' was due to be demolished to make room for further development. My old weights were surplus to requirements and would I like to collect them. With a little help from brother-in-law, Ian, I got them back to the house.

I had now gone full circle and was back to training at home. I had a comprehensive set of weights, dumbbells, a bench and squat stands. I even persuaded Irene to train with me.

Most ladies are wary of weight training. They think they only have to look at a barbell in order to change into a Russian shot-putter. On the other hand, they will spend hours on cardiovascular machines. They avidly watch the little box recording the calories used and think of all that fat they are burning off.

Unfortunately, the vast majority of those calories are not from fat. So, where do they come from? Well, there is a clue in the name of the activity—aerobics [air-robics]. That's right-air-or more specifically, oxygen.

There is a small amount of fat used, but many frustrated trainee falls by the wayside long before any useful results are seen. The other big mistake is that the trainee, in the mistaken belief that they are burning calories at a rate of knots, will think they are free to neglect their diet.

So where does weight-training fit into the picture? The first point is that the term 'bodybuilding' is a misnomer. Everybody has all the muscle they are ever going to have. The point is that the body is extremely efficient and will only use the amount of muscle it is called upon to use in everyday life. If the heaviest thing you lift is a pint, then the only active fibre will be that required to lift said pint. All the other fibres are still there, but are dormant. All weight-training does is gradually re-awaken this dormant fibre.

Women as a gender tend not to have too much muscle fibre. Even if they managed to re-awaken it all, which is highly unlikely, they would look toned rather than muscular. On the other hand, it is muscle that converts body fat into energy. The more active muscle one has, the higher their basal metabolic rate. This means, for instance, that a well toned person is burning fat even when they are asleep. This can't be a bad thing.

Where does diet fit into the picture? Well, it is important, of course, but I don't like the word 'diet'. Apart from being a four-letter word, it implies something that one goes on and comes off. On the other hand, sensible eating is something that you do for life.

As a rule, food intake should approximate the following guidelines :- Carbohydrates 60%; Protein 20%; Fat 20%. The body requires fat for reasons other than stored energy. For example, all the vital organs are surrounded in fat to act as shock absorbers. However, one can easily achieve 20% of total intake without really trying. I am not an advocate of reading labels, nor do I believe in counting calories, but it is important to know the fat content of some common foods. Some cheeses for instance have fat contents around 35%. If you cannot cut these foods completely, at least cut back. A simple rule would be to cut out all food with a fat content over 20%.

I explained all this to Irene before she started training. Our marriage was still in that blissful state where she believed all that I told her. Her weight immediately after Anne's birth was just under 13 stones. Of course, she would have lost some of this anyway, without doing too much. The challenge was, how much more would she lose using the weights, and what effect would it have.

In fact, she got all the way down to her target weight of nine and a half stones. In addition, she was so toned that she could holiday in a bikini for many years to come.

Whether it was a lack of atmosphere in our home gym or the fact that I was over-demanding, I don't know, but Irene decided to join a commercial gym. She found one in Gt. Horton with a ladies-only section, a precursor of things to come. This was in fact 'The Windmill' which had been on the move since its West Bowling home had been demolished.

I accompanied her there on one or two occasions and renewed my acquaintance with Fred and Jack.

Work at home progressed steadily. I knocked through from the lounge to the dining-room, did a couple more jobs in there, and started to decorate. My gym was moved out to the garage which was OK in summer but tended to test your resolve in winter. I had to come up with something else.

There was a new piece of apparatus in vogue at that time, and I decided to give it a try. The Bullworker was being promoted by David Prowse who was to achieve fame as the Green Cross Code Man and later on, as Darth Vadar. The principle behind the Bullworker depended upon static contraction rather than dynamic, but it served its purpose and kept me in touch for the next couple of years.

There was one other free service that Dave Prowse offered. If you sent him your current measurements and a few other details, he would send you a forecast of your potential. I thought it was more relevant to send him my measurements from the day I first started, so I told him that I was 15 years old, weighed 9st 11lb, had a 10" upper arm and a 35" inflated chest along with other measurements. A few days later, I got my forecast back. I was pleased to see that I had already exceeded all of them.

27

MAKING WAVES

At work, I had moved on to the ill-fated Raynor House at the bottom of Manchester Rd. A row of shops at the ground floor, with two levels of maisonettes above, it represented a fairly simple engineering task. There was however a couple of new facets to learn.

With it being a brown-field site, much of the reduced-level dig was in old foundations. If we came across existing cellars for instance, these had to be cleared out and the resulting hole filled with consolidated limestone. One of my jobs was to record this additional work.

One day, we had a visit from the area manager, Mr Limply. He asked me if the Clerk of Works was checking my measurements. I replied that he was. The Clerk of Works is the client's representative on site and is responsible for ensuring all aspects of good building practice are observed. In this case, the client was Bradford Council.

I idly wondered why Mr Limply was concerned about the efficiency of the C.O.W. I knew of course that all materials were accurately recorded in the Bill of Quantities at take-off stage. The only unknowns were what happened below ground.

With the requirement for the fronts of the shops to be open, the structural elements required pad footings bearing columns and supporting concrete beams. Pad footings were merely rectangles of reinforced concrete designed to spread the load of whatever was built on the top. The dig for these footings could be set out from string lines attached to my profiles, but the following job needed to be much more accurate. The standard procedure was to place four short scaffold battens over each pad in a 'noughts and crosses' grid and secure them to the ground. With the aid of a theodolite, the engineer could then drop his grid lines onto these battens so that the centre-lines of each column were depicted by four nails.

The various tradesmen would then be able to carry out the correct sequence. First up was the steel fixer who would use the nails to centralize his steel cage and starter bars for the columns. After concreting the pad, the joiners would follow on and position the 'kicker'

This kicker was very important to the accuracy of the entire building. It consisted of a 3"x 2" timber square constructed to the dimensions of the proposed column. Once this had been concreted and stripped, the shutters for the column could be clamped to the kicker and plumbed-up.

If everything had been done correctly, one could see a neat line of columns emerging from the ground.

One day, I arrived on site and ran my eye along the columns. The last one to be cast was clearly out of line. I asked the joiners what had gone wrong. It seemed that the general foreman, in an effort to gain some brownie points, had gone in on the Sunday morning to prepare the next batch of kickers. Unfortunately, he had strung his line from the edge of the last column to be poured, to the nail on my profile. He was using two different points of reference—the edge of one column lining through to the centre line of another.

With hindsight, I should have checked his setting out, but as they say, hindsight is a wonderful thing. The column was quietly knocked-down and I re-set it in its correct position. On Mr Limply's next visit, I asked if he could stop the GF interfering with my setting-out. His reply was that Mr Byre was too long in the tooth to be making such basic errors.

Shortly after that the building was out of the ground and it was time for me to move on. I found myself on another brownfield site at the bottom of Otley Rd. This was yet another mixture of flats and maisonettes but there were many more of them. So much so that I was given a couple of junior engineers to help out. I elected to set out the three-winged 8 storey blocks as these represented a bit of a challenge. This enabled the two juniors to cut their teeth on more basic stuff.

This time Mr Limply was much quicker off the mark. He told me that when the C.O.W. asked for the value of my temporary bench mark, I was to give him the wrong one in order that we could claim extra for the reduced level dig. I agreed, but of course, I didn't do it. Firstly, I had my professional reputation to think of and secondly, I was a Bradford ratepayer.

The job proceeded quite smoothly. The site agent and general foreman had followed me over from Raynor House. One morning there was a bit of commotion on site and I went to investigate. It was a basic block of four storey maisonettes that was causing the trouble.

The structural elements were quite simple. A concrete ground floor slab with the end and intermediate double lift of walls being 'no-fines'. This was topped with another concrete floor slab, and another double-lift of cross-walls.

The joiners had just stripped the shutters from one of these upper storey walls, and it was clearly out of line with the wall below. John Byre had been up to his Sunday tricks again.

I was summoned to a meeting of the top brass and asked for an explanation. I didn't like telling tales, but I had a duty to protect my junior staff who were responsible for this particular block.

"When I was on Raynor House," I said "I complained that someone was interfering with my setting-out, but Mr Limply told me that this person was too long in the tooth to make mistakes."

Mr Limply turned a deep shade of purple.

"Now listen, Bennett . . . ." he spluttered.

"Wait a minute," interjected Mr Beaumont, the General Manager. "Your name is Eddie, isn't it?"

I nodded agreement.

"Well Eddie," he said. "I think I know what happened. You can leave now. There won't be any repercussions."

Unfortunately, there were repercussions. Mr Limply refused to let me work in his area, and I had to move to a site at Seacroft, at the far side of Leeds. This could have been a bit of a disaster, but my guardian angel was looking after me again.

I would be working with what was known as a pouring gang. Most of them lived in Leeds, but the mixer driver lived in Girlington, very close to our house. He offered me a lift, and although I volunteered to walk down to meet him, he insisted on coming to pick me up.

For the next several months, I travelled to work in the splendour of a three-wheeler car.

That Christmas, we had our usual party at our Geldard Rd headquarters. It had been a good year, so there was plenty of grub and the beer was flowing freely. I was feeling hot so I took a walk in the car park to cool off. I spotted Mr Limply's car and was suddenly overcome with a great desire to pee. I thought of christening his car, but then had a better idea. In those days, petrol caps were not lockable and it was just about the right height. Years later, Ronnie Barker did the same trick in the opening episode of 'Porridge.' I hope my effort had the same result.

The Seacroft job was a 17 storey block and the pouring gang were highly specialized in their construction. I was quickly accepted as an integral part of the team.

The work was once again straightforward. After making sure we were in the right field, getting down to load-bearing strata and bringing the foundations back up to ground level, the job became a routine progression. The floor slabs were constructed in two pours and the walls took two further pours With all the associated jobs of cleaning and oiling the shutters, getting the steelwork in place, fixing the precast stairs, etc, a pouring gang could achieve a rate of one storey per week. My main involvements in the sequence were to ensure that the walls were vertical and that the floors were level.

I was also responsible for quality control, particularly the concrete.

The construction was similar to a standard no-fines building with one important addition. The structural element necessary for multi-storey buildings were reinforced concrete columns. By the clever incorporation of steel slides within the shutters, both of the operations could be carried out. Firstly, the no-fines walls were poured followed by the dense concrete columns. The steel shutters were then raised and the concrete vibrated. This allowed the concrete to leach into the no-fines to give a very strong construction.

The strength of concrete is determined by the proportion of the various ingredients, with the amount of cement being critical. The concrete strength was decided at the design stage, a safety coefficient was factored in, and this gave the final mix. The mixer driver, my Good Samaritan, was clearly a very important member of the gang.

The engineer's part in this process was to take weekly test cubes. There were metal moulds made especially for this purpose, and specific instructions on how to collect the samples and fill the moulds. Three test cubes were taken—one to be crushed after seven days, one after twenty eight days, and the third to be kept on site for reference.

When the block was probably two or three storeys high I got a message that the cube strengths were a bit low, hovering around the minimum level. I was instructed to make absolutely sure I was complying with instructions when I made the next batch. In the meantime, they would await the results of the 28 day test. This was also low, but the block had now gained a few extra storeys. The next step was for someone to come from Head Office and make some cubes. His also failed the 7 day test but they decided to wait for the 28 day result anyway. The block was still growing.

My friend on the mixer was also being investigated but all his actions were to the book. The cement was fed from a hopper to a container on one end of a scale. At the other end a weight was slid along to the point representing the weight of cement required. Cement was released into the container until a balance was achieved. The container was then slid along a rail and its contents deposited into the mixer. The cement hopper was on hire and we got the hire company to come and check it out. A fixed weight was placed in the container which should have corresponded to the sliding weight on the lever-arm. It didn't! The hopper had been giving us short measure.

My mixer friend and I were both exonerated but the fact remains—why have safety measures in place if you are going to ignore them?

By now the block had almost reached its full 17 storey height. To pull it down was out of the question and another solution had to be found. The one they came up with was to replace all the proposed internal breeze-block walls with engineering brickwork. A costly solution but no doubt the hire company's insurance would cover the extra.

Anyway, when I drove past recently, the block is still standing after forty years.

The other Bradfordian on the pouring gang was the tower crane driver, Sean. When not lifting things his other occupation was pulling pints. He was the manager of a pub called 'The Harp of Erin.' Although fairly central, it was tucked out of sight off a side street and I didn't even know it existed. However, now that I'd found it, I got into the habit of calling-in occasionally. The first thing I noticed was the juke-box. Instead of the normal pop-hits of the day, this one was full of Irish fighting songs, with such classics as 'The Wearing of the Green' and 'MacAlpine's Fusiliers.'

One evening I was stood at the bar chatting to Sean when I noticed two rough-looking characters walk in carrying a bucket. They walked round the bar shaking the bucket and the patrons threw money into it. They made their way towards me and I saw Sean give an imperceptible shake of his head. They walked passed me and out of the door.

"Who were they?" I asked.

At first Sean was reluctant to tell me, but finally admitted that they were collecting for the IRA.

"Surely you don't support the IRA." I said.

"No" he replied. "But it's better than getting a bomb through my door."

The block at Seacroft was finished and the pouring gang moved to their next assignment. I was now an integral part of the gang and moved with them. The job was another 17 storey block at Harehills. When we arrived we found there had been a snag. The ground survey results had shown that there was a coal seam beneath the intended site and it showed signs of being worked. The pouring gang moved on whilst I remained behind to oversee the excavation. The hole got deeper and also wider. It was far too big to timber. Plus, it needed access for the diggers and all the wagons involved in the muck-shifting.

Eventually we reached the coal seam. It was six inches thick and showed no sign of being worked. All coal under the ground belongs to the NCB so we informed them and they came to have a look. Not worth the effort to come and collect it they said, so we dug it out and put it on the tip.

As below ground extras go, someone at Wimpey had pulled a master-stroke. Still, the Leeds City ratepayers could afford it.

The bottom of the hole was levelled—off, I projected my setting—out lines down into it and we started to bring the foundations up to ground level. However, my heart wasn't in it any more. First Mr Limply then the test cubes and now this. It was time to move on.

28

OUT OF THE FRYING PAN

I had kept in touch with several of my former classmates from Uni. Roger was a frequent visitor to Duchy Drive. Another friend was Parvis and his wife, Jenny. On leaving Uni. he had gone to work for Gleeson, a Sheffield firm. One day he told me they had won a major contract near Bradford and was looking for site staff. I applied for the position of senior site engineer and was given an interview. By the time this came along, Parvis had done such a good job of promoting me that the only questions I was asked were "When can you start?" and "How much do you want?"

OK. Perhaps not, but the pay offer was considerably more than I was getting at Wimpey. In fact, Wimpey's Chief Engineer tried to get me to change my mind but conceded that they couldn't match the offer from Gleeson.

I spent most of the day looking round Gleeson's various sites in Sheffield including the almost complete Crucible Theatre. The Contracts Manager ran me home as he lived on the outskirts of Bradford.

I worked my notice with Wimpey, had a couple of weeks skiing at Aviemore with Irene, Jenny and Parvis and then it was time to start my new job. This entailed major extensions to the existing Northowram Hall Hospital, situated between Bradford and Halifax. After setting up the site cabins I got stuck into the all—important job of establishing the main grid. The first line was set out parallel to the existing building.

In order to allow for the slope it was necessary to employ a three-foot spirit level. The person at the lower end, usually me, had the job of holding the bottom of the level on the nail, holding one end of the tape against the upper end of the level, watching the bubble to ensure the level was plumb whilst all the time resisting the pull from the chainman at the other end trying to pull the sag out of the tape. These modern surveyors with their laser equipment don't know they're born.

We reached the top corner of the grid and established this major peg with a generous dollop of concrete. Setting-up the theodolite over this peg I sighted back to my original peg then swung through 90 degrees. There was some good news and some bad. The good news—the next leg was fairly level. The bad news—it passed through a copse of trees. I set to and cleared some of the saplings out which certainly helped, but there was some major tree trunks blocking the line of sight. Nothing for it but to it to offset this top grid line to a point that offered a clear line through the trees. By the time I had done this and established the third corner of the main grid, the day had gone and we would have to wait 'til the morrow for the moment of truth.

On the following day we continued on our merry way, setting up over my third corner, sighting back, swinging through a right angle and setting off back down the slope. More action with the three-foot level only this time in reverse and I finally reached the fourth and final corner. I set the theodolite up over this peg, took my back sight and turned it through 90 degrees. I looked through the telescope, adjusted the focus and was relieved to see my original peg come into view. In fact, the nail was about half an inch from the cross hairs. I'll settle for that, I thought.

A few easy days whilst the soil strip was done, some relatively simple levelling for the reduced level dig, then, once the heavy plant had departed it was time to establish the intermediate grid-line profiles. The Geriatric Block as it was to become, was to have a structural steel framework. The construction was similar to concrete columns with a couple of subtle differences. Instead of starter bars the pad footings were fitted with holding-down bolts and with the steel columns being a specific length, it was important to establish the pads at the correct level. It was still necessary to get the footings down to load bearing strata of course, but the difference was made up with mass concrete. There were an awful lot of pad footings on this site. I had a chart pinned to the wall of my office listing all of them and as they were dug I recorded the depths. There was a space alongside each one for the clerk of works to sign his agreement to the extra depth.

One day during the early stages of excavation I had a visit from Gleeson's chief accountant. He pointed to the chart and asked if the clerk of works was actually checking the depths. When I replied that he wasn't he said that I should add a foot or so to each one.

Whoa! Haven't we been here before?

I said I would but of course I didn't. All that extra dig coupled with all the extra mass concrete could probably buy the NHS an iron lung.

Structural steelwork is a very exciting way of construction. Once I had established line and level, the block grew quickly. However, the sheer size of it kept me there for a considerable time. Additionally, there were perimeter roads to set out and drainage runs to establish. Floor slabs were concreted and internal and external brickwork and blockwork was started. The external facing brickwork was proceeding at a pace when it became obvious that there was a problem. The face of the bricks was spalling off. The architects came all the way from the sunny south to have a look. It transpired that they had miscalculated the severity of the northern winters. All the existing external brickwork was taken down and replaced with a much denser facing brick. I hoped that the geriatrics who would eventually occupy this unit were made of sterner stuff.

29

BOYS TOYS

I could never understand people's obsession with the motor car. It seemed to me that its only function was to get you from A to B relatively cheaply and safely. The fact that it could go from 0 to 60 in three seconds was totally irrelevant. Likewise, to quote a top speed of 120mph when the speed limit is only 70 could be construed as completely irresponsible. The only important statistic is how many miles to the gallon will the thing do.

It was only when I got posted to Leeds that I realized I could not rely on other people's generosity for ever. I signed-up for lessons.

After about eight my instructor said he would put me in for my test. It wasn't that I was a fast learner, far from it. His theory was that the tests took a while to come through, and by the time I had got mine, I would be ready.

The following week he came for my lesson beaming all over his face.

"Good news," he said. "They've had a cancellation and your test is next week."

"Why is that good news?" I asked. "I've not had all my instruction yet."

He considered this for a moment, and then said "Well, just consider it as experience."

The test was going quite well until we came to the part where I had to reverse round a corner. We'd only covered this a couple of times in lessons. I managed to select the reverse gear, looked over my left shoulder, lined the kerb up correctly, engage the gear smoothly and set off. As I approached the junction, I began to turn the wheel. We finished up in the middle of the road. I had turned the wheel the wrong way.

"Drive back to the Test Centre, Mr Bennett" said the examiner.

My instructor wisely decided to complete my lessons before putting me in for another test. Come the day and I was feeling confident and prepared. All was going well until he asked me to drive up Crow Tree Lane. The junction it makes with Duckworth Lane must be the worst in the World. An already steep road steepens even more as it approaches the stop line. The driver is sat gazing up into the sky. The sight line to the right is obstructed by a high wall and the view to the left is equally obstructed by safety rails and parked cars.

In the 40 years since this ill-fated day, Bradford's traffic engineers have installed traffic signals at every crossroads. The ones they missed have been given one or even two mini roundabouts instead. Every other road has suspension breaking humps including a number of bus routes. Ambulances going to Bradford Royal Infirmary can no longer use Girlington Rd, having to take a much longer route instead. Yet no one has tackled the problem at the top of Crow Tree Lane. Improving the sight lines is a relatively easy task, as is taking out the hump, but the easiest solution by far is simply to change the priorities.

Anyway, back to the test. I had been asked to proceed across the junction to Daisy Hill. After five minutes of stalling and sliding backwards my examiner said "Drive back to the Test Centre, Mr Bennett."

For my third test, my instructor came up with a cunning plan. What was needed was a test route that had no hills. He booked me in for Horsforth. I don't suppose the natives of Horsforth consider themselves as living on a plain, but in the context of Crow Tree Lane it was the equivalent of the Bonneville Flats. Happily, I passed.

The next job was to obtain a car. The husband of one of Irene's customers had one for sale. It was a 1956 Ford Popular with 48,000 miles on the clock. The owner assured me that there were many more miles left in it. Four days after I had parted with my thirty quid, the engine blew up.

My brother-in-law, Ian, was a motor mechanic and said he would look out for a replacement engine. After about a week he found one and I went over to Clayton to help him fix it. We unfastened a few nuts and bolts, lifted the old engine out by hand, lifted the replacement in and tightened-up the nuts and bolts. Job done.

I went to close the bonnet, but it refused to close. The engine we had put in was different to the one we had taken out. Ian had the solution. He cut a hole in the bonnet so that the offending engine part stuck through.

I drove around in this hybrid for about a week then visited the second-hand dealers. I chose a 1960 A40 on the principle that this was the car I had learnt on. It had even more miles on the clock than the Ford Pop. I pointed out the uniqueness of my existing car and the dealer allowed me £35 in part exchange.

This car turned out to be a good buy. Not only was it economical, but the boot was extremely roomy. The work at Duchy Drive was still ongoing as it would be for many years to come and the car ensured a steady supply of building materials. In addition, we could fit our skis in if we needed to pop up to Scotland for a weekend's escape.

30

STILL GOING DOWNHILL

Irene and I had kept our love affair with skiing going for the previous few years but had left Anne at home with one or another of our parents. However, now that she was four we considered her old enough to come along. We had chosen Voss in Norway and in our ignorance had picked a date in the middle of winter.

The first part of the journey involved a boat trip from Newcastle to Bergen. The boat wasn't over-big and the North Sea was extremely rough. We asked a passing matelot what the slapping sound was and he told us it was the stabilizers lifting out of the water and then crashing down again. We concluded that the safest place to be was in the bar. I find it easier to match my staggering to the roll of the ship when I've had a few, but perhaps more research is needed.

From Bergen to Voss the journey by train was much more civilised. At Voss we were met by a chauffeur-driven car. The chauffeur was wearing a natty peaked cap. We arrived at the small family hotel and the driver carried our bags inside. He hung up his peaked cap and put on a green visor. Going behind the counter, he proceeded to book us in. We went for our evening meal which was a typical Norwegian smorgesboard. There was a gentleman cutting the meat dressed in a tall chef's hat. It was our friend the proprietor. In the evening we made our way to the cellar for a disco. The DJ was wearing a John Lennon style leather hat. Yes, it was our multi-talented owner. We wondered if he wore his various hats just to remind himself which job he was supposed to be doing.

Voss was in a deep valley which never saw the sun during the winter months. There was a permanent mist in the air over the frozen lake and the temperature at night plunged to minus thirty. However, we were cosy enough in our triple glazed hotel, and the snowfields were at the top of the mountain. As we made our way there in the cable car on the first morning we were met with brilliant sunshine. It was to remain sunny up there for the rest of our stay.

Our first job was to get Anne enrolled in the kindergarten. This was situated within the upper cable car complex and was run by a young Norwegian girl called Inga. Anne had a tremendous time playing with the other children, sledging, snowballing and generally having fun. We met up with her at lunchtimes for a bite to eat, and Inga took her back to the hotel in the evening so that we could ski back down to the village.

Irene had enjoyed her time in the beginners' class in previous years so much that she elected to go in the beginners' class every time we went. After several years of this, she was so good that she was rivalling the instructor for the precision of her snowplough turns.

I had now progressed to parallel turns and our lessons consisted primarily of following the instructor down various slopes, trying to match his exact moves.

All too soon our holiday came to an end and it was time to make our way back home. Inga had become quite close and she asked if she could accompany us on the train to Bergen. Once there we said our farewells and boarded the boat. If anything, the return journey was even more stormy than the outbound one. We had just settled down in the bar to get our usual injection of sea-legs when there was an announcement over the tannoy.

"Will Irene Bennett please proceed to the wireless room on the upper deck."

Highly concerned, I accompanied her onto the deck. Waves were crashing over the side and the spray made the deck extremely slippery. We needed to climb a steep companionway next to the side rail to gain the upper deck. With the continuous rolling of the ship, we found ourselves one minute high in the air and the next minute, staring down into the swirling foam. At last we reached the radio cabin and announced ourselves. "There's a ship to shore message for you" said the operator indicating a hand set. Irene picked it up with trepidation.

It was Inga. "I'm missing you already" she said.

31

FOREIGN PARTS

Eventually Northowram Hall Hospital reached the stage where the Engineeer was surplus to requirements and it was time to be moving on. Gleeson had won another very interesting contract which had one small drawback—it was in darkest Lancashire. Bolton to be precise.

The job was to become a post office surmounted by offices constructed in an L shape and bordering the Town Hall Square. The construction for the most part was standard reinforced concrete floor slabs and columns. The interesting bit was the front and side elevations. These consisted of huge precast concrete window units with a variety of shapes. The construction involved many novel problems including line, level, waterproofing and stabilising. The young architect responsible for the design had rented an office on the other side of the square and we had a number of brainstorming sessions to iron-out details.

This all took place in the days before the M62 was opened. Even at the crack of dawn the journey took a minimum of an hour. The return journey tended to catch the evening traffic and took even longer. Coupled to the long days required by the construction industry, it was becoming all bed and work. I decided to compromise and stay over on Monday, Wednesday and Friday. The site agent, Keith, was from Sheffield and was already in digs during the week, so I moved in with him. The general foreman was from Scotland and he had found himself some permanent digs,

The old problem of filling in spare time now re-appeared. Once again I was lucky. There was a gym just along the road from our B&B and I joined up. It was yet another old mill as they all seemed to be in those days. This time the ground floor contained all the weights and machines, and was extremely busy. The upper floor was devoted to two activities—a karate class and a weight based circuit. As I was now playing rugby regularly, I decided to give the circuit a try.

The principle is quite simple. The circuit consists of a series of resistance machines and free weights usually covering twelve to fifteen exercises. The layout must be such that the same muscle is not exercised at two consecutive stations. The participant firstly presets all the machines/free weights to a pre-determined poundage. He then notes the time and sets off from one exercise to another doing a pre-determined number of repetitions, usually ten. The idea is to try and complete the circuit within a target time. Once this time has been achieved, all the poundages should be raised margininally and the circuit procedes once again. The theory, which is quite sound, is that the person will gain strength from the resistance element whilst gaining cardio-vascular benefit from the non-stop action.

I usually did three circuits with about 10 minutes rest inbetween. During these rest periods, I would watch the karate class going on alongside. I became quite an expert. In fact, I'm the only person to gain a black belt without raising a foot in anger.

Bolton was a good place to be if you were a drinking man with an interesting variety of city centre pubs. Keith was a teetotaller and spent his evenings reading, so the general foreman, Jock, became my drinking companion. "Ye Old Man and Scythe" for instance was the place to go if you liked folk singing, as I did. I believe there were organised nights at weekends with recognized artistes, but during the week when we tended to go, the singing was entirely spontaneous.

Yate's was another regular haunt. We used the upstairs bar and one night there was a bit of a disturbance in there. Two rough-looking guys on a table near us started arguing. This esculated as they stood up and started wrestling. They stumbled over towards the banisters and I thought we might see one or both of them take a header over the top. Suddenly it was all over as they started cuddling and kissing. It was just a lovers' tiff.

Following that, we concentrated our drinking in "The Swan" over the road. After a while we got to know the manageress quite well. One night after closing, I volunteered to drive her home. Once there, she made it quite clear that I didn't have to leave. I thanked her for her kind offer, but told her that I was happily married. The following day at work, I told Jock this story. That night he ran her home and shortly after, he moved in with her.

At that time there was a film being shot in and around Bolton. The star, James Mason, was staying in a country hotel out in the sticks, but most of the lesser actors and crew were staying at "The Swan." At the conclusion of filming, they were to hold a post film party in the banqueting suite of "The Swan." Staff members of the hotel were invited, and they were permitted to take one guest. The manageress naturally asked Jock. On the given night I went down to to have a couple of swift ones before it all kicked off. They then made their way upstairs and I left.

As I exited the front door, a large limosine pulled up opposite. I walked over and opened the rear door.

"Good evening, Mr Mason," I said. "Follow me please."

James Mason, his wife and daughter followed me through the front door and up the central staircase. Two large bouncers stood at the top of the stairs. As we approached I announced "Mr Mason and party." They leapt into action and held the double doors open wide. We swept in imperiously.

32

RISE AND FALL

Because of the unique nature of the Bolton building, I managed to stay on site for quite a while, but eventually it was time to move on. I had dropped several hints that I thought I was ready for higher things. At last I got my wish. I was to be the site agent on my next job. This was to be a development in Prestwich, north of Manchester. It was to be yet more flats and maisonettes, but at least I would be able to break a young engineer in gently. I made a start on the setting-out and waited. Eventually it dawned on me that I wasn't going to get any help—I was expected to do both jobs.

There were a couple of benefits though. The obvious one was the increase in pay, but I also learnt that I was to get a new firm's car. I had been allocated a well-used Ford Anglia when I first started at Bolton. Coupled with a petrol allowance, this represented a significant perk. Ford had now brought out a new model called the Escort and I was to get one. In fact, I asked if I could go and collect it on a Sunday as I didn't like the idea of some mechanic hammering it up the M1.Gleeson were happy to oblige as it saved them a day's wage for a driver.

The storage depot was south of London, close to Gatwick. I took Irene with me armed with a street map of London, to act as a guide. We found the place OK and did the exchange—an old Anglia for a brand new Escort with only 3 miles on the clock. I was even prepared to accept the colour—beige!

Compared to the previous cars I had owned, the control panel of the Escort looked like something from Cape Canaveral. Irene now had a new job—to read the instruction manual as we drove through London. As we entered Oxford Circus it began to rain. I reached for what I thought was the windscreen wipers and turned on the indicators instead. The drivers behind me pulled back and I felt obliged to do another circuit or two of the roundabout until we got the controls sorted out.

The job at Prestwich proceeded serenely enough until one fateful Saturday. In those days, Saturday morning was still a working day. There was also a good chance of working on Saturday afternoon too, especially if the job was behind schedule. We were paid extra for any Saturday afternoon worked, although it was only at flat rate.

On this particular Saturday I put in a claim for an afternoon's work. I got a snotty letter from the chief accountant asking why I was claiming overtime when no-one else on the site was. I sent an equally snotty letter back telling him that I had kept the site open so that one of the sub-contractors could work over. I had employed my time catching up on all my paperwork. I reminded him that I was doing two jobs which must be saving them a fortune, and I thought it was extremely petty of him to quibble over such a relatively small amount. I suppose in retrospect, I did lay it on a bit thick.

We would get a weekly visit from head office by a quantity surveyor. His job was to keep a running check on the work completed. From this, the firm could claim a monthly payment from the client and also work out the amount of bonus each tradesman had earned. I had become quite a good friend of this QS over the years. On his visit after my outburst, he told me what a stir it had caused. It had been discussed at the Directors' meeting and it seemed that the knives were out.

Eventually the job reached the point where the engineering content was complete. In spite of the fact that I was now the site agent as well, it appeared I still wasn't to be allowed to see the job through. I was moving on again.

The good news was that the next job was at Halifax, virtually on my doorstep. The bad news was that it was yet another high-rise block and I was to be both the site engineer and the site agent again. The site was on Gibbet Street, named after the gallows that once stood there. This had been the place where many a poor sheep stealer or coin-clipper met an untimely end, and was to prove very prophetic in my case.

I was given a fairly young looking general foreman who wasted no time in letting me know that he was the son of one of the directors.

I got the reduced level down to rock and started bringing the block out of the ground. We had reached the ground floor slab and was ready to set out the kickers for the first lift of columns. I strung a building line between my profiles in order to offset the measurement. The GF was acting as my chainman. Normally, I would get the chainman to hold the tape on the datum so that I could be at the business end. This time, the GF insisted on being at the kicker end, claiming he had already worked on a number of these blocks and was familiar with them.

The kickers were duly concreted followed by the columns. The particular column in question was concreted on the Saturday morning. When I arrived on site on Monday there was a small posse to greet me, including the chief accountant. The column had already been stripped of its shutters. The chief accountant took great pleasure in telling me that it was 2 inches out of position and as the site agent/engineer, I was to be held responsible. I had been stitched-up.

One could believe that the GF had accidentally held the tape to the outside of the 3" x 2" kicker instead of the inside, but that didn't explain why the column had been stripped on the Sunday. Nor did it explain why the chief accountant and the posse of witnesses, including the clerk of works, had got there so early.

The outcome was, I was told to clear my desk as I was to be dismissed instantly. Even if I had been guilty, this would have been a harsh punishment and only added further proof that I had been railroaded for having the termerity to criticise management.

I still had the firm's car, of course. It was agreed that the GF would accompany me home and then drive it back. I let him know that I was aware of his part in the charade, but as you would expect, he denied it. The rest of the journey passed in stoney silence.

33

AND RISE AGAIN

There is never a good time to be sacked, but this one was particularly unwanted as my son, Mark, had been born a few months earlier. On the positive side, I had always been a saver and there was no chance of us starving. Also, Irene was still doing good business in her home hair-dressing shop. Besides, as so often happens, fate intervened.

We were still in touch with Roger, and whenever he visited, he would sleep-over on the divan in the lounge bay window. Shortly after my enforced idleness, he came over to commiserate and stayed as usual. In the morning he awoke at a strange angle. One of the divan legs had gone through the floor. Upon investigation I found that we had got dry-rot. I decided to tackle it myself—a job so big as it turned out, that I could never have managed it whilst being in full-time employment.

The first thing to do was get rid of all the affected timber. I took the floorboards up for about one third of the room and burnt them. Similarly, a couple of floor joists. Next, I carefully went round everything below floor level with a blowlamp to kill-off any spores and liberally splashed Cuprinol around. I had decided that the cause of the dry-rot was two-fold and elected to tackle them both.

From the outside it was clear that the ground level was the same as the damp-course instead of the minimum 6" below. I needed to lower the outside ground level. The front wasn't too bad. I dug out the old tarmac footpath and relaid it at the required depth in stone setts. The side of the house was different. There was no way I could lower the whole drive, so I constructed what I refer to as my moat. This involved digging down to about a foot below DPC level and then concreting the base. About 18" away from the wall I concreted an upstand to contain the drive. As there was a slight fall towards the road on my drive, this upstand gradually got bigger. By the time I reached the rear of the house the difference was quite substantial. I built a nice stone retaining wall to contain the back garden and flagged a patio next to the house.

Whilst this was going on, I also made a start on the second cause of damp entering the house—to clean the cavity of all the mortar droppings. In fact, I decide to go the whole hog and replace the old dampcourse and brickwork whilst I was at it. Starting at the front corner, I carefully took out a short stretch of the old brickwork, cleaned out the cavity, including what was left of the old felt dampcourse, replacing it with a slate one and finally, replacing the bricks with Staffordshire Blues, the densest brick available and completely impervious.

My nephew, Nicky, told me many years later that one of his earliest memories as a child was sitting in our lounge, watching me down the hole laying bricks. Years later, he did an apprenticeship in joinery and obtained a job in London with a property developer. After mastering all the skills, he returned to Skegness to set up in business for himself and is doing very well, thank you.Its nice to think that I may have been a subconscious influence.

I gradually worked my way across the front of the house and down the side. The going was of necessity slow because I had to wait for the mortar to set before taking out the next section. Additionally, once I started along the side of the house, another problem presented itself. The floor joists were bedded in the brickwork on this side and they all showed signs of advanced wet-rot. There was nothing for it but to cut the offending ends off, which meant building a subsidiary wall inside to carry the joists.

All this work not only took up a great deal of time, but also took a lot of materials. I had built up a store over the years and I still had good friends in the industry, so I managed to keep my costs down. Professional builders would have charged the earth and not done such a good job.

I was signing-on, of course and going for interviews. I had qualified myself as a site engineer/agent, but all of the jobs I applied for were with small builders who never used the services of an engineer and their site agent tended to be an older tradesman who could drop back on the tools if the situation required it.

The big job on the house was coming to an end and I was about to cast my net wider when my guardian angel did her stuff again. An advert appeared in the local paper stating that Bradford Council Engineers Department was about to embark on a new iniative and was looking for an engineer to head it up. I applied and got an interview.

This was conducted by Mr Mathers, the Deputy City Engineer. After a bit of small talk, he asked me if I read the trade journals, and if so, did I know anything about this new Government iniative?

I was a regular reader of the Construction News, known to one and all as 'The Jackers' Journal.' I had read something in there recently that I thought must be the one, so I rabbited-on at length about it. Mr Mather listened patiently until I finished, then said "That's very interesting, but that's not the Act I am referring to." He then went on to explain the rational behind General Improvement Areas, whereby the Government would make money available to refurbish older houses rather than demolish them. The City Engineer's job was to enhance the environment to compliment the internal work done on the houses

He then asked me what I thought of the idea and how would I carry it out. I have always been a conservationist and launched into another five minute ramble, only this time I could see that Mr Mather was impressed. I had put on my application that I was still working for Gleeson. I thought if I told them I was out of work, it might prejudice my chances. Mr. Mather asked me why I wanted to leave my present job. I told him that I had two young children, and with the long working hours and all the travelling, I was missing seeing them growing-up. Well, this was partly true.

Mr Mather was obviously a compassionate man and I could see that this had struck home. One final question—how much notice did I have to give? When I told him one month, he said "Put it in because the job is yours."

A month to kill, but there was still plenty of work to do at home. I had floorboards to replace, bits of bare brickwork to re-plaster and skirting-boards to refix. It occurred to me that all the work I had carefully done would be hidden from any potential buyer. Still, I had the satisfaction of knowing that we were now home and dry.

The new job was a real cultural shock to me. The hours for a start. Nine to five with an hour's lunch and no Saturday mornings. Luxury! My working companions were all engineers or technicians and were a great bunch. There was work to do, of course, but I never felt any pressure, although our office was situated on the top floor of the City Hall immediately behind the clock tower, so there would be no sleeping on the job.

I was doing the other side of engineering now—designing rather than building. This involved working closely with colleagues in the town planning department, another good bunch. They would come up with the basic idea and I would turn it into a working drawing.

The first GIA to be tackled was Barkerend. This was so large it was sub-divided into four phases. As soon as the first phase was drawn up, the work got underway. This, along with many of my subsequent jobs was allocated to the Direct Works Department. Contrary to popular opinion, these were very skilled and hardworking tradesmen, and I got to know them very well. At my interview, I had been told that the job would entail approximately 50% of my time in the office and the other 50% on site. In practice, it didn't quite work out this way, with the majority of my time being in the office. I was called upon to give the occasional line or level and sometimes there was a problem to resolve, but I did encourage the tradesmen to use their initiative as well, and they in turn valued being given the opportunity.

At the conclusion of the job, the City Engineer, Jim Hayton, asked me to write a report to submit to the Government, presumably to determine whether their initiative was working. As a result of this, the scheme was awarded a gold medal. Not bad for the c.v. or to massage a slightly battered ego.

We had been told that Barkerend was the biggest GIA in the country, but my next one was to be even bigger. Lidget Green GIA reached all the way from the outer ring road down to the university.Another four phases taking several years to complete, although I was also engaged on other jobs during this time, including probably the countries smallest GIA. Chain Street contained the oldest alms houses in Bradford, and in order to have them upgraded, the architect had declared the area a GIA. Next door to this site was one of my old stamping grounds. I called into 'The Harp of Erin' to enquire after Sean's health but he had moved on.

The GIA programme had grown so large that other colleagues were drafted in. This enabled the administrators to create a new post of senior engineer with special responsibilities for GIA's. I got the job.

34

SOWING THE SEEDS

Financial security, doing a job I enjoyed, the house beginning to look more like a home than a building site and the family all fit and well.I was now finding more time to indulge in my hobbies.

Starting work at Bradford enabled me at last to link-up with the Univesity gym. This was situated within the Richmond building in the spot I had suggested many years previously.There was one innovation awaiting me. The bars and weights were all competition standard. The bars in particular were engineered to a high standard, with the central part being knurled for a better grip, and the ends rotating independently on bearings. They made training a pleasure and encouraged heavy lifting. A world away from my old wooden bar and home-made weights.

There weren't too many regular trainees, and the majority of these were competitive lifters. They seemed to be divided equally between the two sports of weightlifting and power lifting. In those days, weightlifting consisted of the three overhead lifts, the press, the snatch and the clean and jerk, although subsequently the press was dropped. The lifts require speed, precision and flexibility. Many atheletes who need explosive power in their sport, such as sprinters, utilize these lifts in their training. Carl Jennings had been the British shot-put champion for instance and certainly knew the value of these movements. When he became the conditioner for the Bradford Bulls, he set me on to teach these lifts to the academy side. Can I take some credit for this also being the Bulls' most productive period? Why not?

Weightlifting is a very old sport, having been included in the very first Olympic Games. Power lifting on the other hand is much more recent, having evolved in the 50's from standard bodybuilding movements. In Britain it was known as the strength set, but when they got together to draw-up some international rules, they adopted the American term of power lifting. Well they would wouldn't they, although it is something of a misnomer. The engineering definition of power is strength applied at speed, and the powerlifts are slow and deliberate rather than fast. Ironically, weightlifting is the one that actually employs power, but let's not go there.

Whatever, the three powerlifts that became accepted were the squat, the bench press and the deadlift. I was certainly using the first two as part of my regular training, and occasionally did the deadlift. I remember doing a session one time and I was repping 100kg on the bench. One of the powerlifters was watching and suggested that I took up the sport. I told him that I was happily playing rugby, but the seed had been sown.

The guy in charge of sport at the University was Frank Murray. I got to know him very well following yet more coincidences. Firstly, I found out that he was a neighbour of mine, living a few doors further up the Drive.Secondly, he was a rugby player and he joined my club. We had many games together where he played winger to my centre.

We were aware that a purpose-built sports centre was taking shape further up Great Horton Road. We also knew that it was to have a free-weights room. Frank was so pleased with one piece of apparatus that he allowed us to train there even before the official opening. This was called 'The Universal machine' and was the forerunner of the modern gyms stuffed with complicated apparatus. There were ten different stations situated around a central frame, and it was possible to do a full workout entirely on this one piece of apparatus. There was also plenty of room left for a number of weight-lifting platforms, a bench press station and squat racks. All in all, a very pleasant little gym and one that was destined for great things in the coming years.

After a while it was decided to extend the Sports Centre further and a pool was added. Irene had decided at last that hairdressing was not really a healthy occupation, standing in an un-natural position for long periods and breathing in hair spray all day. She did a short College course and got a job at the pool as a swimming teacher/lifeguard.

It was nice to be training at the same place that my wife worked. It was also nice that, after many years of peripatetic training, I at last had a settled base. My training now was aimed at getting stronger for my rugby. I was doing a bit of running to take care of my aerobic fitness, but had come to the conclusion that rugby wasn't really an aerobic sport. Rather, it is a series of anaerobic movements,[so is football, but don't tell them], and so strength training is more beneficial.

I continued with this idyllic situation for the next several years, enjoying my work, my training and my rugby.

35

BRADFORD SALEM

So where was all this rugby taking place? Well, it was a bit of a non-contest really. From the day that I moved into Duchy Drive, I was aware of there being a club on the opposite side of the main road. In the early days, I was too busy working at home to do much about it, but eventually I got on top of the work and took a stroll down. I was offered a game with the 2nd team.

My first appearance was almost my last. Halfway through the first half, our full-back joined the attack. Like a good centre I dropped back to cover him. The attack broke down and the opposition kicked through. I gathered the ball and made to clear my line. As I put boot to ball my feet flew from under me and I fell flat on my back. The captain had a few choice words to say. I looked at my boots in dismay. Several of my studs had disappeared. I had forgotten to tighten them up!

At half time I got my stud spanner and rearranged the remaining ones so that I could at least stay on my feet. During the second half we were attacking and I had the ball. I could see that my winger was covered so I chipped ahead. As I ran through, the ball stood up for me nicely. I gathered it, raced-on and plonked it down between the posts.

Towards the end of the game the match was poised and could have gone either way. I had a word with my winger suggesting a move that we might try if the opportunity arose. On our next attack we went for it. It was just a simple run-around move, but it worked and I dived-in at the corner.

Two tries in one match! I may have managed it again in all the subsequent years of playing, but this was probably the most significant. As a result, I was selected for the 1st team the following week, a position I was to hold for several years to come.

One Saturday some years later, we all got changed in the old wooden pavilion at the top end of the site and walked down to the pitch only to be met by a sight that resembled the Somme. The pitch bordered Garden Lane and the Yorkshire Ripper's house was behind one of the goalposts. The police had been out with metal detectors and spades looking for evidence. I idly wondered whether to ask them if they had found my studs.

At that time, Salem had no club house of its own, and after the game we would go down to 'The Fountain' on Heaton Road for our post-match pie and peas and a few jars. No doubt Edgar, the landlord, was happy with the arrangement but Salem were not getting much out of the deal. What was needed was our own club house.

After a great deal of searching, we found a possible location. It was off Shay Lane next to the upper part of Heaton Woods. It was immediately next to a council recreation area that would accommodate two additional pitches; there was room for a decent sized car-park and most important of all, the owner was willing to let us have it on a long lease. In fact, the only negative was that the area designated for the first team pitch would need an awful lot of work in order to get it up to standard. Then, as so often happens, fate stepped in. At work, the GIA period had drawn to a close, but there were plenty of other initiatives to keep me busy. For example, I was involved in a number of land reclation schemes and through these, I got to know a number of specialist sub-contractors. I was chatting to one of them one day and mentioned our problems. He said he might have the solution.

Apparently, he had just won the muck-shifting contract for the proposed Yorkshire Clinic at Cottingly. He had seen a sample of the stuff he would be removing and it was a beautiful sandy sub-soil, ideal for our purpose.

We quickly worked out a plan and set-off. The first job was to remove what topsoil there was and store it for future use. During the week his lorries would come and deposit their loads on this cleared area.On the Saturday he would send a machine to the site to level and consolidate it. I would meet the driver there armed with a theodolite, dumpy level and ranging rods that I had 'borrowed' from work. I had set up my base-line, equal to the full length of the pitch plus a working margin, on the top side of the proposed pitch as this was more or less the finished level. From each corner I would swing the theodolite through 90 degrees, measure across and place a ranging rod in the ground. This gave the machine driver his parameters. The land within this rectangle would form the future playing surface and this had to be brought up to level evenly and consolidated to prevent any future settlement. Outside the rectangle were the embankments and these had to be constructed within rules to ensure their stability. The work continued for three or four weeks as the lower side was gradually brought-up to finished level. At last the site was ready for the final operations. I set up profiles at the four corners and with the aid of a travelling profile, I made sure that the finished surface was level and to the predetermined crossfall. The topsoil was respread and my friendly contractor supplemented this from his own stockpile.

Throughout all this, my 7 year old son, Mark, had helped me as my chainman. I was slightly miffed at this as I thought that someone from the club might have given me a hand. To be fair though, a number of them were helping with the building of the clubhouse which was going on at the same time. The main contractors were the Brumfitt Brothers with various others chipping-in at the weekends. It took a little longer than anticipated as the first effort blew down. For their second attempt, they decided to build the walls before they put the roof on.

There was one fly in the ointment. One of our members was a QS for a local building firm, and he thought he knew a bit about site procedure. He told our president, Geoff Pennett, there was no way a contractor could find a free tip and that he must be slipping me a nice little wedge. Instead of trying to explain to Geoff, I brought my contractor friend to meet him, and hopefully convince him.

He explained that, far from being a free tip, it had actually cost him money. Firstly, he had supplied a machine and driver every weekend at his own expense. Secondly, he had donated some of his own topsoil to make up the shortfall. Thirdly, and this was the clincher, he had turned down an offer from Shipley Golf Club for the same sub-soil. This would have been a shorter haul and they were prepared to pay him to spread it.

Geoff gave him free life membership of the club. I didn't even get an apology.

There was one important accessory that the new clubhouse had to have—a stage. Salem's Easter socials were renowned. It was great for we younger members to see some of our staid seniors getting up on stage and making fools of themselves. The format always followed the same routine. Two major sketches, one based on a pantomime, the other based on a TV show. Inbetween, there was one or two minor acts which gave budding thespians a chance to shine. The grand finale was the sextet, more of which later.

In the pre-clubhouse days, the venue was where ever would accept us. Among the places I can remember are The Pile Bar, Bradford Cricket Club and Dudley Hill Working Men's Club, a truly eclectic mix.

After a few years some of the older members began to fall by the wayside and others were drafted in to take their place. The rule was that whoever wrote the sketch would also get to play the roles. I was asked to join one of the script writing teams and was highly delighted to accept. I loved writing, loved dressing-up and, as I was to discover, I loved acting.

One year our team might be doing the pantomime. We did such classics as 'Throbbing Hood', 'Pleasure Island', 'Sinderella' and my favourite 'Jack Bean and his Magic Stalk.' On other years, for our TV based sketches, we had plenty to choose from. Our 'Coldtits' was a holiday camp rather than a POW camp and the twist was that people were constantly breaking in. Crash Craven played the camp commandant, Herr Oberleg Von Topp and John Grundy was his beautiful secretary, Heidi Dildo. I played an airman, Bummer Harris, and daughter Anne had sacrificed her pigtails to make me an authentic moustache. I had fastened it with an elastic band to a long cigarette holder, but every time I spoke, I took the holder out and off would come the moustache. Visual gags were a big part of the evening.

I think my favourite must have been the sketch we based on Kung Fu. Of course, we had to call ours Fu King. The storyline had him searching the old Wild West for his brother, Wan King. We weren't too bothered about pinching characters from other TV shows. For instance, I played the sheriff, Wild Bill Twitchcock and John Grundy played the barmaid, Fanny Pokely. Come to think of it, John always played a girl. The scene opened in the bar of the local saloon. I am playing cards with a stranger and Fanny is standing behind me looking at my hand. We give each other knowing looks as the tension mounts. Finally, the stranger speaks.

"Have you got Mrs Bun, the baker's wife?"

I leap to my feet and draw my gun.

"Doggone it! There's only one varmit can play cards like that, You must be Handiball Haynes, the outlaw. But say, where's yer partner, Kid Curry?"

"He's yella. That's why we call him Chicken Curry."

Just then Kid Curry walks in and I make to arrest them. Fanny intervenes.

"Calm down, boys. Let's all have a little drink."

"Thanks Fanny" says Handiball. "I'll have a raisin wine."

Fanny climbs a ladder to a top shelf to get a bottle. She is wearing an extremely short skirt and showing all her frillies. She comes down, pours a drink, then back up the ladder to replace the bottle. We men are enjoying the view. Back down, she asks Kid Curry what he wants.

"I'll have a raisin wine too" he says.

Back up the ladder to collect the bottle again, but this time she is thinking ahead.

"Is yours a raisin too, Bill?" she calls down.

"No ma'am" I reply. "Just a-twitching."

Well, what do you want? We were only amateurs.

The sketch proceeded as the plot developed. Fu King made his entrance followed by the Indian, Chief Ironside. Eventually, Wan King made his entry and the brothers were re-united. Wan only had one line, "Fu King [pause] Hell, it's good to see you."

In rehersals we had emphasized the importance of the pause. However, it was his first time on stage and, on the night he had downed several pints of Dutch courage. He blurted out" FuKing hell, it's good to see you."

We all shouted spontaniously "Pause!" It got the biggest laugh of the night.

The crowning glory was always the sextet. I don't know whether I was invited on for my singing or my writing ability. Probably the latter as the others used to tell Irene that they would wait for me to start and then join- in in whatever key I had chosen. Whatever the reason, I was certainly glad to accept. The basic idea was simple. We would recount the year in song, mostly covering the antics of our recalcitrant colleagues, but anything was fair game really.

The curtain would open to reveal six empty chairs. Bob Dinsdale, our chairman, stood to one side behind his podium. In true Leonard Sach's style he would do a two minute intro using the appropriate superlatives. The audience would greet each new one with 'oohs' and 'aahs'. After that, he would bring us on one at a time and introduce us as the character we were representing. Every year we had a different theme. For instance, if the theme was musicians throughout the ages, Bob would say "We now bring on Mozart." Pete Breaks would walk out wearing the appropriate costume and Bob greets him with "Good evening Mr Mozart. Tell me, are you still composing?"

Mozart replies "No. Decomposing" and takes his seat.

Once all six of us had been introduced we would stand and sing our opening number, 'Hello Salem' to the tune of Hello Dolly. The evening would proceed with us delivering the year's misdeeds through a number of well known tunes. 'At The Salem Rugby Club' was sung to the tune of 'Much Binding in the Marsh.' It was a relatively easy task writing verses for this one as the long lines gave plenty of opportunity to develop the story. Next, each member would do a solo with a Limerick. The audience would respond with the chorus 'That was a bloody good song. Sing us another one, do'

The trick here was to try and find a verse that no one had heard before. No reason why you couldn't write your own, of course. Between numbers we would sit down whilst Bob introduced the next one with some more jaw-breaking vocabulary. We then launched into another series of verses sung to the tune of 'The Eton Boating Song', another easy melody to write to.

After this, we sat down and waited for the thunderous applause to die down. At a signal from Bob, we would stand and perform the final number, 'Goodbye Salem' sung to the tune of 'Goodbye Dolly.' This brought an end to the night's entertainment and it was then a rush to get our make-up off and get changed before the bar closed.

On our 'musicians' year, Graham Scarborough was dressed as Shakin Stevens. He was so much into the part that he decided not to get changed. At closing time, a number of us set off for a curry. We pulled up outside a curry house on Oak Lane just as the staff were leaving for the night. Seeing four car loads of customers arrive, they about-turned, switched the lights back on and fired-up the ovens.

We introduced them to Shakin Stevens and told them we were his minders and the rest of his entourage fresh from a gig in the City. They looked suitably impressed, but thankfully they didn't ask him to perform.

Another social occasion was our annual Twickenham trip. Down on Friday and return on Sunday meant two nights on the town. The stroke of genius though was arranging a fixture against Harlequins on the Saturday morning. The early kick off meant that our coach could arrive at their car-park when it was relatively quiet. Our 1st team would play their select fifteen, although they always picked a strong one, with a sprinkling of former internationals. It wouldn't do to be beaten by a set of Northern oicks. There was always time after the game to have a few swift halfs in the bar, then as the kick-off time approached for the International, we would stroll across the road into Twickers. After the game, we would walk back to Harlequins' clubhouse and remain there for an hour or so until all the traffic had dispersed. Then it was a smooth drive back to our hotel, a quick wash and brush-up, then out on the town for an assault on Soho.

One of the important aspects of rugby union was the after-match socializing. Some teams would go home relatively early, but others, particularly if they had come in a coach, would make it clear that they were out for the night. There were standard games to play which relied on the participants being slightly the worst for wear, and then there was the singing of the rugby songs. Shades of being back in the NAAFI all those years ago.

Irene had joined with some of the other wives in a duty rosta for pie and peas. There was a small kitchen next to the bar and once all the eating was out of the way, the shutters would come down, and we would tend to forget the ladies were still in there. One year whilst holidaying on Menorca we met up with another couple. One evening, after we had sunk quite a few, we discovered we were both rugby players, so he challenged me to a singing contest. The rules were quite simple—we would alternate on verses of Limericks and the winner would be the one to keep going when the other had run out. He obviously fancied his chances; otherwise he wouldn't have challenged me. However, I'd been around a bit myself, and was quietly confident. After something like thirty verses had gone, I was beginning to have my doubts. Seeing I was struggling, Irene began to help me by singing the first line. Once prompted, I was able to finish the verse. Between us we managed to win the competition, but I was amazed at Irene's knowledge of risqué songs. She told me that as they sat in the kitchen, they could hear every word and would often sing along with us.

As the years rolled by, I slowed down a bit and moved into the pack at wing forward. More chance to get involved and more chance to utilize my weight training. I was also gradually sliding down the teams. Possibly my most rewarding time was my final few playing years as captain of the 3rd team. This consisted of older players like myself and youngsters just starting out. It was interesting blending the two together and a taste of things to come.

One week, a new young winger scored seven tries on his debut. It took all my skill to persuade the selection committee that he was still a bit rough round the edges and I would need to keep him a bit longer to hone his skills. With subterfuge such as this, I was able to rack up an impressive games won against games lost balance sheet. So much so that at our annual dinner, I was awarded the 'Player of the Year' trophy.

However, I was also getting my fair share of injuries. I remember going home one Saturday night and Irene actually screamed at the sight of my face. Come to think of it, she still does! I had my nose broken three times, usually by my own players. The first time it went over to the left of my face and the second time, it went to the right. For the third time, it finished up almost central. I decided to quit whilst my nose was in front.

36

CREATING A STINK

As mentioned, the work on GIA's had come to an end, but there was plenty of other work to take its place. One of my favourite jobs was land reclamation. I enjoyed working with large plant and I have always regarded landscaping as an art form. The sites themselves ranged in size from being just an odd corner to being quite large. One that fits the latter description was Pit Hill at Holmewood.

As the name suggests, this was once the site of an old coalmine. The hill was formed from the old workings and consisted mostly of shale. There were various requirements to take into consideration in my design. I was to provide four level areas within the site boundary. Two of them were for Council housing, one for private housing and the final one was to establish a football pitch. The local populace wanted to retain a high point and the final requirement was that no material was to be taken off site.

There was some new technology becoming available at that time known as computer aided design {CAD} and Pit Hill was perfect for the purpose. Our survey team had done an up to date survey of the site and this was transferred electronically onto a computer screen. I was now in a position to start my design, the first job being to locate the four level areas. In this context, the term 'level' is relative. The areas had end fall to tie in with the bordering roads and crossfall to facilitate drainage. Once these had been established, I could concentrate on the other requirements. I managed to maintain the hill peak at roughly the same height and position as the existing one. For the remaining condition, I had a considerable amount of surplus material to use up. In order to do this, I designed ridges that radiated out from the high point. There was one long one that formed the spine of the site and two shorter ones that borded the football pitch. The final job was to see if my cut and fill balanced, and the computer made this job extremely simple, churning out cross-sections at the touch of a button. No doubt the computer could also have done the calculations if I had known which buttons to push. Anyway, it was no big deal to do them by hand and after about three attempts at moving my contours slightly by a process known as successive approximations, I achieved a balance.

The next job was to draw up a Bill of Quantities. Architects have quantity surveyors to do this for them but we Engineers are made of sterner stuff. Since we also have to supervise the work, it is important that we are familiar with every aspect of it.

The final job was to go out to tender and to facilitate this, we had various select lists of contractors, depending on what type of work was required. In this case the bulk of the work was muck-shifting and we needed contractors with heavy plant expertise. After first telephoning to check their availability, we would send out a copy of the Bill, usually to six firms. Invariably, the firm submitting the lowest tender would get the job.

Several years earlier, shortly after I had joined Bradford City Engineers, Mr Mather came to see me. He told me that my former employer, Gleeson, had applied to go on the select list, and what did I recommend. Well, what was I to do? Clearly, the Gods of Retribution were on my side and I couldn't let them down, but how was I to handle it? I told Mr Mather that I wasn't happy with their integrity. When he asked me to explain, I told him of the incident at Northowram Hospital when I was asked to add extra depth to the pad footings.

"Oh dear" said Mr Mather. "We don't want that sort of thing. I'd better turn them down."

Mr Mather had spent all of his working life in Local Government and was unaware of the fact that every contractor was up to this same skullduggery.

The lowest tender for Pit Hill was in the order of £750,000, a considerable sum for the 1980's. The job required a resident Engineer, and the common practice was to allocate this to one of the younger ones in order to broaden their experience. Chris Bedford was nominated and he turned out to be more than adequate. I had warned him of some of the tricks that contractors got up to and, sure enough, they tried them on. However, Chris was up to the task and they didn't get any change out of him.

One of the first tasks was to find the old mine shaft and cap it off. This turned out to be rather simpler than it sounded. There was a depression at the side of one of the slopes which suggested that the material was subsiding. Sure enough, when we excavated below the depression, there it was. It was certainly bigger than I had expected and lined with stone. Since it fell within the proposed football pitch, we took it well down before capping it with a substancial concrete slab and then backfilling the hole.

The contract was drawing to a close and there was only one task left to do. We had recovered what topsoil we could and stockpiled it for reuse. However, the bulk of the site was now covered with the original shale which is an inert material. It was clear that we would need some form of amealioration, but what to use? Our colleagues from the Landscape Architects Department came up with the solution—Human excrement!

This wasn't as strange as it sounded. In fact, many sewage works sell bagged-up versions for manure using the brand name 'Humax'. We approached the nearest sewage works and told them our requirements. They were happy to accommodate us, but first, one little precaution—the stuff had to be tested. Disaster! We found there were too many heavy metals in the sample to be used for our purpose. What was going on? Apparently it was alright for humans to eat food containing these poisons, but once they had passed through our digestive systems, it was too toxic for grass to feed on.

We cast our net wider and tried other sewage works but they all had the same tale. Eventually we found a small one some considerable distance away that was suitable and the scheme was set up. This required the works to mix the waste with straw and leave it out in the open to rot down. At the appropriate time, this was delivered to site and ploughed into the shale. There was a bit of a pong but nothing too bad. However, the job was progressing faster than the sewage works could process it, and towards the end we were spreading virtually raw sewage. The smell was horrendous.

All calls to the City Hall switchboard were directed to me, but I played innocent and blamed the stables at the bottom of the site.

37

A DEGREE OF SUCCESS

After I had been working for Bradford for a few years, I started to think about further qualifications. My initial move was to write to the Institute of Civil Engineers to inquire about getting my Part 3 and eventually becoming chartered. They wrote back to say that I had to submit a major engineering scheme that I had been involved with in a substantial way. It turned out that none of the jobs I had worked on to date met this criterion. Bradford did do major highway schemes, but to head up one of these, I would need to be chartered. Catch 22 or what?

Time for plan B. The fact that I had been denied a degree still rankled slightly. I went to see Jim Hayton, the Chief Engineer, with my proposal to do an Open University course, and ask if Bradford would finance it. He responded that funds were in place for employee's further education provided that the subject matter was relevant. I agreed to those terms.

The concept behind an OU degree was simple. All that was required was six credits, but how you obtained these credits was very flexible. Some courses were valued at a half credit—very useful for people with very busy lives. Most courses were worth one credit and some brave souls would tackle two of them per year. However, by far the most popular option was to do one credit per year and that was the option I chose. One of the few rules was that you had to do two first levels known as foundation courses, with one of these being compulsory in your first year.

Bearing my promise to Jim Hayton in mind, I prepared to do my first foundation course. There were no engineering courses available, and, even if there were, there was no point in going over old ground. I chose a Social Science module called "Making Sense of Society". We could all do with a bit of that I thought.

There were set books to buy and study, TV programmes to watch, and, in the case of foundation courses, a tutorial every week. This took place at Bradford University, so it was back to 'D' floor after 17 years. Afterwards we would all retire to the 'Biko Bar' in the link block to meet up with other OU students and make out like under graduates.

The greatest bonus of all was the course booklets. No frantic copying down of notes during an entire lecture and then finding them illegible when you come to read them. The module booklets would drop through your letterbox at regular monthly intervals. This gave you four weeks in which to read and digest them and then prepare a set project, usually an essay. These would be marked by the course tutor and the average mark counted as 50% of the overall assessment. The other 50% came from the end of year exam, but if you already had good marks from the continuous assessment, this certainly took some of the pressure off the final exam.

At the conclusion of my first foundation course it was decision time. Many students go straight to their second foundation course in order to get it out of the way, but I was keen to get my teeth into something more relevant. The foundation course gave you a taste of all the directions you could take within that particular faculty. I would have loved to have followed-up on the Psychology module for instance but my path had already been decided. Bearing in mind my promise to Jim Hayton, I chose to follow the direction of human geography. Fortunately, I found this subject totally fascinating, but I also assumed that it would be the basis of any town planners' course. Since I was working with them, it wouldn't do any harm to think like them. There were two 2nd level courses dealing with geography on a human scale, so one year I did one then the following year, I did the other. They were as interesting as I had anticipated and very relevant to my job. Well, I thought they were.

We had access to two tutors. The course tutor was a full-time employee of the OU and was based in Milton Keynes. Although he could be contacted if required, our main contact was with our local tutor. He took us for our tutorials, marked our papers and was normally a full time university lecturer doing a bit of moonlighting. If the OU had a fault, it was the vetting of these local tutors. Of the six I had, two were good, two were adequate and two were absolutely diabolical.

Another aspect of OU life that generally went down well with students was summer school. A week's residency at a selected university with your days spent in intense learning and your nights spent in the student bars putting the World to rights. Many students chose a course based entirely on where the summer school would be held. One of the favourite destinations was York University with its beautiful campus set round a lake.

The courses usually started on a Saturday with the weekend being included in the working week. The following Thursday evening would be the farewell dance as students would make their way home after Friday's morning lecture. One year I found myself at York and being close to home, I suggested that Irene should drive over and join me at the dance. She said that she would try but did not promise. The rest of my class had decided to go in fancy dress, but in deference to Irene, I declined. We made our way to the bar and started getting a few down. Time passed and no Irene. Obviously she couldn't make it. I didn't want to let my classmates down so I went back to my room to get changed. I put on a pair of wellington boots, some baggy shorts, an old tee shirt and I painted my face blue. As I strolled back into the bar, I walked into Irene, dressed to the nines and looking like a million dollars.

Too late to get changed again, I thought, we'll have to do some dirty dancing. As it happens, we never made the dance floor. The conversation was flowing as only it can when aided by copious amounts of libation. Before we knew it the dance had finished and the bar was closing. However, there was a rumour of a party going on in one of the common rooms, so we made our way over. Sure enough, we found a guy with a guitar working his way through the Tom Lehrer song book. I had once owned the record 'An Evening Wasted with Tom Lehrer' and was a big fan, so we stayed. The bonus was, there was another guy there with crates of beer and he was selling them at cost, so that clinched it.

We made our way back to my room just as dawn was breaking and had a couple of hours together. The ducks on the lake had already started their dawn chorus, so we didn't get much sleep. Soon it was time for our fond farewells. I followed her home a few hours later.

My fourth year was something of a crossroads. I had exhausted the appropriate 2nd level courses and could now do my outstanding foundation course before setting off in another direction. Alternatively, I could do a 3rd level course. There was no real need to do 3rd level if one was only taking a basic degree. The only time it was relevant was if you intented to do honours which required eight credits, with at least two being at 3rd level. I had vague thoughts about taking honours so it wouldn't do me any harm to get a 3rd level under my belt.

I chose a guided project in human geography. There would be no broadcasts, no summer school and no final exam. Instead, there were masses of literature to be read before the project could properly begin. The first job was to choose a subject from the three on offer. For someone living in an industrial city, there was only one real choice, to test for a correlation between deprivation and pollution.

There were test cases to read through and lots of information on how to obtain data. We were given a fairly free hand on which data we chose to use, but we had to justify it. For instance, the deprivation information was obtained from the National Census statistics and could include such things as educational achievement, type of work, age structure and number of persons per household. The statistics for pollution could have proved more difficult, but once again, fortune was smiling on me.

By this time, we had moved from the City Hall and were ensconced in the Jacob's Well office block. A few floors below us were the Environmental Health offices. I made a few inquiries and was directed towards a very helpful young man. He informed me that Bradford had several monitoring post throughout the city, set up with the sole purpose of measuring pollutants, and he made masses of information available to me.

I followed this with a trip to the County Council offices in Wakefield where they provided me with traffic counts for all the major highways in Bradford. This was to give me a measure of the noise pollution as the exhaust pollution had already been picked-up by the monitors.

There were many ways in which this information could be progressed, and we were encouraged to contact our local tutor for guidance. The one I had been allocated lived in Sheffield. I rang him at an early stage of the project and requested a meeting. He invited me down to Sheffield University and at the subsequent meeting his sole interest seemed to be in talking about his holidays. Eventually, I managed to steer him onto the project and told him I was having trouble deciding which convention to use. He told me to use neither, but to use a third one which he proceeded to outline. Since this was not described in any of the supporting literature, I came away more confused than ever. A 60 mile journey and a wasted day!

I phoned the course tutor at Milton Keynes and got the guidance I was looking for.

Sometime later, I needed to see him again, but being a bit wary, I suggested that we meet in a more central location. He agreed but left it to me to arrange. Fortunately, I had a friend at Huddersfield College and he made a room available for us. The format of the meeting followed much the same pattern as the first one—a lot of talk about his holidays and no help whatsoever with my problem. Once again, I rang HQ and got the help I needed, but this time they told me to ignore the local tutor and liaise directly with them. Under this arrangement, I progressed quite well.

In addition to the main assignment, we had been given the further task of outlining a secondary associated project. Seeking inspiration, I went to see my friend in Environmental Health once again. He told me that they had recently tested the blood of every first-school child in Bradford for traces of lead, and he was prepared to make the results available to me. The lead of course came from the exhausts of cars, and I already had the traffic counts. By comparing the traffic passing a particular school with the lead counts from the children attending that school, I was able to show a positive correlation.

At the end of the academic year I submitted my final work, one copy to the local tutor and another to Milton Keynes, and awaited the results. The Milton Keynes one arrived first. It had been marked by Philip Sarre, the Head of Department. He spoke in glowing terms about my work and was particularly impressed with the section on levels of lead in schoolchildren. He awarded me 90%. After a long wait, the results from Sheffield arrived. The page for comment was completely blank, and he had given me 60%. Following the rules of the OU, he had also sent a copy to Milton Keynes. A short while later a letter arrived from Philip Sarre. He told me that he was disgusted with the pathetic script from the local tutor, { his words } and if I wanted to appeal against the low marking, he would support me.

My average mark was still a respectable 75%, and I was just pleased to come through a difficult year with a solid pass. I wrote back to Philip thanking him for his concern, but turning his offer down. I came to regret that decision.

In the following year, I did my second foundation course. After all the trauma of the previous year, it was nice to get back to something relatively easy—weekly tutorials again and fellow students to share ideas. I had chosen the faculty of technology, and with all of its design content, I felt I was once again fulfilling my promise to Jim Hayton. I had also learnt the subtle difference between the required answer and the correct answer. These two were not necessarily the same. The OU had definite political leanings, standing as it did just to the left of Karl Marx. Using this acquired knowledge, I managed to gain a distinction at the end of year exam.

One more to go for my degree and I chose a second level technology course. Once again, this was marred by a rather indifferent course tutor. At our first tutorial everyone had the same question—Why had we been marked so low on our first assignment? He replied that we had all used the wrong convention. We told him we had used the one we had been told to in the course module. His reply was that he had not read the course module and had no intention of doing so. It appeared that he thought the OU was an easy way of obtaining a degree and he intended to make it as hard as possible. As someone who had done both, I could attest to the fact that it was at least as hard as a full-time degree. The fact remained, with his attitude, what on Earth was he doing as a course tutor?

In spite of this, I tried not to let him ruin what was a very interesting course. With the use of small manikins we learnt the art of ergonomic design. One assignment was to design an improvement for a bicycle which is supposed to be the most over-designed piece of apparatus in history. Nevertheless, I managed a rather novel suggestion. There was another assignment that was right up my street. We were given the plans of an old cottage and asked to improve it for modern living without altering the external appearance. Even our surly tutor gave me reasonable marks for that one.

Another assignment that I enjoyed was to come up with an idea for a 'greener' car. I had noticed that most car journeys were undertaken by lone drivers. My idea was to make the rear passenger seat easily removeable in order to reduce weight and hence, save fuel. For the same reason, I placed the engine at the rear to eliminate the heavy transmission system. The boot was moved to the front to provide a crumple zone. Over the ensuing years, cars have probably got heavier rather than lighter although some promising trends are discernable. As an afterthought, I threw in one more idea. I placed a small camera in the rear bumper to facilitate reversing. {especially round corners?} The other day, I read that one of the big motor manufacturers was incorporating this idea in their new models. I wonder if I am entitled to any royalties?

My degree was now complete and Irene and I had a great day out in Leeds at the awards ceremony. The question still remained—what to do about honours? I sent off for details in order to make-up my mind. It transpired that there were 1st, 2nd and 3rd class honours, and the marks you obtained in both of your 3rd level courses determined which honours you attained. It appeared that the 75% I had already gained in my first 3rd level course was not sufficient to give me 1st class honours. Coupled with my two bad tutor experiences, I decided to call it a day.

38

FRIENDS UNITED

When Irene decided on her change in direction and went to college in Halifax to gain her qualifications, she met up with another georgous young lady and they became firm friends. Irene used her charm on our neighbour, Frank, and got Krystina a job with her at the University pool. Before long, we were invited for tea at her house in Cullingworth and this gave us a chance to meet her husband, Jacque.

These meetings can sometimes be a bit fraught. Just because the wives hit it off doesn't necessarily mean that the husbands will do likewise. However, in this case there was instant rapport. We found that we had so many interests in common. Jacque was a French national, but was working permanently in this country representing a company called Schlumberger whose headquarters were in Alsace, very close to Jacquie's home village. This firm had many interests, but the relevant one here was that they manufactured machinery for the textile trade. Although textiles were now a dying industry in this country, there was still enough going on in Bradford to keep Jacque fully employed. His job was essentially that of a trouble shooter. Although every mill had its own team of fitters, occasions would arise when they were unable to solve a breakdown and Jacquie would be called in. He told me that his approach was to dismantle the machine to its many thousands of parts, give each one of them a thorough clean and then re-assemble all the parts. Invariably, this method would work. Eventually, I got to see this approach in action, but that was someway off in the future.

Like us, they had two children who were now growing up and afforded us adults a large degree of freedom. One of the things we had in common was a love of walking and one of our early targets was to walk the Dalesway. The initial legs were in Wharfedale and presented a short drive for us. As we progressed to the more distant legs we would book into a country pub for the weekend. This would enable us to do one leg on the Saturday, spend an enjoyable evening eating and drinking in the pub, and then do a second leg on the Sunday before returning home. The Sportsman in Dentdale was one of our favourites with another one being The Bull in Sedburgh. In fact, we used this latter one on a couple of occasions as, strangely enough, there was a shortage of suitable country inns on the final few legs in the Lake District.

Our method of determining our walks became standard. We would purchase a book of walks covering a certain area then gradually work our way through them before moving on to another one. This way, we got to know Upper Wharfedale, Littondale, Ribblesdale and many, many more. In all this time, we had only once been denied access to a public footpath and that was by an irate gamekeeper waving a shotgun. It seemed that the annual slaughter of pheasants was imminent and he didn't want us disturbing potential targets. Did the 'Right to Roam Act' supercede the various 'Enclosure Acts' that took away common grazing land from the peasants so that the rich could have their pleasure? I don't know, but it is an anachronism that needs resolving. Unbelievedly, even Bradford Council sell the shooting rights on Ilkley Moor.

> They hang the man and flog the woman
> That steal the goose from off the common
> But let the greater villain loose
> That steals the common from the goose
>
> Anon

By this time, Krys and Jacquie had moved to a large house on the moors beyond Haworth, and this opened up a whole new area for us to explore. To the south was Bronte country itself with its strange waymarker signs written in both English and Japanese. Apparently, the Bronte novels are big in Japan! To the east is Emmott moor with the Pennine Way meandering over it towards the distant monuments known locally as 'the salt and pepper pots.' To the west is Boulsworth Hill with its flanking footpath still flagged with Yorkstone paving, recalling the days of the packhorses carrying their bundles of wool to the fledgling mills. To the north is the Forest of Trawdon containing the hamlet of Wycoller with its clapper bridge, haunted ruins and unique vaccary field boundaries. Although less than half a mile from the main Haworth to Colne road, it remained out of sight and unspoilt until the coming of the ubiquitous motor car.

It was but a short drive to our next destination, Pendle Hill. Its distinctive profile is made all the more dramatic by the fact that the surrounding countryside is relatively flat. We bought yet another book of walks covering the surrounding area, but the king of all these walks was the assent of Pendle Hill itself. There are many ways of making the climb, but my favourite involves following the track from Barley that passes the two reservoirs before becoming a footpath. This then winds its way along the valley following the course of the stream. Eventually the valley gives way to more open ground were some thoughtful authority has laid a Yorkstone path to protect the peat. The summit is defined by a trig point which gives some measure of protection from the inevitable wind. However, a better option is to cross the ridge and decend the escarpment slope slightly before nestling back into the heather. Here you can devour your sarnies and pop in peace whilst admiring the magnificent panoramic view.

The decent is via the stone steps built into the escarpment slope and is growing increasingly harder on my ancient knees. I've often thought that a zip line would get you from the top to the door of the 'Barley Mow' in a matter of minutes!

Pendle of course will forever be associated with witches, and the present tourist board makes much of the connection. However, it was no fun for the poor souls that were hanged on no more evidence perhaps than the say so of a jealous neighbour. The so-called witches had once been valued for their knowledge of the curative properties of herbs and other plants, but once mass hysteria took hold, fuelled by religious fanaticism, their days were numbered. This probably set the practice of pharmacy back for many a year.

Our final book of walks took us into the area known as the 'Forest of Bowland.' Like the 'Forest of Trawdon', the term 'forest' is some what of a misnomer. The area was once owned by the king and certainly use by him and his court for hunting, but the idea of endless tracts of trees cannot be sustained by any contempory accounts.

On one of our Bowland walks, the girls dived into a nearby health spa for a day's pampering, leaving us fellows to complete the walk on our own. Towards the end of another one, we popped into a handy pub as usual for a quick refresher. The girls decided to stay there, leaving us to retrieve the car and pick them up on the way back. To prove we were not feeling our age as the girls obviously were, Jacquie and I ran all the way to the car and were back before they had time to miss us.

Another pastime that we had in common was our love of skiing. Jacque once told me how he first got started back in his home village of Lautenbach-Zell which is situated in a side valley of the Vosges Mountains. These are a ridge of mountains running northwards from the Alps and bordering the river Rhine.In winter he and his friends would set off walking up the valley with their skis on their backs. Once they had arrived above the tree line, they would find a suitable field, climb to the top and ski down, then repeat the whole process until it was time for the long walk home again. Of such dedication are champions made.

Krystina too had become a good skier under Jacquies guidance. My own skiing had settled into a rut. Once I had mastered parallel turns, I thought that was it. However, trying to keep up with Jacque meant pushing myself to new limits. The bonus was that Krys managed to drag Irene away from the beginers class at long last, and do the level of skiing she was capable of.

We worked our way through many resorts in the Alps with Italy probably being our favourite due to the lower cost of living and the more laid back après-ski. We started casting our net wider, and one year found ourselves at Borovets in Bulgaria. At that time, Bulgaria was still under communist rule and currency control was very strict. There were a small number of shops selling Western goods, but these would only accept Western currency, and the black market in currency exchange was rife. It was possible to get four times the official rate for sterling, but unfortunately, there was not a lot to spend it on. In those days, it was usual to take a two week skiing holiday. That way you could take an odd day off from your skiing without feeling you was missing out. We decided one day to take an organized bus trip to Sofia, and after a two hour journey, we reached the Bulgarian capital.

Our first stop was at a former departmental store, but the communist model was run slightly differently. In this case, the store was broken down into various small units with the local populace renting these spaces to sell their own particular goods. So, for instance, we might find one stall stacked with cans of motor oil whilst the stallholder next to him was selling home-made cakes. In addition, each stallholder was responsible for providing the lighting for their own pitch, so that if one was unoccupied it would be in a pool of darkness. I bought three plaid shirts for about £1.

From here, it was back on the coach for a conducted tour of the city, stopping at various places of interest for a more detailed look. Next, we drove to a nice restaurant for a super three course meal with wine. The final stop saw us at the Grand Opera House, sat in the front stalls and watching the National Ballet Company performing Swan Lake. The whole day out had cost us £10 each.

Some years later, we found ourselves in Borovets yet again, only this time the Iron Curtain had come down. The difference was noticeable right away. On the bus from the airport, the driver's wife was doing a steady trade selling drinks from a cool box. The hotel was brand-new and the entire ground floor was given over to retail outlets. The slopes, which had once been the exclusive province of the skier, now boasted stalls every hundred yards or so. From Communism to Commercialism at the drop of a curtain.

We also enjoyed many summer holidays together, mostly at our time-share on Lanzarote, but more of that later. Probable our most memorable holiday was the one we spent in that totally delightful part of France known as Alsace. The official reason for going was to attend the wedding of Jaquie's niece, but we elected to go for ten days and see something of the surrounding countryside at the same time. Little did I realize what a full programme this would be.

We set off by car, taking the ferry from Hull to Zeebrugge, and then motored across Belgium and Luxembourg into France. Jacque had chosen a scenic route that avoided the motorways and gave us a chance to appreciate the countryside. We picked up the road that follows the spine of the Vosges Mountains until we reached the head of Jacque's valley, and then dropped into it. We drove through dense pine forest until eventually reaching the village of Lautenbach-Zell, a picture-postcard place far away from the usual tourist haunts. It didn't even possess a hotel, but we needn't have worried, arrangements had been made. Our first call was on Jacque's mum to let her know we had arrived safely and to have a chat, then we were taken to the village hall. In an upstairs room was the biggest bed I have ever seen. The only other piece of furniture was a large wardrobe. This was to be our home for the next ten days but the lack of furniture didn't really matter as we were hardly ever in the room.

For walkers, this place was Paradise. Paths radiated out in every direction through the pines, but there was no chance of getting lost. The paths themselves were well maintained and waymarked by a series of coloured discs. Each walk was allocated a colour and the appropriate disc would be nailed to trees or posts at regular intervals, but particularly where footpaths intersect. Of course, with a good map it was possible to change from one path to another and the possibilities became endless. Jacque told us that the villages themselves were responsible for maintaining the paths in their particular area, and it became a matter of pride to make a first class job of it.

Not all of the walks were through forests. There was one at the head of a neighbouring valley where much of the path had been cut into the shear face of a cliff. The views as one would imagine were fantastic. In the distance we could make out the township of Munster. Later, as we drove into the town for some refreshments, we could see what made it famous. Attached to the chimneys of most of the houses were large metal wheels. These were to tempt storks to build their nests there as this was judged to be lucky, and, indeed many did contain the fragile looking bundles of twigs. As we sat outside a cafe enjoying a drink we watched these great birds slowly wheeling about above us.

Another one that was of interest to me as an engineer was known as the two reservoirs walk. This followed paths winding their way down from an upper reservoir to a lower one. As we walked, Jacque explained the rationale behind the set-up. During the day when demand was high, water was released from the upper reservoir to a generating station on the lower reservoir. At nightime when demand had dropped, the water was then pumped back up again. I was familiar with this technology having recently visited a similar set-up in Wales which was being constructed in an old slate mine. I thought at the time that the technology was cutting-edge. As we approached the pump-house on our walk, I glanced up at the datestone over the door. It read 1935!

Following our walks, Jacque would drop us off at our digs with the instructions 'I'll be back in half an hour. We are dining with so-and so tonight.' Half an hour for a triple 's', it was like a military operation! We gradually worked our way though Jacque's extended family for our evening meal, and then started on his friends, including Maurice the Mayor. Finally it was our turn and we took over the local restaurant as we hosted the hugh family gathering.

Not all of our days were spent walking. On a few occasions we drove down the valley and out onto the floodplain of the river Rhine. Here there were country parks and medieval villages to visit, not to mention the odd hypermarket so that Irene wouldn't get homesick. Even after these visits, it was still the same old military operation once we got back to base.

At last the day of the wedding arrived. First up was the civil ceremony, and for this we all crowded into Maurice the Mayor's parlour. After the formalities we gathered outside for the next stage. This involved a procession of couples winding their way down to the church, led by the bride and groom. Jacque had given me the task of videoing the whole event which meant taking up strategic positions along the route. This would have left Irene partnerless, but, as it happened, there was an aging French Lothario present who was a distant relative of one or other of the happy couple. He was looking for an easy conquest, and he didn't have far to look.

The church ceremony was a very informal affair. The wedding itself was fairly standard but then it began to get unusual. Firstly, the bride strapped on an accordion, was joined at the altar by her group, and gave us an impromptu set. Not to be outdone, her sister went up into the balcony and gave us a beautiful rendition of 'Ave Maria.'

The procession formed up again outside to make its way over to the village hall for the reception. I was still videoing and Irene was still with Charles Boyer. The hall was crowded and the champagne was flowing. As soon as I took a sip, someone was at my elbow to top me up. I confessed to Jacque that I wasn't a big fan of champagne as the bubbles tended to blow me up. He produced a bottle of liquid that resembled blackcurrant juice and said it would kill the bubbles. It appeared to be working, so I carried on drinking this mixture. The local youth took over the stage and gave us renditions of French folk songs. I remembered many of these from my schooldays, and impressed everyone by joining in. Irene disappeared for a while with old leather face, but claimed she had only gone to look at his car.

Eventually, the afternoon's festivities drew to a close and we were given our usual 30 minutes to get washed and changed for the evening entertainment. This consisted of a superb meal washed down with lots more champagne, but I was now making sure it was well diluted with plenty of blackcurrent juice. After the meal, the dancing started and I asked Irene to give it a whirl. She replied that I was too drunk, and she danced with the hunchback of Notre Dame instead. I resented this as I had done some of my best steps when a little squiffy. Anyway, I decided it was time to sober up. The next time the waitress came round I told her to forget the champagne and just give me the blackcurrant juice.

"What blackcurrant juice?" she asked. "That red stuff you have been drinking is called chasse and is 30% proof."

39

GOING WEST

In the early 80's, a young town planner, Sue Webber, went to see her boss to outline a scheme she had been working on, little knowing that it would be her final job. In those idyllic days, officers could take the lead, unfettered by Council's party bickering. What changed? Well, possibly the greatest mistake was to introduce obscene expenses for councillors. Where once we had dedicated men serving the community, we now have career polititions serving themselves. Jo Steel was impressed with what she showed him and advised her to take it a stage further by forming a working party comprising officers from various relevant departments. I was chosen to represent Highway Design. Others included an officer from Estates to advise on land acquisition, and one from the Traffic Engineers in case of any road closures. The head of Landscape Architects, David Nunnerley, thought the scheme so important, he nominated himself as their representative.

We met on a monthly basis, and Sue's first job was to outline her thoughts to us. Bradford's Media Museum and the Alhambra theatre were attracting a good number of visitors. Her idea was firstly to upgrade what was a rather grubby area and secondly, to provide a third major attraction. This hopefully would encourage visitors to extend their stay from a day's visit to at least a weekend. For an authority that was trying to promote itself as a tourist spot this was a positive step forward. Sue told us that her working title for the project was Bradford's West End, and we all agreed that this should be adopted.

One of our primary considerations was what to do with the Odeon. We had a visit at one of our early meeting from a representative of Top Rank. He told us that bingo players tended to be very loyal, whereas cinema goers were more fickle. The Odeon therefore would remain open until a replacement bingo hall was built, at which time, the Odeon would be surplus to requirements.

The working party agreed that the Odeon must be refashioned in order to make the all important third major attraction. Many suggestions were put forward for its change of use ranging from a planetarium to a concert hall. The suggestion of an electronic zoo was treated with much mirth in the local press, but this idea has now been converted into a reality by the City of Bristol.

The Alhambra itself had come perilously close to being demolished. The front-of-house facilities were non-existant and the stage area was considered too small for modern productions. However, it was saved by some very enterprising architecture. The architect herself had come up from London to supervise the work, and she proved to be quite formidable with all of the sub-contractors. I had been given the job of designing the paved area surrounding the building and came up with a good solution involving the use of brick paving. The architect wanted me to change my plans to reflect the curving walls of the building. I told her that bricks wouldn't bend and neither would I. After that, we became good friends. I even got her temporary membership at the Uni gym so that she could do her aerobics.

One of the other so called 'pump-priming' schemes that I became involved with was the stone cleaning of the old Winsor Baths complex prior to it being remarketed as a series of commercial outlets. I was given a key and spent an hour or so exploring the maze of rooms given over to the Victorian art of deep cleansing and relaxation. These rooms were all down in the basement as one would expect torture chambers to be. I worked my way upwards, this time through a maze of offices. When I finally reached the top floor, I solved one of life's great mysteries—where do pidgeons go to die? The floor was literally covered with them. The building was cleaned and converted, and it appears today to be a commercial success.

The West End scheme gradually took shape. David converted our ideas to some rather splendid drawings which were then presents to the Council. They were sufficiently impressed to invite a major developer on board. This was to be Arrowcroft who had been instrumental in developing Liverpool's dockland amongst others. Their first involvement was to widen the scheme's boundaries even further by extending along Thornton Road. This is an area of mostly derelict mills and certainly required some regeneration but it was departing slightly from our original brief. Never mind, if they could swing it, good luck to them. Even though these additions brought the scheme's final estimate to £200 million, we were given the go-ahead to proceed with the next stage. In retrospect, perhaps things had become a little too ambitious, but at that moment in time, all looked rosy, so what could possibly go wrong? In the event, plenty.

Our final task as a working party was to flesh out the details of the scheme. To aid us in this task, Arrowcroft hired a small local publicity firm called '3D'. They organised a number of well- attended public meetings, and we officers obtained some useful feedback from them. The scheme was completed and all the legal documentation was in place when an inexplicable rift developed between the main contractor and their publicity company. In a fit of pique, 3D offered to take over the whole project. What did a small publicity company know of major development projects? Well, according to Bradford Council they knew enough because they were given the contract.

They had evidently learnt something because they actually made a start by building the office block at the end of Aldermanbury. This wasn't a part of our original scheme, being one of the additions that Arrowcroft had included. Never mind, our bit would be sure to follow, but then, the work ground to a halt. It appeared the idea was for the office block to be sold, and the money raised would finance further development. In the event, the office block remained empty for many years and the whole project floundered.

It was heartbreaking to all those officers who had spent so much of their valuable time on the scheme, but this was literally true in the case of Sue Webber. She contracted cancer, and after a short illness, she died at a very young age.

Will her vision ever be completed? I have no confidence at all in Bradford Council as it appears to have degenerated into a name calling shop. However, the scheme itself was too good to die completely and sections of it are gradually being addressed, albeit piecemeal. The Photographic Museum has been extended and improved. Vacant plots on Thornton Road are slowly being developed, and derelict mills are being converted into flats. The refurbished Alhambra and the Winsor Baths complex continue to attract numbers of visitors, but what of our third major attraction? To its everlasting shame, Bradford Council has overseen the rundown and decline of the former Odean building. Our colleagues in 'The Theatre Preservation' group inform us that it is the last remaining example of its genre in the Country. In that case, why on earth hasn't it got a preservation order on it? Meanwhile, Bradford ironically made a bid to become 'The City of Film.' No wonder voters treat their task with such apathy.

40

LARK'S NEST TO COUNTY COURT

We tend our children, watch them grow
Then all too soon before you know
From helpless babe to fully grown
They leave your nest to build their own

Daughter Anne was a bright student but a very impatient one. She finished her regular schooling at Belle Vue Girls School but declined the opportunity of further education, preferring instead the lure of commercialism. She had a number of different jobs ranging from a checkout girl at Morrisons to a nanny for a Greek millionaire living on the island of Corfu. Finally she did get to go to University—she obtained a job in the registar's office at Bradford Uni. Still, it maintained the family connection.

As soon as she reached 21, she asked if she could move into a place of her own. I advised her that rented property was dead money and that it made better economic sense to buy her own place. Sound advice, but there was also method in my madness. I reasoned that to find a property for sale that she could afford would take some time and we could maintain her in the safe bosom of the family for a while longer. This was a strange decision in view of what I had been through by the time I was her age, but parents can be very protective.

However, fate was at work once again, but was it on my side or not? Only time would tell. A colleague at work had heard of my interest and told me he had a house for sale. It was in Bingley which was one of Anne's preferred areas, and it was also in her price range.

Anne and I went to look at No 5 Lark Street. It was in a terrace of back to backs, which was a promising start—easy to heat and low maintenance. The external door led directly into the lounge with a narrow kitchen off to one side. A flight of stairs led from the lounge to the first floor which contained a good sized bathroom and a large bedroom. A second flight of stairs led up to two further large bedrooms. As if this wasn't enough, a further flight of stairs led down from the kitchen to a large cellar.

An eight roomed house seemed a lot for a young girl to rattle around in, but Anne was taken with the place and Dad had a cunning plan, so we started negotiations. A price was agreed, a building society loan arranged and all the other legalities completed. It was then time to reveal my master plan.

As it stood, the cellar had a very low ceiling height and could only be used for storage. On the other hand, the lounge had a very high ceiling height. My proposal was that we raise the floor level in the lounge by about a foot and convert the cellar into a large kitchen/dining area. The existing small kitchen would become an entrance hall. Anne agreed to my suggestions, and we set to.

The initial work of removing the few units in the small cellar head kitchen was soon done and the way was paved for the first major job, repositioning the entrance door. For this, I required help, so I enlisted the aid of a builder friend of mine. He removed the kitchen window, took away the stonework beneath, and inserted the new casing. Next, he took down the existing door and hung it in its new location. Finally, he sealed the former door opening with an inner skin of blockwork. A good day's work which left me in a position to complete this particular phase. This involved completing the outer skin of the old doorway. With the house now being secure, I had resolved to do it properly and tooth the new stonework into the existing walls. In fact, there was only one slight problem. The walls were of gritstone and the majority of old Bradford was constructed in sandstone. Would this be a holdup?

Well, not really. With my usual slice of luck, the problem was solved fairly quickly. I was visiting one of my sites and I noticed that a nearby building was being demolished. The gritstone was exactly what

I was looking for. After a quick word with the demolition contractor and money changing hands, I had my stone.

It was a relatively slow job bearing in mind I could only work at weekends. Even with Anne mixing mortar for me and helping with the sizing of the stone, I was only managing about two courses per visit. Still, the finished effect was worth it, and it will take a keen eye to spot there had once been a doorway there.

It was now time for the second major job, the raising of the ground floor level, and for this I enlisted the aid of my nephew, Nicky. The ex- kitchen cum entrance was to remain at its existing height to tie in with the new threshold level and the level of the cellar steps. This meant sawing off the existing 10" x 2" joists at the partition wall which ran from the cellar up to first floor level. They were prevented from crashing to the floor by some well-placed acrow props that I had 'borrowed'. The other end of the joists were bedded into the party wall, but with a bit of easing they were slid out. Once all the joists had been lowered we rawlplugged the partition wall and the party wall and bolted some 4" x 2" runners to them. The ends of the joists were then notched and lifted back into place in joist hangers fixed to these runners. This operation needed to be accurate so that the new floor level would exactly match the second tread on the staircase leading up to the first floor. The floor was then covered in some tongue and groove sheeting and the job was complete in one day. It's surprising what a difference a professional can make.

There were still other jobs to do, of course. The connecting door between the new hallway and the lounge required lifting to its new height and providing with a couple of steps. The fireplace also needed raising. In fact, I finished up building a new one in stone.

In the cellar/kitchen were a number of jobs that were beyond my capabilities. The flagged floor required asphalting, all the walls required plastering and the one external wall needed damp-proofing. As this work would require payment, Anne went back to the Building Society for an extension on her loan. They agreed, but informed her that each additional loan would incur a fee to themselves.

Anne had got herself an evening job working behind the bar at 'The Mucky Duck' in Frizinghall. She was explaining her predicament to one of the regulars who professed to be a builder, and he claimed he could do all three jobs and therefore, only require one loan. I invited him up to the house, and after several minutes conversation, it was obvious he was a cowboy. I tried to warn Anne off but she was very headstrong and gave him the go-ahead.

To be fair to John Wayne, he did make a reasonable job of the asphalting and plastering. However, the damp-proofing was another matter. What was suppose to happen was a series of holes were drilled into the stonework, sloping in a downwards direction. Into these holes was poured a silica solution, which would disperse into the stonework. The liquid would then evapourate, leaving the silica to seal the stonework. I inspected the cellar and found plenty of holes, but when I tested them, I found them all to be horizontal, and they clearly could not hold any liquid.

I had told Anne not to give Butch Cassidy any money until all the work was complete but he had managed to con her out of most of it. There were a few pounds outstanding however and Anne started getting threatening phone calls. Once Anne made it clear she was acting on my instructions these phone calls were directed to me. I even began receiving them at work, but it was clear that I wasn't going to move, so he changed his tactics and paid me a visit. It was early one morning and as I gazed out of the window, I saw his old van pull up outside. I shouted up to Anne that her friend had come to see us.

He stood outside the patio door looking at me, so I opened the door to hear what he had to say. Instead of speaking, he pointed back down the path. Like a lemon, I stuck my head out to see what he was pointing at, and the next thing I know, I received a blow to the side of my face. He ran off like a startled rabbit and I rang the police. They came quite quickly and could plainly see my swollen and bleeding lip. They seemed to know all about Jesse James and went to pick him up. Initially, a cafe owner on Legrams Lane gave him an alibi, but he cracked under the rubber hose treatment and they charged The Cisco Kid with assault.

Eventually, the case came to trial, and Anne and I had to appear at Leeds Crown Court as witnesses. We were kept outside the court until our turn came, then we were led in individually. I was up first and explained what happened that fateful morning. I faced a barrage of questions from two barristers. I believe one of them was supposed to be on my side, but I couldn't be sure. One of the jurors decided to get in on the act. He asked me if I was wearing my glasses when I was punched. I told him I was and he duly made a note. Finally, it was the turn of the judge to have his say.

"Mr Bennett," he intoned, "did this punch hurt you?"

"No your honour" I replied. "To be honest, I was more impressed with his running than his punching."

A little titter ran round the court. (Supply your own punchline.)

Next, it was Anne's turn to tell what she had seen through the kitchen doorway. The same juror asked her which way the kitchen door opened. She told him and he duly made a note.

The Lone Ranger was found guilty. It turned out he was on a suspended sentence for a similar offence, and he was sent down for three years.

Anne still had to get another expert in to finish off the damp coursing, but at least my cunning plan had worked. The conversion had taken so long that by the time she eventually moved in, she was somewhat older, and hopefully, a lot wiser.

I was telling this story to a friend sometime later and she asked whether I had been in touch with the Criminal Compensation Board. I had never heard of them, but I found out where they were based and sent them a letter. They replied, sending me a form to fill in and asking me to supply a photograph of my injuries. I got a friend at work to take a head shot, but when it was developed, there was little sign of the scar on my lip. It had healed so much that it was almost invisible. I decided to touch it up a bit with a dab of Tippex, and my mate took another photo. This time I looked like I was disfigured for life so I sent it off. The people at CCB obviously thought the same because they sent me a cheque for £300.

Anne took in a lodger to help with the mortgage. Robert was a schoolteacher which should have acted as a warning to me. It soon turned out that he was giving her more than the rent, and our first grandson, Dominic was born. He was followed two years later by grand-daughter, Gabrielle.

And so the wheel of life moves on
Now our daughter has bourne a son
Thanks to Dominic and to Anne
We'll now be known as Gramps and Nan

A house is not a home they say
Without a child or two at play
So down from Heaven an angel fell
To fill our lives, sweet Gabrielle

With two growing children, Anne decided that she needed a house with a garden, and No 5 Lark Street went on the market. She quickly sold it for six times the original price, making all that graft worthwhile. They moved to a large semi with plenty of garden in Crossflatts. By this time, Robert had decided he didn't like teaching so he told them he had had enough. Bradford Education Authority said OK and gave him a fat pension, at which point he elected to become a kept man. Anne decided someone else could keep him, and booted him out. This made my role as Grandpa even more important.

41

FUN IN THE SUN

In addition to our skiing trips, we usually managed to squeeze in a summer holiday as well. After sampling the delights of the Spanish Costas for a few years, we moved on to the Baliarics. We then had a couple of interesting trips to Malta, including one year watching the film 'Popeye' being shot. Eventually we made it to the Canaries.

First up was Gran Canaria where we stayed at the resort of Playa del Ingles. Just along the beach from us was the area known as Maspalomas, which had the reputation of being the largest nudist beach in the World. Well, I didn't mind getting my white bits brown as long as Irene rubbed plenty of cream in. As we walked passed the sunbeds which were filled exclusively with males, I was aware of hungry eyes watching us. Suddenly, two of them got up and ran into the sea. One turned to the other and said "Oooo, splash me, Tarquin. Splash me!"

I had been worrying about the wrong person.

The following year we went back, taking the children with us, but this time we were careful to avoid Maspalomas beach. Instead, we decided to take a trip on a square—rigged sailing ship. Mark, who would be 11 or 12 at that time, had befriended a younger lad staying in our hotel. He was there with his grandparents who didn't fancy the trip, so asked us if we would look after him. The ship sailed round the coast, and then moored-up in a quiet cove. The girl in charge of entertainment proposed a swimming race round the ship. There were to be two prizes—a tumblerful of brandy for the winner and a bottle of champagne for the loser.

Everyone got into the water and we set of in a flurry of splashing and kicking. I quickly found out that our young charge wasn't much of a swimmer, so I stayed with him as he slowly dog-paddled his way round the ship. Eventually, we got back to the starting point long after everyone else had finished. I followed him up the ladder and was met at the top by the entertainment officer who presented me with a bottle of champagne. At this point, Mark challenged me to a diving competition, and I reluctantly agreed. He went in off the side rail of the ship which was quite a height above the water. I followed. He got out, climbed up to the first rung of the rigging and dived in. I followed. He repeated the procedure, only this time going off the second rung. I followed. As he climbed up to the third rung, I was contemplating conceding the match when I was saved the trouble. The Captain had been watching proceedings and he forbade us to go any higher.

I turned to Irene and asked her what had got into Mark. She replied "He won the swimming race, was presented with a tumbler of brandy and knocked it back in one go. The little sod's drunk!"

The following year saw our first visit to Lanzarote. The island is barren compared to the others in the group, but it is interesting nevertheless, especially to someone like me, keen on the power of nature. We stayed at Peurto del Carmen in an appartment opposite the beach. There were enough bars, shops and restaurants to keep us busy when not swimming or sunbathing. Plus, the island's volcanic topography meant plenty of interesting trips. So much so that we decided to return the following year. In order to save a few bob, we booked what was known as a 'sunsaver' ticket. All this meant was, although we knew we were going to Lanzarote, we didn't know our final destination. From our previous visit, we knew this must be somewhere in Carmen. At that time, there was nowhere else. At least, that's what we thought.

We boarded the bus at the airport and set off. At the main road, instead of turning left, we turned right. We then turned inland, drove across the Island and dropped down towards the rocky West coast. We drove down a long, straight road, and in the distance we could see a large, white building standing on a rocky promontory on its own. Our representative told us it was called La Santa Sport, and that was to be our destination. We protested that we wanted somewhere with shops and bars, not a monastery. She asked us to give it a try for a couple of days, and if we still felt the same, she would move us.

Once we had got settled in and had a chance to look around, the picture began to change. The apartments themselves were formed around a central square, within which were bars, shops and restaurants, more of which later. However, it was the parts outside the complex that were really exciting.

To the east was a tartan track, a grass football pitch, tennis courts, a golf driving range and the bikesheds. To the south was a lagoon with windsurfing and canoeing, a recreational swimming pool, a beach volley ball pitch and a crazy golf course. To the west was a badminton hall, squash courts, a five-a-side pitch, an Olympic swimming pool, a basketball court and, most important of all, a superb gym. The bonus was, not only was all this sporting activity free, there was free instruction too. Most instructors were experts in their own field. Indeed, the young guy, Torben, who taught us to water ski was not only the Danish champion, he was also No. 3 in the World. Because the uniform they wore was predominantly green, their official title was the Green Team, but this inevitably got shortened to the 'Greenies.'

Children were well catered for too. They had their own playgroup run by specialist Greenies. There was a paddling pool and a children's playground, and in addition, numerous small sandy beaches around the lagoon. The bonus was, parents could leave their children, knowing they would be safe within the complex. All of this was academic at the time as our children were quickly becoming adults, but who knows what the future might bring in the way of grandchildren.

As veteran travellers on the continent, we were used to being pestered by time share touts. It came as something of a surprise therefore to find out that this place was indeed, timeshare. No pressure on us to buy. In fact, we had to go looking for a salesperson. We bought a couple of weeks in November, and as a thank you, we were offered a further two weeks free the following year. We chose to take them in the April, and this time we took the children with us. They loved it as much as we did, so we bought another two weeks.

One advantage of going in April was that it coincided with the British athletics squad doing their warm-weather training. In the gym I found myself rubbing shoulders with many household names and found most of them to be very friendly, although one or two were a bit stand-offish.

I was in the gym as usual one day working at the squat racks when I heard this deep brown voice behind me.

"Can I join you, man?"

Well, I wasn't going to say no to Linford Christie, was I?

He was completely different to his public image. He was one of the few "stars" to appear on the weekly guest show, for instance. I have a photo of him playing pool with a young child happily perched on his shoulders.

One year I was there as usual and he walked into the gym. After a few pleasantries, I asked him the whereabouts of his coach, Ron. He explained that he was out there for five weeks, and that Ron would be joining him for the final two, but in the meantime, he was on his own. I did the usual thing and offered my services, not really expecting him to take-up my offer. Instead he replied "Right. Meet me on the track at 10.00 tomorrow morning."

The following morning I turned up feeling a slight trepidation. Would I be able to cope with whatever he had in mind for me? He explained that he would be doing something called three- hundreds. He would line up at what would normally be the finishing line and I would give him the starting signal, at the same time pressing the stop-watch. He would sprint round the bottom bend, down the back straight and round the top bend. In the meanwhile, I would run down the homestraight and stop the watch as he crossed the starting line. In other words, he would be running 300metres whilst I did 100. Could I cope, bearing in mind I was now well into my fifty's.

We tried it and it worked OK. Linford looked at the watch and I saw him frown. After a rest, we repeated the process and the stop-watch got another frown. When it happened for a third time, I had to speak.

"What's up? Are the times too slow?" I asked.

"No, man" he replied. "They're too fast."

Huh!

He explained that he was aiming to peak at Barcelona at the end of the year, and his fast times meant that he would peak too early.

I had done some psychology training as part of my BAWLA coaching course, and now was the time to put it into practice.

"No," I said. "It doesn't mean that at all. What it does mean is that you will still peak at the required time, but you will reach a higher peak."

Linford immediately brightened up.

"Yeah man, you're right" he said.

In Barcelona later that year he won an Olympic gold medal in the 100 metres.

In addition to all the sporting activities being free, so was the entertainment. The complex had a nice disco set away from the apartments to minimise disturbance. The Green Bar had a number of pool tables and sponsored a weekly tournament. Not to be outdone, the Sports Bar ran a weekly quiz. However, the piece-de-resistance was the nightly activities in the square. This open area in the centre of the complex was bordered by shops, bars and restaurants as mentioned, but the central area was where it all happened. In this was a performance space modelled on a Roman amphitheatre with a stage at one end, fronted by a circular floor. This in turn was enclosed in tiered seating leading up to a level area which contained tables and chairs to accommodate clients of the Sports Bar and the Bodega restaurant. On show nights, these areas would be full of bodies, and you needed to book early in order to secure a table.

In the very early days, the square was used almost exclusively for dancing, with a live band providing the music. It was very pleasant to dance beneath the stars. One evening, Irene and I sat watching the proceedings when the band struck up a popular Danish number, and there was a rush for the floor. One young Dane came bounding down the stairs, took a flying leap onto the floor, and promptly fell on his back. He stood up, but immediately fell over once more. He tried again, but the same thing happened. He was helped to his feet and looked down in dismay. His left foot was at right angles to his leg where he had dislocated his ankle. The dance floor did tend to get wet with condensation in the evening, and shortly after that, a roof was built over the square.

With the passage of time, the entertainment in the square began to change to give a greater variety. There is something happening every evening with many of them being paid acts. A number of these are singers, either solo or part of a group, but we have watched many other acts such as magicians, jugglers and acrobats. However, the highlight of the week is inevitably the three variety shows. Two of these are performed by the Greenies, and known as the Green Team Show. It became a requirement when applying for a position on the Green Team, not only to be proficient at your chosen sport, but also be capable of performing on the stage. The third and probably the most popular of the variety shows is known as the Guest Show. As the name implies, this is performed by the timeshare owners themselves. Sometimes we will be lucky and have a guest with genuine talent, some groups might give us a dance, and occasionally, we will get a sketch, but by far the most popular act is to dress-up and mime to a record. The Greenies in charge of entertainment have a room full of costumes, and can usually accommodate every request. As an old ham, it was going to be difficult keeping me off the stage.

My first chance came somewhere around our third or forth year, when the Guest Show was still in its infancy. We had booked a meal at the Bodega and sat at a table overlooking the stage. During one of the acts, I could hear the familiar clanking of iron plates backstage. As the act finished, the compere called forward a young giant of a man from behind the curtains, and introduced him as the Junior Mr Denmark. Whilst this was going on, the stage hands brought a barbell and a number of weights to the front of the stage. The compere then announced that Mr Denmark was about to try and break the Danish deadlift record by lifting 300kg. As an afterthought, he added "Does anyone want to challenge him?"

It was a rhetorical question, of course, so he must have got something of a shock when I shouted back "Yes, I will." I was probably giving away about 30 years in age and about 20kg in bodyweight, but what the Hell! It would certainly be more entertaining for the spectators, and I thought I may have a couple of things going in my favour. I had recently broken the British Masters record with my 255kg, so I knew I would be able to put on a decent show. Secondly, although he was bulging with muscles, he was after all, only a bodybuilder, and they train in an entirely different manner to we powerlifters. They tend to use lighter weights and higher reps, and also take shorter rests. The idea is to force the body into using more energy in order to complete the sets. This energy is supplied in two ways. Firstly, extra glycogen is stored in the muscle and secondly, more capilliaries are formed to get this glycemic energy into the muscle. Both of these processes add bulk to the muscle without necessarily adding power. When a bodybuilder 'pumps-up' he is essentially engorging these capillaries with blood.

Anyway, all this theorising was shortly to be put to the test. The bar was already loaded to 150kg as my opponent had done some warming up backstage. To be fair to him, he did ask me if I wanted to do any warm-ups, but I brashly declined. I went first and lifted the 150kg quite comfortably, and he followed. He allowed me to choose the next weights, so I went 180; 200; 220; 240. Each time, he followed me, and each time, I watched him closely to detect any sign of weakness, but without success. I may or may not have had one more lift in me, but it was the first day of our holidays and I daren't risk an injury, so I made an honourable withdrawal. However, I did remain on the stage to give my erstwhile rival some help and encouragement. He proceeded with further lifts of 260 and 280 and then put on the all important 300kg. Although he made a gallant attempt, the bar wouldn't budge. Anyway, it didn't really matter. It couldn't count as a real record without referees being present, but we had achieved the prime objective of entertaining the crowd.

We became good friends during the remainder of his stay, and had many a chat about aspects of training. When I thought I knew him well enough, I asked that all important question. "Bodybuilders aren't supposed to lift all that heavy a weight, and the deadlift isn't a normal bodybuilding exercise, so how come you are so strong?"

"Well," he replied. "It is true that I am the Junior Mr Denmark, but I am also the European Heavyweight Powerlifting Champion." The compere forgot to tell me that little gem, but would it have made any difference? Knowing my impulsive nature, probably not.

With visiting the place twice a year, we got to know the staff pretty well. One year, the entertainment Greenie told us she was a bit short of acts for the Guest Show, and would we be able to do something. Of course, we said yes, but with the show being the following evening, I was prepared to fall back on the old standby and mime to a record. In fact, I thought the pair of us would make a passable Kenny Rodgers and Dolly Parton, and perhaps do "Islands in the Stream." However, Irene would have nothing to do with it on the grounds that everyone does a mime. She proposed that we do a ballet dance instead. What! In addition to all the other possible excuses I could have come up with, we only had one day to prepare. Never the less, we found a tape of the pas-de-deux from Swan Lake, and Irene set about devising some cheoreography. We spent the whole day in our room rehearsing, and come the evening, we made our debut, suitably dressed in tutu and tights, and calling ourselves Rudolph Nearinuf and Dame Vera Zadinuf. It went down a bomb—I think the entire complex must have been present. Well, all except one.

For the previous three or four mornings, we had been awakened in the wee small hours by a young child in the next apartment click-clacking her way around the tiled floor in her mother's high heels. Finally, I had to ring her mother and ask if she could stop her child from making this racket. She reluctantly agreed, but the following morning, she went to the reception to complain about us. The gist of her complaint was that, in retaliation for her child waking us up every morning, we had played the same record over and over again just to annoy her. Yeah, right! We'd give up a day's activities for such pettiness.

In order to try and fill the place, we were allowed to take additional weeks whenever space permitted. Moreover, we were allowed to take friends with us and order additional apartments at time share prices. Jacquie and Krystina were frequent visitors, as were nephew Nicky, initially with his friends and then with wife, Sue. Many of my weight lifting companions have also sampled the delights of La Santa Sport, but this idyllic state of affairs was to come to a sad end.

The original time share contract had dropped an almighty clanger. It had forgotten to include the clause stating that time share weeks must be paid for whether they are occupied or not. Many speculators had seized on this omission and bought multiple weeks. Of course, they couldn't occupy all these weeks and the complex was very rarely full. Since maintenance was based on 100% occupancy, this meant that it was losing money. In fact, we learnt that the Danish owner was subsidising it to the tune of two million pounds per year.

The current owner died and his business interests were inherited by his daughter. She quickly made it clear that she wasn't prepared to carry on subsidising the place. Her initial move was to ask the owners if we were prepared to renegotiate our contracts and pay maintenance regardless of occupancy. This didn't go down too well, especially with the speculators.

Her next move was to suggest that unoccupied apartments could be relet to ordinary holiday makers. This proposal was accepted, and now-a-days the occupation rate is close to 100% all the year round. The complex is finally making money, much of which is reinvested in upgrading and improving the facilities. It also hosts many International events, including the Lanzarote Ironman.

Ironman events are the pinnacle of achievement for triathletes, consisting of a two mile swim in the sea, a 100 mile bike ride and concluding with a full marathon. The Ironman was to prove a significant part of our lives, but that was some way off in the future. Our son, Mark had finished his time at Belle Vue School with an impressive list of qualifications. However, like myself many years previously, he didn't know what to do with his life. He got a succession of temporary jobs, but nothing that really stretched him.

We were using our November timeshare weeks one year when a potential disaster struck. The DJ from the disco quit! Fortunately, Mark was able to step into the breach. Amongst his many jobs, he had been running his own mobile disco back home and he was extremely talented. In addition, it was the time when kareoki was just making an appearance, and with his excellent singing voice, he could always get the evening off to a good start. Indeed, he made such a good job of it, he was offered the job permanently.

After returning home with us to collect some things, he made his way back there and remained for the following eight years. He had enough adventures to fill a book of his own, so I won't steal his thunder, except to say that he met his future partner, Caroline, out there.

Meanwhile, back at the University gym, I was coaching my lifters as usual. Between sets, I got into conversation with one of them, and asked what course he was doing. "Electronic Imaging and Media Communication" he replied. Being a bit of a dinosaur, I asked him to explain. As he did so, a bulb lit up in my brain. This was all the stuff that Mark was passionate about. I got a few more details and gave Mark a call. He agreed with me and flew home for an interview.

It was getting very close to the start of term and the course was essentially full. However, after Mark had recounted his adventures over the previous eight years, the interviewer told him he was just what they were looking for, and he was on the course. Four years later he graduated with honours.

He returned to Lanzarote, bought and converted an old farmhouse, set up home with Caroline and gave us our third grandchild, Jacob.

Initially, he worked for Lanzarote television, but then he became freelance, working on a commission basis. One of his regular jobs is to film the Lanzarote Ironman which is then sold to international television. He will engage eight or nine cameramen and give them precise duties. For example, for the swimming section, he has utilised underwater cameras giving a unique perspective on the race. He will usually also do a great deal of filming himself, perched precariously on the back of a motor bike zooming round winding roads and holding a heavy camera. He sometimes employs a professional actor to do the commentary and interviewing, but he has been known to do this himself. One year, I asked him how he got Richard Burton to do the commentary and he replied that it was in fact him. He had modulated the voice electronically.

The real work begins when the race is over. He needs to look through many hours of filming and edit it all down to about one hour of entertainment. He then has to add in pre-recorded interviews with the winners, make sure that the commentary is relevant and, finally, do the selling. Hopefully, this last job will prove easier as his reputation precedes him.

Ode to Jacob.

As we wait to watch you grow
There's one thing that we surely know
With such a gifted Mum and Dad
You're bound to be a likely lad
Will you be artistic like your father
As you climb your Jacob's ladder
Or be linguistic like your mum
Gifted with the proverbial tongue
Or at sport will you find fame
A Worldwide star, a household name
Perhaps them all, but then again
Does it matter what you attain
If love is your criterion
Then Jacob's already a No 1

42

THE PIONEERING SPIRIT

Bradford Council's Recreation Division started organizing skiing holidays and I joined in with enthusiasm. Although they were ostensibly for staff, family and friends were also welcome, and Irene, Krystina and Jacque joined in as well. It was nice to let someone else do all the work of booking flights and hotels, and I'm sure we got to many locations that we otherwise may have missed. It was also possible to meet up with colleagues from other departments. That was how we got to know Sue.

Sue worked for Social Services, and one day told me about one of her projects called the Bradford Pioneers. These were a group of children with various disabilities, mostly Downs Syndrome. The idea of the group was to get them together at regular intervals for social activities. This served the dual purpose of providing fun for the children and giving their parents a break.

Sue asked if I was interested in helping out and I agreed immediately. Most of the trips were one day affairs such as the Nell Bank animal rescue centre near Ilkley or the Birds of Prey centre at Settle. However, one day Sue came up with the idea that we could take them for a week's skiing. We proposed the idea at one of our regular meetings with the parents and got a tremendous response, which meant we would need an equally large number of volunteers. I roped-in Irene and a couple of guys from the weights club, and with some more Council employees, we were in business.

I was asked if I could find a large inner tube to take with us, and went to a garage that specialized in lorry repairs. I asked the proprietor if he had an old one we might have and he replied "No, lad. I've nowt like that." He then asked why I wanted it anyway, and I explained about the Pioneers. "Hang on," he said "and I'll see what we've got." He came back with the biggest inner tube I have ever seen. When I asked him how much, he said it was on the house.

We made our way to Valoire in the French Alps, high enough to almost guarantee snow, but with plenty of slopes to suit beginners. We booked the Pioneers in for lessons with two of the most patient instructors ever. They had lessons every morning whilst we volunteers did our own thing. We then linked up with them in the afternoon to practice what they had learnt. In the evening, after an early meal, I found out what the inner tube was for.

We all trooped off to the nursery slopes which were floodlit. We dragged the inner tube about 100 metres up the slope, got as many people inside as possible and let it speed down to the bottom, trying not to lose too many bodies on the way. Actually, it was better to try and 'fall' out if possible as the tube usually came to rest in a large puddle at the bottom. After about an hour of this, our charges were ready for their beds and we were ready for some liquid refreshment.

We were staying at a small family run hotel, and the only other people staying there were a party of adults from Cheshire. We naturally got chatting, and after a couple of days, one of the ladies asked Irene and me which one of the children belonged to us. We replied that none of them did and explained the situation. "Oh," she said. "I don't think I could do anything like that."

On the final evening, we had planned a big party for the children, and the hotel had laid on a special banquet. The two instructors turned-up looking resplendent in their full regalia, and presented the children with their certificates. The party that followed was fancy dress, and knowing what was coming, we had all brought something with us. The Cheshire party joined in the festivities, but had to make their fancy dress out of whatever they could lay their hands on. Our friend from the previous evening had particularly gone to town, and must have spent a considerable amount of time putting it all together. She joined in every game and really endeared herself to the children.

Not only had she found out that she could indeed do it, but she also found out how rewarding it was.

Back in Bradford, things got back into the normal routine. By now, I had become chairman of the Pioneers.

This involved going to regular meetings with the parents for feedback and to plan further outings. One of these was to be a long weekend at an activities centre called Lakeside, situated on the shores of Lake Windemere. Once again, I recruited a couple of my weight-lifting buddies to help out.

The camp itself was absolutely first rate. Activities included an obstacle course, abseiling, a zip line, canoeing and archery, a very full programme. Hopefully, enough to ensure that the kids slept soundly, but we had been warned that Downs Syndrome children can be a little promiscuous, so we patrolled the corridors in the dormitories until all seemed quiet.

The brochure had said that everyone must be off camp by 4 o'clock on the Sunday, and so I had advised the parents I would be dropping the kids off from about 6.00 onwards. At 4.00 on the Sunday we were sat on the top of a hill admiring the view, and our guide didn't seem in any hurry to get rid of us. Eventually we got back to camp and I told the children to 'phone their parents and let them know we would be late.

At the following parents' meeting I was preparing myself to be suitable embarressed by all the thanks. Instead, all I got was complaints, "Why hadn't I got them home at the promised time?" and "Why had I allowed them to climb in and out of each others bedroom windows?"

I reluctantly handed in my resignation.

The kids were great. Shame about the parents.

43

MAJOR DISASTER

Bradford Council loved reorganizations. Some were thrust on them, others were self imposed. One of the former happened about three years after my arrival and it was quite substantial. It saw Bradford move from a borough council to a metropolitan district council by absorbing all the surrounding urban councils. This didn't go down too well in these areas as they could see their rates subsidising Big Brother Bradford. In this, they weren't too far wrong. In all my years with Bradford, I don't remember doing a single job in Ilkley for instance. Of course, one could argue that all the money in up-market Ilkley had been made in Bradford's smokey mills anyway, so justice was being done.

There was one other important implication to this move—all the major highway schemes were to be designed and contracted out by the County Council. This body had been set up to represent the five Metropolitan districts of Leeds, Wakefield, Huddersfield, Halifax and Bradford. In effect, one level of beaurocracy had been replaced by another. The theory was that with a bigger pot of money to spend on each district in turn, this would enable larger schemes to be completed.

The theory may have been sound, but the practice was definitely stacked against Bradford. With the other four districts being Labour controlled, Conservative Bradford was sure to be well down the pecking order. And so it proved.

Leeds was naturally first to have its inner relief road built. This was followed by Wakefield, Huddersfield and then, Halifax. Finally it was the turn of Bradford. Nothing could go wrong now, could it?

Well, yes it could. The County Councils were disbanded!

Bradford re-formed its own major works section and resolved to carry on alone. In fact, Bradford's inner relief road makes an important link between the M62 and the M6 via the A65, which should have given it a much higher priority in the first place. However, this makes the huge assumption that people in high places actually know what they're doing.

Not withstanding this, Bradford established the desired line from its boundary at Chain Bar all the way to its northern boundary at Kildwick, then broke the road down into manageable sections and set about the detailed design.

The rural sections were the first to be designed and constructed, having the least disturbance value. These included the stretch from Chain Bar to the outer ring road at Staygate and designated the title M606. This was followed by the sections from Kildwick to Keighley and from Keighley to Bingley, and it was time for the first real urban stretch. Saltaire was nominated for this honour, being a complete bottleneck.

The obvious solution to this daily snarl-up is a tunnel under Nab Wood. At 2.5 kilometers, it is approximately 2 kilometers shorter than the existing circuitous route. Additionally, it cuts out eight sets of traffic lights and the notorious Saltaire roundabout. However, this solution was scuppered even before it got off the ground, ostensibly because of the cost.

Cost of course, is a relative concept and it would all be recouped in a relatively short time by the savings in time and fuel. Additionally, the 'green' benefits are inestimable, but government ministers are clearly colour blind. The box on wheels is going to be around for a long time to come, whatever the fuel, but there are many more practical ways of saving money rather than cutting down on roadworks. Engine size can be capped by legislation and top speeds can be built into engines. It seems strange to have a top speed of 150mph when the legal limit is 70. This will bring squeals from the 4x4 brigade and the boy racers, of course, but the benefits would certainly outweigh this minor inconvenience. In fact, the most important statistic for a car is not its rate of acceleration or its top speed, but its fuel consumption. This isn't usually prominently displayed, but can normally be found among the small print. Two figures are usually given—the urban and the non-urban. By the use of judicious design, the highway engineer can bring these figures closer together.

Meanwhile, back in Saltaire an alternative was drawn up following the route of the canal and the railway, and this was submitted for public inquiry. There were two objectors at this meeting. The first was a local smallholder who didn't want the sound of cars disturbing his pigs. The second was an itinerant trouble maker whose sole purpose in life was to travel from one highway inquiry to another, objecting on principal to any form of development. I found out many years later that his services had been obtained and paid for by the Bradford Rail Action Group. Their reasoning was that if they could keep Saltaire a bottleneck, people would abandon their cars in favour of train travel.

Complete nonsense of course, but obsessive people are always blinkered. The outcome was that the government inspector, to his undying shame, took notice of these two dubious objectors and the people of Saltaire are suffering the unhealthy consequences.

The next section to be considered was the Bingley relief road. This presented a number of engineering problems, including diverting the Leeds/Liverpool canal, crossing both the north and south bogs and spanning the River Aire. Engineers love solving problems and the design was quickly drawn up. The inquiry must have had a more enlightened inspector because the plans were accepted and the scheme got underway. The construction was not without its problems however, as it was targeted by 'Swampy' and his fellow loonies. Yet more idiots who thought that traffic was designed to choke up towns and villages. His chosen methods of obstructing the work was firstly to perch in trees that needed to be felled, then, once the work was more advanced, he would dig tunnels under the new highway. Strangely enough, he was never heard of again once the job was completed. Maybe he's buried in one of his tunnels. More likely he's something in the City and drives a large, gas-guzzling car.

The road was completed and the centre of Bingley was reclaimed by its residents. The relief road itself is mainly in cutting. Many more trees were planted than were taken down and when these trees begin to mature, they will form a green tunnel which will act as a noise barrier and a filter for greenhouse gasses. We engineers are not the vandals some people depict us to be.

The link road was slowly taking shape, but there were still some important gaps. The second stage of the M606 from the Staygate roundabout to the inner ring road at Croft Street had run into its own problems. In my early days with Bradford, our major works department had upgraded Manchester Road and Wakefield Road to dual three lane carriageways and the Ministry of Transport now used this fact to deny permission to procede with the M606 Stage two. They claimed it was impractical to have three major highways in the same sector. In that case, and knowing that the M606 was in the pipeline, why had they given the go-ahead for the two radials? Anyway, Manchester Road has since been severly reduced again by the inclusion of a permanently empty bus lane and parking bays outside shops. Will our Council reapply for planning consent? Not really as the plonkers have sold off all the land for redevelopment.

Anyway, all this speculation suddenly became secondary. In the early 90's Mrs Thatcher was in power and her paymasters in the construction industry complained to her that highway design work was being given to local authorities instead of them. They didn't have the wit to realize that the design work was non-profit making whereas the construction in which they would be involved, gave plenty of opportunity for money making.

The implications of all this was that new legislation was to be introduced known as Compulsory Competative Tendering. Conservative Bradford, in full appeasement mode, jumped on this particular bandwagon with alacrity. The outcome was that Bradford decided to have a cull of all senior engineers in order to make the division more competitive when tendering for new work. To facilitate this major transition, the Council put together what was, essentially an attractive package. We were offered the remaining years of our service to be added to our existing years for superannuation purposes with this amended amount to become payable immediately. Even with this amended amount, my pension would only amount to three eights of my current salary, a hugh drop.

More importantly, I loved my work and couldn't imagine not doing anything worthwhile for the rest of my life. I went to see the boss.

He was very sympathetic, but told me the offer was non-negotiable. However, he did promise that once the legislation was in place and Bradford began to win a few contracts, there would be an opportunity to re-enlist.

In the event, Maggie faced her own night of the long knives. She was ousted, firstly by her own party and then by the electorate, and CCT never found its way onto the statute books, although, by then the deed had been done and I was a gentleman of leisure. However, Bradford were as good as their word and did give me a steady supply of work over the following ten years. Moreover, in order not to compromise my superannuation, I was employed via an agency. In other words, Bradford were paying me twice, but I forced myself to accept. Well, serves them right for playing politics.

With so many senior engineers gone, the highways design section was once again farmed out to an agency. This body had no real interest in the welfare of Bradford and its traffic problems, and after a few desultory attempts at getting the relief road moving, they gave up, and the incompleted scheme remains a monument to ineptitude.

There was an interesting aside to all these machinations. Two of my fellow early retirees, Hugh and Mike, suggested we should all keep in touch, and to this end, they formed a walking group. An appropriate acronym was formed from the words Bradford Retired Engineers Walking Society, and we became the BREWS. We meet on the middle Wednesday of each month with spouses and friends being welcome. An average turnout will be in the region of twenty bodies. The winter walks are designed with a lunch stop at a local pub in order to give our old bones a chance to thaw out, whilst the summer walks rely on sandwiches to keep us moving. Anyone can volunteer to lead, which gives us a large pool of knowledge. Even now, I find myself going on new walks. We have a newsletter called, naturally enough, the BREWS NEWS which describes the previous walk, gives details of forthcoming ones, and interesting titbits about members.

After 18 years, we are still going strong, although 'strong' might not be an appropriate word. Now-a-days we resemble the lost tribes of Israel, and I'm sure I've seen a couple of vultures following us, ready to pick off stragglers.

Irene shows neice Dianna the art of ab control

Everything comes to those who persevere

House warming in the Larks Nest

We have hiked from Alsace to the Dales (But not literally)

From the forest to the hills

Linford Cristie at work

And play

Rudolph Nearinuf and Dame Vera Zadinuf

The BREWS at a compulsory stop

Dominic at La Santa

Gabby looking cute

Mark celebrates with Anne, Dominic and Gabrielle

Dominic and Gabrielle become stars

Did I mention that I love dressing up

Jacob looking mischievious

Jacob with his Daddy

Jacob at La Santa beach

Jacob and Dominic

One of the many groups we took to La Santa

Are they really abs or is it trick photograph

The hair is greyer, the figures are fuller, but the look remains the same

Section Five

Power Lifting

44

GETTING STARTED

Although I had finished playing rugby, I maintained my active association with Bradford Salem for a while longer. The first job I took on was as a referee for the third team home fixtures. In order to do this, I acquired a rule book and studied it. It was surprising how much I didn't know in spite of playing the game for many years. Mind you, I watch a lot of internationals now-a-days and they seem pretty clueless about the rules too.

The second job involved setting up and running a minis section. There were plenty of participants but not too much help from the other parents. Most of them would drop their kids off then return home for a quiet Sunday morning in bed.

After teaching the kids the basic skills, we organized a few matches against other minis. Whilst refereeing these, I quickly found out what many another ref has discovered, both before and since. There is nothing more frightening than an angry parent who thinks his precocious child has been treated unfairly.

I tried running a few fund raisers such as treasure hunts in order to buy a set of shirts, but even these were poorly attended, and my enthusiasm began to wane. Although I enjoyed watching the kids develop, I grew tired of being a babysitting service. Once more, it was a case of—great kids, shame about the parents, and again I found myself resigning.

Although these activities were keeping me involved, I was missing the competitive side of playing and my thoughts returned to the possibility of powerlifting. By now, we were well ensconced in the new gym and I was regularly training with other lifters. I had always used the squat and bench press as part of my training, but now I started to include the deadlift as well.

Looking back at my training diaries of that time, I can see that I fell into the usual beginners trap, that of over training. The powerlifts in particular use big muscles and require lots of energy and lots of recovery time. In fact, I was training all three powerlifts on Monday and Friday and doing twelve assistance exercises on Wednesday, including heavy cleans and front squats. Doing squats and deadlifts on the same day is particularly bad as both exercise the same muscles—the quadriceps, the hamstrings and the gluteals. By performing one exercise to near failure means the following one cannot be performed to its full potential. In addition, I was doing heavy singles every alternate session. Conventional wisdom has it that singles are only performed at competition. However, there was no recognized coach in those days and it was a case of finding out by trial and error.

After training for a while, I was persuaded to enter my first competition. In those days, all competition was run by the British Weight lifting Association and ranged from World championships all the way down to Divisionals. My debut was to be the Yorkshire and North East Divisionals held at the Huddersfield Sports Centre.

The first job was to weigh-in. There are twelve different weight classes for men, ranging from 52kg to 145+kg. Working on the principle that it is better to be at the top of one weight category rather than at the bottom of another, I had got my weight down to just under the 82.5kg class limit. As we stood on the platform to be introduced to the audience, I took a look at my fellow competitors. All three were shorter than me, with the eventual winner, John White, being a good eight or nine inches smaller and built like the proverbial brick outhouse. I was to get my first practical demonstration that powerlifting is all about leverages.

My top three lifts of 137.5kg squat, 112.5kg bench and 200kg deadlift reflected well on my training poundages, and were enough to give me 3rd place. However, when compared with John's winning lifts of 275kg, 155kg and 260kg, it was clear that I still had a long way to go.

I thought that I had one thing going for me though. This first competition had fallen just seven months short of my 40th birthday, at which point, I would become a Master and be able to compete against other golden oldies.

In deference to the competition being on a Sunday, I had taken the Friday off from training. However, I was back in the gym on the Monday, lifting heavy weights. Once again in mitigation, there was no one to tell me the importance of cycling ones training, and the value of rest and recovery breaks. As in all sport, powerlifting is fuelled by adrenelin, and this is naturally high after competition. Trainees must learn to ignore this and force themselves to stay out of the weights room for a week or two.

The other aspect of training that I was slowly coming to terms with was the mental side. When lifting maximal weights, it is natural to have feelings of negativity. One must train to overcome these feelings by encouraging positive thoughts. Now-a-days, I tell my students that training is 50% physical strength and 50% mental strength. One of the many benefits of heavy training is that this mental strength carries over into everyday life.

These criteria help to explain why there is such a discrepancy in the perception of the different lifts. In the squat and bench press, the bar is taken either across the shoulders or at arms length, and slowly lowered to the starting point before the lift proper commences. During this lowering stage, the trainer has time to register the enormous weight and negativity could set in. The deadlift is just the opposite with the lift commencing straight from the floor. The lifter psychs himself up for a big pull and the bar is well on its way before the weight begins to register. Most beginners tend to under perform on the first two lifts, but exceed their expectations in the deadlift.

I probably wasn't aware of all this philosophizing at this stage of my fledgling career. One thing was clear though, I would need some more bodyweight in order to compliment my long levers. Most lifters learn to manipulate their bodyweight using the appropriate training. We already use heavy weights for low repetitions and work the largest muscle groups in the body, so that part of the plan was already in place. In the case of gaining weight, two further things were required—keep the cardio to a minimum and eat plenty of good wholesome food. I had always had an appetite like a bird. It was time to stop being a tit and become a gannet.

Looking back at my training diaries, I can see that I still continued to train in the same crazy fashion. In fact, the only concession I made was to reduce my assistances from twelve to six, and this was probably more due to exhaustion rather than reasoned thinking.

The following year, I once again competed in the Divisionals, but this time my bodyweight was just under the 90kg limit. My lifts were 160, 125, 227.5 which was a good improvement over a year. Of course, there would have been some improvement anyway, but the additional bodyweight certainly helped. My total was enough to win me my first Masters 1 title, but unfortunately, the competition was too small to run to trophies for masters and I had to content myself with yet another third place trophy for the open event.

I ploughed straight on with my training as previously, but at least, I introduced a couple of innovations.

The first one was to include the concept of cycling into my training. Instead of plunging straight back into lifting maximal weights, the cycling principle advocates starting again after a competition with a relatively lighter weight utilizing the principle of active rest. This allows both the body and mind to recover whilst still giving the body a decent workout. As the cycle progresses, the trainee will eventually reach their previous best {PB}. If the timing has been correct, the trainee will be able to have a couple of weeks or so of improving on these PB's before competing again and hopefully, consolidate these new maximums.

The second innovation was to finish doing all of those silly singles as part of my training and stick to something like five reps. Once again, the logic for this is undeniable. The body is naturally self protective and lactic acid will start to build up as the set progresses. This is a sign that further repetitions will cause damage to the muscle. However, for improvement, this muscular trauma is in fact a requirement. I tell my students that trainees will grow stronger whilst they are resting, not training, and this is easily demonstrated. When training the multi set system to near failure, the number of reps will fall as the sets progress. However, after a good 48 hour minimum rest, if this same exercise is repeated, the chances are that MORE reps will be possible. What in fact is happening, is that the body is repairing the damage the lifter has inflicted on it, but making it that fraction stronger so that the next time you ask it to lift a heavy weight, the muscle is up to it. Of course, the next time, you ask the muscle to do even more reps or lift even more weight. That is why it is called progressive weight training.

Lifting a maximum weight for a single rep would actually cause some muscle trauma and hence some further growth, but it would be very hard both physically and mentally to train this way. Far better to use a weight that will enable you to do a few reps. The early ones will act to pre-exhaust the muscle and the final one or two will do that all- important job of traumatisation. Trial and error has suggested that the optimum number of reps is five, which drop down to threes and finally twos immediately before a competition, but keep those singles for the platform.

Both of these innovations were a step in the right direction, and my steady progress continued. At my third Divisionals, I had increased my bodyweight once again to 94kg which enabled me to squat 170, bench 127.5 and deadlift a creditable 240. My total of 537.5 was enough to give me a second place in the open category. At 42 years of age, I should have been looking forwards to several more years of progress, but, unbeknown to me, clouds were gathering on the horizon. In fact, although I subsequently managed to push my squat and deadlift marginally higher, I never managed to surpass that 127.5 benchpress.

I wouldn't find out the shattering reason for several years to come.

45

TEAM BUILDING

We were now firmly established in our new training room. It was necessary for all users to join the weights club in order to train, regardless of their aims. The very nature of weights dictates that these uses can vary greatly. By far the largest group would come under the loose heading of bodybuilding. Having been there myself, I could advise if ever I managed to get them away from the mirror. The second group comprised of those that were weight training in order to improve their chosen sport. Once again, I'd been there and done that, and was able to help out. This left the third group comprising the lifters themselves. The Uni had teams from both the competitive elements of weightlifting, Olympic lifting and powerlifting, and both would devote time to training newcomers.

In the case of the Olympic lifters, my good friends Dave Dargue and Joe Graham were the senior exponents and were called upon to pass on their knowledge. However, the Olympics, comprising the snatch and clean and jerk lifts is a difficult sport to master, requiring a great deal of flexibility. The best lifters are those that are recruited when they are fairly young, before their joints have a chance to seize up. The powerlifts on the other hand, comprising as they do of three standard exercises, are much easier to teach, and I tended therefore to get the bulk of the new recruits. Even if the bodybuilders ever stooped to ask my advice, I would tell them that the best way to get big was to exercise the body's large muscle groups, such as the legs, the chest and the upper back. I then went on to explain that they should be doing plenty of squats, bench press and even deadlifts. By such devious means was I able to spread the word about the benefits of powerlifting.

Having talked newcomers into taking up powerlifting, it now befell me to supervise their future development. In effect, I found myself drifting into coaching rather than making any conscious effort. This had the positive effect of making me think about my own training from a deeper prospective. For instance, I became interested in the psychological aspects of lifting. In certain sports such as football, competitive matches are played every week and training for them is an inconvenience to be bourne. Powerlifters on the other hand may only compete a maximum of four times per year. It is important therefore that they enjoy their training and look forward to it. This is yet another reason why cycling is so important. The lifter is essentially competing with himself week upon week. Furthermore, if the lifter is performing a PB for reps, it stands to reason that his top single will also be a PB and there is no need to constantly prove it.

These insights had been hardwon by myself, learning from the perspective of trial and error, and I was happy to pass them on. I did manage to get a steady stream of lifters over the years, some with great potential and others, like me, destined to be hardgainers. It used to upset me when students, particularly those with the potential, fell by the wayside. With the passing years, I have become more philosophical and concede that lifting, in spite of its many benefits, is not for everyone.

The main recruiting effort was done at the beginning of the academic year at the athletics association fair. The dance area within the student communal building was taken over and each club and society was given a table and a notice board for posters, etc. On the day of the fair, freshers and other students would stroll around seeing what was on offer. It was our duty to try and encourage them to join our club.

There were display areas where clubs could set up their apparatus to futher encourage recruitment. One year, we availed ourself of this facility and took an Olympic bar down with a 15kg disc on each end. The accompanying poster read "If you can lift this, the weights club need you." Underneath was another one which read "If you can't, you need the weights club."

Although the fair gave us a flying start, recruitment carried on throughout the year. The till roll on the desk gave the destination of every customer and Sue, the sports centre manageress, told us that the membership of the weights room in general was second only to her own pet project, the aerobics classes. I'm sure if we started to train in tight fitting Lycra, we could have beaten even them.

I was constantly on the lookout for potential lifters, and one that I'd had my eye on was Tim Litt. I'd seen him training several times and one of his main exercises appeared to be doing countless repetitions of the wrist curl. This is probably one of the least productive of all exercises, and my curiosity was raised. When asked, he informed me that his hobby was sailing, and he needed a strong grip to cope with all the rope pulling. I told him that I thought he had an excellent shape for powerlifting, and, as a crafty afterthought, I mentioned that deadlifting was the single best way of improving your grip. Tim tried the lifts and confirmed my thoughts—he had the musculature and leverages to make a superb powerlifter. Indeed, Tim went on to become my first student to gain International honours.

Tim pointed me in the direction of a pal of his, Don Fleming who was also using the gym. I had seen him, of course, but hadn't paid too much attention as I thought him the wrong bodytype. Now that I had a closer look, I could see how wrong I was. At a bodyweight of 52kg, he was benching close to 100kg. A double bodyweight bench is international standard and Don hadn't even started the specialized training yet.

A third member of this particular triumvirate was Andy Rignall, known to one and all as Arthur. He had joined the club a few years earlier and reminded me of a smaller version of myself—very slight with long levers. However, through sheer persistence, he had built himself up and was now posting creditable totals.

With these three on board, plus one or two others, I could begin to cut back on my own involvement. The previous year, for example, I had competed eight times, usually league matches, which is far too much, and probably contributed to my lack of progress.

In those league matches, the University had usually been the whipping boy, although, as I was to find out later, we hadn't been competing on a level playing field. Now, however, we actually began winning things. At that time, the British Student Sports Federation ran an annual powerlifting competition. The culmination of this was a trophy presented to the highest scoring three-man team worked out on a bodyweight formula. My three of Tim, Don and Andy began winning this on a regular basis, and there was an audible groan from the other competitors whenever we arrived at the venue.

One year, Tim was awarded the Victor Ludorum trophy for the best sporting achievement at the University Sportsman's dinner. His acceptance speech was very short. He stood up, said "I nominate my coach to make my speech," and then sat down again. No big deal. I can waffle for England, especially when I've had a jar or two. At a subsequent dinner, I found myself making another speech, only this time, it was on my own behalf. I had been awarded the AA presidents prize for services to University sport. There wasn't a trophy as such, but what he had done was to arrange for me to become a free life member of the Uni gym. In fact, I had been paying my entry fee religiously every visit, in spite of my unpaid coaching, so this was indeed a perk.

One of the many additional benefits of weight training, as already mentioned, is the mental discipline which rubs off onto other aspects of life. As if to prove this, Tim, Don and Arthur all got good degrees and stayed on to do their doctrates. The bonus of this for me, of course, was that I had their services for seven or eight years instead of the normal three or four. Now-a-days, they are all married with families and are living near to one another in the Midlands. We are in regular communication and try to get together at least once a year. The brotherhood of the weights is strong.

46

JOBS GALORE

And still they gazed
And still the wonder grew
That one small head
Could carry all he knew

Thomas Gray

There could have been another reason why I was doing my coaching for free, of course. I had no formal qualifications. I had always worked closely with the AA president, and one year, I got particularly pally with the current imcumbent, possibly because O.J. himself was the karate coach. He mentioned the fact that the Student's Union would pay for me to get qualified as a thank you for all the years of unpaid coaching I had done. Well, I was happy doing a job I liked, but if there was any money going, I may as well have some of it.

BAWLA did three levels of certificates at that time, with the first level being known as the Leaders course. This took place over two days, usually a weekend, and focussed primarily on the business of teaching exercise. As I had already been doing this for a number of years, I was given permission to go straight onto the second level, the Instructors Certificate. This took place over two weekends and comprised of more teaching practice combined with some basic physiology. There was also a chance to do some practical teaching, and our instructor had recruited a number of local youths to act as guinea pigs for us. No health and safty issues in those days, of course. This was tremendous stuff, and of all the studying I had done, this was certainly the most satisfying. I was now a fully qualified instructor, and as good as their word, the University began to pay me.

Shortly after this, I was approached by Bradford's Recreation Division. They ran a number of free-weights classes at various sport centres and it appeared that one of the current instructors was leaving. They had contacted BAWLA who had given them my name, and was I interested in the part time post? A chance to spread the word whilst getting paid was no contest really, and so I found myself working two evenings per week at Manningham Sports Centre. Some weeks later, I got another 'phone call, this time from Thornton Recreation Centre, where the same thing had happened, and would I like to take over there as well. Their two evenings were different, and being a boy who can't say no, I found myself working four evenings a week. In addition, I was still doing my own training and coaching at the Uni. It was good for the taxman, but once again, I wasn't seeing much of the family.

I stuck it out for a while then decided to offload the Manningham job on to one of my colleagues at the gym. However, I kept the Thornton job going for a number of years. In fact, my eventual departure was brought about by some mistaken happening that was very current at that time. Many a gym, both commercial and municipal were getting rid of all the free weights in favour of the new resistance machines that were becoming the fashion. The theory was that these machines are more user-friendly and also safer, thus requiring less supervision. All this is no doubt true, but many a trainee prefers to train with free weights and lots of gyms are re-establishing free weight areas to run alongside their machines. This was not to be the case at Thornton where they gave many of their weights to a local school, and I claimed the remainder for the University.

Losing the Thornton job was no big deal in spite of the fact that I had found two World class lifters there, as I already had another job. Delivering courses was, in theory at least, a big money spinner for BAWLA. I was to find out later that it wasn't bringing in quite what it should.

In our YNE Division, the courses were run by two likely lads, Bill and Bob. For some unknown reason, the two of them did a disappearing act, leaving the Division without a course coordinator. In addition to the courses being an excellent source of income, they were also a good recruiting ground for new lifters. It was essential therefore that they were replaced as quickly as possible. I was asked to take on the job, and once again, I was happy to oblige.

I received the teaching material, with which I quickly familiarised myself. Next, I organised a course at the University for staff and colleagues to break myself in gently amongst friends. I found that I liked teaching, and had an aptitude for it. Very soon, I began receiving calls for courses. These were split into two types. Firstly, there were the large institutions like other universities, colleges, sports centres and even prisons. They required me to agree a suitable date, turn up and deliver the course—all very straightforward. The second type were the individuals, and in their case, I put them in touch with their nearest institute that was running a course. I quickly built up a collection of contact names, and places such as Carnegie College would probably put on three courses per year. On average, I was doing about twenty each year, mostly the Leaders Certificate, but occasionally, we would do the Instructors. The area I covered stretched from Sheffield in the South to Berwick upon Tweed in the North, and from Hull in the East to Halifax in the West. If the course was nearby, I would travel to and from the venue on the Saturday and Sunday, but if the venue was any distance, I would stay over night. Although I was on expenses, I tried not to abuse them and my digs would usually be lowly B&B's. The courses cost the students £100 for the leaders and £200 for the Instructors, and with class sizes varying from eight to thirty, the money was rolling in. The Divisional treasurer express surprise, and said this was far in excess of what had been coming in in the past.

After a while, Bob reappeared as suddenly as he had disappeared, and asked if he could help out on the courses. As far as teaching was concerned, it did not matter how many where in the class, the lessons took the same time. However, roughly 40% of the courses consisted of practical work and this could be very time consuming for a single person as every student required personal attention. For that reason, I took Bob on. In fact, we got into a routine wereby I would do some of the smaller ones, Bob would do others, and we would share the larger ones.

This idyllic situation carried on for a year or two, and then I got another offer of help from Gavin. He lived in Durham and was prepared to do all of the courses in his part of the country to save me a lot of travelling. I agreed although it meant a considerable loss of income for me. Additionally, I was still spending a considerable time on the telephone organizing the courses. The final piece of this particular jigsaw fell into place when Bill reappeared and asked if he could do some courses for me. As it happened, I had a large one coming up at Carnegie and I knew Bob was going to be away, so I said he could help me with that one.

I had heard that he was something of a wizz kid at teaching, so I let him take the lead, hoping to learn something. I was disappointed. His style was far too bombastic and confrontational for my taste with no anecdotes or levity to relieve the situation. Eventually, we came to the practical exam and one young lady was clearly very nervous and made a mess of her presentation.

"That was rubbish," shouted Bill. "You've failed."

"Hang on," I said. "You can't fail her. The practical is continuous assessment, and we continue working with them until we get them all through."

"Well, you better get her through then because I can't be bothered."

By this time, she had disappeared into the toilet in floods of tears. I managed to coax her out, took her to one side and gave her indivual coaching. Gradually her confidence returned, and eventually I considered her delivery good enough to pass. It only remained to do the written exam.

I had been in the habit of sending these off to an independant marker so there could be no suggestion of collusion, but Bill elected to mark them himself. The following morning, I got a 'phone call from Bill.

"You know that woman you pushed through the practical. Well, you needn't have bothered because she failed the written exam," he said triumphantly.

For a moment, I was flummoxed. Recovering my composure, I replied "Will you send me her paper so I can see what she is weak on, and persuade her to do a re-sit."

"Can't do that," he replied. "I've destroyed all the papers."

"What!! Don't you know it is illegal to destroy exam papers?"(I felt like adding' you pillock,' but restrained myself.)

I rang head office for guidance and spoke to Wally Holland, our General Secretary. He confirmed my view that it was illegal to destroy an exam paper, and instructed me to give the young lady a pass.

Some weeks later, I had one of my regular team meetings with Bob and Gavin. The meeting was in Ripon, very close to Bob's house and I arrived early. I decided to call on Bob to pass a bit of time. He opened the door looking a bit sheepish, and when I followed him in I could see why. Gavin was already there, as was Bill who had not been invited. On the table were half empty cups of tea and plates of biscuits. What on Earth was going on? I was soon to find out.

We trooped across the road to the hall and I started the meeting. I had an agenda, but it soon became clear that they had one of their own. One after the other they began attacking me with what looked like a well-rehearsed plan. Some of the things they accused me of were frivolous, some were outright lies. There was only one point they made that was relevant. Courses are supposed to be delivered by BAWLA Coaches and I was only qualified to Instructor level. I made the point that no one cared about that some years previously when I had got the Division out of a hole.

I noticed the Bill was sat to one side smirking. I suspected he may have coordinated the whole thing.

"You shouldn't have passed that girl," he sneered.

"The situation won't arise again because you won't be working for me anymore," I replied.

"You can't talk to Bill like that," spluttered Bob.

"I can and I have," I replied.

One of them proposed a vote of no confidence in me and all three hands shot up. So that was their plan, to get me out, but I still didn't fully understand why. I was doing the job conscientiously, and they were getting a far bigger share of the work than I was.

When I returned home, I wrote my letters of resignation and sent one off to Head Office. A few days later, Wally Holland was on the 'phone wanting to know what was going on, so I told him the story of the meeting.

"I'm not accepting your resignation," he said. "I'd rather those other three idiots resigned."

He then went on to tell me what had been happening. Apparently, in prisons, qualified officers were allowed to give courses to the inmates in the hope that maybe they could find gainful employment upon release. To this end, they had been given their own supply of certificates. Some prison officers had abused the system by using this supply of certificates to run courses outside the prison and pocketing the money for themselves. Both Bill and Gavin were prison officers.

No wonder the Divisional treasurer had been so happy with me—he had never seen so much money. I had been like a breath of fresh air.

I explained to Wally that there were still a couple of problems to overcome. The first one was that I was indeed under qualified to be running courses, and the second one was that I had also sent a letter of resignation to our Divisional President, Mike O'Carroll. Wally replied that he would take care of both problems.

He was as good as his word and organized a Coaches course for me in Manchester. There were six other Instructors on the course to make the class viable, and we spent another two interesting weekends with the emphasis this time being on the psychology of coaching.

In the meantime, Mike called for an Executive meeting to discuss my letter. I didn't go, of course, but my friend Fearless gave me a blow by blow account. After a bit of discussion, the motion was put not to accept my resignation. Gavin was there in his capacity as Prisons' Officer and Bob was there in his role of Schoolboy's Officer. The motion was carried unanimously. Hypocracy or what?

I carried on as courses coordinator, but my heart was no longer in it. How can you work with people who tried to stab you in the back? At the next AGM, I didn't put my name forward for the post and it was given to Gavin. The postscript was, Bill was sacked from his prison officer job, and Gavin stopped using him. Bob did another of his famous disappearing acts, and Gavin was left without any representation at our end of the Division. He asked me if I would help out, and like a plonker, I agreed.

47

BREAKING RECORDS, BREAKING HEARTS

I continued to compete throughout the early 80's without setting the World alight. My squat made a slight improvement, but the other two were fairly static. At least, the Division had started a Masters competition, so I was able to compete on a level footing, although I always thought that the ten year gap between age categories was too great.

As I approached the big five-O, I became more motivated, and my poundages began moving upwards once again. The first competition after my birthday was, in fact, the YNE Masters, and, as a now Masters 2, I had prepared well.

I had one other competitor in my class, Roy Teal from Hull. We had had a number of clashes over the years, and we were pretty well matched. Roy was also an Olympic lifter, and in common with all who follow that code, he had a good squat. His top lift with 200kg opened up a 15kg lead. In the bench, I managed to pull back 5kg of this lead in spite of the severe pain in my shoulder, which had been growing worse over the previous few years. For his opening deadlift he took a solid 222.5kg, so I went 225kg, firstly to register a total, and secondly, to keep the pressure on. For his second, he took an excellent 235kg to extend his lead. It was now time to make my move. I called for the 247.5kg I needed for the outright lead. It was in excess of my previous PB, but I had had a good training cycle and was feeling confident. It was hard going, naturally, but in doing it,

I managed to convince myself, and hopefully Roy, that there was a little bit more there.

Roy called for 240kg for his third in an effort to regain the lead, but it wasn't there on the day. This meant that I had already won the class and had one lift left, but what was I to put on? The M.C. saved me the trouble of deciding by suggesting that I go for the British record. I didn't even know what it was, but he told me it stood at 255kg—so close! In competition, the smallest incremental jump is 2.5kg, but for record purposes it is permitted to take a minimum of 0.5kg, and that is what we did.

As my final turn approached, I began my preparation. The first job is to pull the weightlifting belt as tight as possible. This not only gives a reassuring solidity to the mid section, it also provides a surface for the abdominals to flex against. The abs are one of the body's most important fixator muscles, and maintain the body in an upright position.

The next job is to chalk-up. Plunge your hands into the bowl of magnesium carbonate powder and work it well in. This is an aid to gripping, certainly a physical help, but also possibly a psychological one. As mentioned, the psychological aspect of lifting is as important as the physiological one. In fact, at this stage the mental preparation should begin. Visualize the lift you are about to perform, rehearsing the movement in your mind, and imagine the euphoria of success.

If your timing is correct, the announcer should be calling 'Bar loaded' about this time. This is your cue to mount the platform and approach the bar. Walk slowly towards it, focussing on the bar and trying to ignore those hugh lumps of metal on either end. Keep those positive thoughts going as you take your stance with your feet under the bar and about six to eight inches apart. Bend the knees and grip the bar with the 'over and under' grip universally adopted by powerlifters. Move the body into the optimal starting position with the arms vertical, the shoulders over the bar, the back flat or even slightly concave and neck in line with the spine, so that the eyes are looking forward and slightly down. The knees and hips are only flexed sufficiently for this position to be adopted. One more mental reheasal and then it is time to start the pull.

What's happening! It's not moving!

Don't panic. The initial pull is to overcome the inertia of the bar. Keep pulling and the bar will move, slowly, almost imperceptibly, up the shins. The secret now is to keep it moving in spite of the heaviness which is beginning to register. The knee joints will straighten first, allowing a smooth passage past them by the bar. This will effectively eliminate the quadriceps from the equation, but the big muscles of the hamstrings and gluteals are still working. As the bar slowly slides up the thighs, stop thinking of the lift as a pull, and concentrate on pushing the hips forwards. This will straighten the spine, raising the shoulders, which in turn, lift the arms with their unyielding load. As the hips complete their forward movement, there is just one more thing to check—that the shoulders are braced back. Then it is just a case of waiting for the centre referee to give the 'Down' signal. Remember to maintain control all the way to the floor and not drop the bar. In fact, if you are confident of your grip, you can do a bit of showboating by lowering the bar extra slowly and gently placing it on the floor.

Wait for the three referees to give their verdict. Two white lights would be sufficient for a successful lift, but three are nicer, especially when you have just broken your first British record at the grand old age of fifty.

As a result of all these exertions, I was invited to the British Masters a few months later. Once again, I prepared well, hoping to push my 560kg total even higher. I opened my squat with an easy 180kg, with the intention of taking a PB 190 for my second and who knows what for my third. Disaster! I got two red lights for my opener. You can put the weight up anyway for your next attempt, but it is not advisable, and I took the 180 again. Another two red lights! The referees aren't obliged to tell you why they are failing your lift, but most of them will. Apparently my left knee wasn't flexing sufficiently for me to reach the required depth. I was aware of a lump that had been forming at the back of this knee, and decided this was the cause of the trouble. For my third and final attempt with 180, I made a conscious effort to push down through the pain. I was awarded with three white lights, but my big total was already falling apart.

In the bench, I took 120 for my second, but a third with 122.5 wouldn't budge. Similarly in the deadlift, I followed my second of 250 with an attempt at 257.5 in order to push my British record a bit higher, but someone had nailed it to the floor.

In spite of having a day that was well down on my expectations, I had still won my class. Another milestone achieved late in life by becoming a British champion.

I had always been a great believer in shunning doctors' surgeries. Well, they are full of sick people. However, after this latest scare, I called in to see my GP. He in turn referred me to a consultant, and on the appointed day, after the inevitable delay, I was summoned into his presence.

"What appears to be the problem, Mr Bennett?" he asked, gazing at some X-ray films.

"My shoulder hurts when I bench press," I replied.

"Well, don't bench press then," he said.

As usual, my mouth was working faster than my brain, and I let him have a broadside. "You people are supposed to encourage exercise, not prevent it," I said, followed by a few choice remarks about his own corpulant frame.

There were three young nurses in the room whose sole purpose was to gaze at the great man in awe. They all looked suitably distressed. The consultant, for his part took it in good spirit, but of course, he knew he was holding the trump card.

"Don't give it up if you don't want to, but it's never going to get better," he responded. "You have got arthritis!"

What a bodyblow. For someone who prided themselves on their fitness, to find out they have such a debilitating disease. It turned out that the lump on the back of my knee is known as a Baker's cyst, and is also a symptom of arthritis.

Twenty plus years later, I am still lifting, albeit in a restricted fashion, but more of that later. The point I am making here is that whenever I go to my GP nowadays, he always asks me if I am still training, and encourages me to continue.

How times change.

48

ODD BEHAVIOR

In addition to the three powerlifts and the two Olympic lifts, there are a further 22 other lifts that are recognized by BAWLA for record purposes. Their official title is the 'All Round lifts', but they are known to one and all as the 'Odd Lifts.' In fact, there used to be 44 of them, but they dropped the oddest of the lot.

In the late 90's, our Division decided to instigate a competition utilising these odd lifts. The idea was that each competitor would choose three lifts to perform, and these would be scored against merit tables. As usual, I was up for anything.

The first thing to do was to decide which three lifts suited me best, so I initially tried for a top single in all 22. By comparing my results with the merit tables, I was able to arrive at my best three. In view of my long levers, the results were somewhat surprising.

My best overall result was obtained in the straight arm pullover. Admittedly, I had used this exercise for many years as part of my assistance work, but the competition style was much stricter than the loose style of the gym. It required the competitor to be lying flat on the floor with arms extended behind the head and grasping the barbell. At the start signal, the bar had to be raised in a smooth arc until it was over the lifter's chest. To make things more difficult, there was a maximum disc size of eleven inches diameter, which meant the bar was very close to the ground.

There was however, an alternative way of performing the movement. This allowed the competitor to start with the bar over the chest and slowly lower it to the start position, at which point, there must be a discernable pause before the 'start' signal is given. This, in fact, is exactly what happens in the competition benchpress. I had spent years telling my students that, although the bar is lowered until it touches the chest, it mustn't rest there. Instead, the weight is still maintained on the stretched muscles of the pectorals and the triceps. That way, once the start signal has been given, the elasticity stored in these muscles can be utilized to get the bar moving.

I decided that the same principle must apply to the straight arm pullover, and that is the way I trained. In addition, there are many muscles that contract statically in the body in order to maintain a particular body position. These are known as fixator muscles and are also activated during the lowering phase. Once again, by remaining tensed in the lowered position, these muscles can aid the lifter.

The second lift to be included in my specialized training routine was very similar in many respects to the straight arm pullover. Its competition name was the lying lateral raise, but it was known in bodybuilding circles as dumbbell flying. Once again, the competitor lay on his back on the floor with arms stretched out to the side and grasping two dumbbells with the maximum disc sizes again applying. At the given signal, the dumbbells were brought in a smooth arc over the body. Again, it was possible to start with the dumbbells held over the body, and using the same logic as before, this is the way I trained.

My third choice was the two hands curl whereby the bar is raised from the hang position to the shoulders in a continuous smooth movement using an underhand grip. Again, this is a standard bodybuilding movement, possibly the most popular of them all, but the competition version was much stricter than the gym version. This can vary from a slight lean backwards to ease the bar through its sticking point, to a full-blown swing of the body to literally throw the bar up. The competition version requires the body to remain in the upright position throughout. This led me to think about what is actually happening to the body during the lift. The extreme position occurs when the forearms are at right angles to the body and the centre of gravity of the bar is furthest away. This position encourages a backwards lean in order to bring the combined centre of gravity of the body and bar back over the feet. However, there is nothing in the rules that state the arms have to remain clamped to the side of the body throughout the lift, and I began experimenting with a version where the elbows swing backwards during the movement, and the bar remains close to the body. This seemed to work, removing all tendencies to sway backwards, and allowing the lifter to concentrate on the lift proper.

By this time, I had passed my 60th birthday and was now lifting as a Masters 3. At my first competition, I managed to break all the Divisional records for my three chosen lifts. By the following year, I had gone down a weight class and made some marginal improvements to my poundages. So much so that I recorded British records in all three of my lifts.

Not bad for a physical wreck who was told to give-up lifting ten years earlier.

49

THE RISE OF THE DRUGGIES

Anabolic steroids were discovered in the 1950's and used initially as an aid to people recovering from major operations. However, it didn't take the sporting fraternity long to realize their possibilities. In the early days they were tolerated, possibly because there was no method of detecting them. Eventually this problem was solved and they were banned in most sports. This only served to drive them underground.

Weightlifting, of course, was a prime candidate for drugs with its emphasis on pure strength. I was aware of it going on throughout my early lifting career, but niaively thought that people in their mature years, lifting in relatively minor competitions wouldn't be bothered. I was about to be rudely awakened.

My first indication of how widespread it had become was at an Olympic weightlifting event. This was the English Natives being held at Huddersfield. Although testing had been carried out at the full British, they had never bothered with this particular event before and people clearly thought they were safe. When the word went round that the drug testers were on their way, lifters suddenly began developing all sorts of injuries and other reasons why they couldn't lift. Eventually, out of an original entry of 24, only 8 lifters competed. The testers took their samples, but they would have been better testing the audience.

Drugs weren't only confined to lifters, of course. I was reminded of this one year at La Santa Sport. We had gone early in the year, and as usual, the place was full of athletes doing their warm weather training.

One day, Andy Norman, the secretary of the AAA, rang to say the drugs testers were on their way. I have never seen a place empty so quickly. They were all jumping on 'planes regardless of destination. When the testers arrived, the place was deserted with the exception of the pole vaulter who couldn't find a 'plane long enough to take his equipment. He was tested and found positive.

Meanwhile, back in the world of powerlifting, things began to get closer to home. Stuart McConman had been a member of the University club for a long time, and also worked for the Uni as a lab technician. He moved on from this job to become a fireman and also changed clubs, but he still kept in touch. One day he appeared in our training room bearing what was to become his trademark white plastic bag. "Do any of your lads want any gear? "he asked. I was shocked to learn he was talking about drugs. "No they certainly do not," I replied, "and I will be obliged if you don't come back."

"All your competitors are taking them," he replied, and ran through a list of names. I was annoyed to find that just about everyone I had ever lifted against, with the exception of Roy, was on his list. We found out later that the drugs were being manufactured by some of his relatives in the pharmaceutical industry. For many years after that, we would see him at competitions with his tell-tale plastic bag. Occasionally, he would wander off into a dark corner with one of the lifters and emerge some minutes later with the bag looking somewhat lighter.

Eventually, the police caught up with him and his family and they appeared in court. After the inevitable guilty verdict, the relatives were sent down, but Stuart somehow escaped with just a fine. The fire service got to hear of it and sacked him. BAWLA also thought they ought to do something and threatened to ban him for life, but Stuart told them that if they did, he would publish the names of everyone he had ever supplied. He is still lifting to this day.

I got a further reminder of how widespread it was one weekend when I was doing one of my courses in Sunderland. Being a fair old haul from Bradford, I had elected to stay over night. I was sat in the bar of a local hostelry enjoying a quiet pint when in walked one of the biggest blokes I had ever seen. Even his muscles had muscles. He came over and sat next to me and we naturally struck up a conversation about training. I asked if he knew any of the powerlifters from the Sunderland club. "Know 'em," he replied. "I supply them."

He then went on to list all the lifters in the North East he was supplying. Not only did he name the entire Sunderland club, he also named most of the Gateshead club too. Guys we were regularly competing against, supposedly on an equal footing. I now understood why my lifters were being chosen every time for testing in what was supposed to be random selection. The Divisional Secretary, Micky Finn, himself a member of the Sunderland club, was nominating them because he knew them to be clean and he was protecting his own lifters.

The same thing was happening to our colleagues in the University weight- lifting squad. One of their number, Paul 'Fearless' Furness is one of those who lift for pleasure rather than glory. In spite of this, he was constantly being chosen to give a sample. He once gave eight of these within a five month period! By this time, the concept of 'out of competition' testing had been introduced, whereby testers could call at your home at any time and request a sample. On this particular evening, Fearless had arranged to go to the cinema with some friends. They pulled-up outside his house and Paul walked down the path to meet them. As he did so, he met a chap coming the other way, and he introduced himself as a Sports Council drugs tester. Paul explained that he had just been to the toilet as one does before going out for the evening, and it would be some time before he could perform again. He did what we understood to be the correct procedure and invited the tester to accompany him to the cinema. The chap refused and told Paul that if he didn't remain at home until he could produce the required sample, he would enter it as a refusal. Unwilling to spoil an evening out, Paul told him to go ahead.

A refusal is the equivalent of a failure and Paul was given two years compulsory suspension. Of course, he could carry on training, but he wouldn't be able to compete. Ironically, if he had been a druggie, this would be an ideal time to take them, as he wouldn't appear on any register, but that is another story.

One day whilst sat at home, Paul was listening to a programme on '5-Live' about drugs. He rang up to tell his story and finished-up telling it to the Nation.Of course, the BAWLA supremos got to hear of this and his two year sentence became a life ban.Once again, Paul was not unduly upset. In fact, it was the ruling BAWLA Council themselves who quickly came to see the error of their ways.

As the senior partner in the marriage of the weightlifters and the powerlifters, the weightlifters had always had the controlling interest on the various committees. Paul had been a leading light on the North East Counties committee, but with his ban, he had been forced to step down from his position of Divisional Secretary and the post had been taken up by a powerlifter, thus changing the balance of power. Too late, the Central Council saw their mistake. They contacted Paul and told him that if he would be prepared to take up a position again on the Divisional Executive committee, they in turn would recind his life ban. Paul of course agreed, but the ethics of the Central Council leave a lot to be desired.

It was primarily the drugs issue that led to my eventual defection.

50

THE LITTLE AND LARGE SHOW

Over the years, I have coached a number of lifters of varying ability and promise and two of these came through my connection with Thornton Recreation Centre. The first to appear on the scene was Gerald, at that time just 14 years old, but already showing signs of his future potential. He had the extreme muscle mass of a mesomorph, and he didn't take too much persuading to take up the sport. I like to get my students competing early, firstly to give them a taste and secondly, to maintain their interest. I organized a grading test for some of my beginners followed by an in-house friendly. At these Gerald in particular stood out, and I decided to test him in front of a larger audience. I approached his school, Rhodesway, to see if they would be interested in putting on an exhibition, and they agreed. On the appointed day, I carried a bar and a boot-full of weights up to the school hall and set them up on the stage.

We had planned the exhibition for one lunch time, and I thought we may be lucky enough to half-fill the hall. How wrong could I be? The hall was so full it was standing room only, with probably every pupil and every master in attendance. Gerald didn't let them down. As a now 15year old and weighing 95kg, he squatted 200kg, benched 107.5kg and deadlifted an outstanding 227.5kg.

It was round about this time that I found my second promising lifter. I had seen Peter around the University on numerous occasions and I found out that he was visiting his brother, Steph, who worked with Irene on the poolside. Peter was a dwarf and I knew from my reading that other dwarves were making a big impact on the sport of powerlifting. I persuaded him to have a go and the poundages he posted at that initial trial convinced me that I had another winner. Even so, he took some convincing, but eventually, I wore him down.

He started competing almost immediately, and within a year he got an invite to the British Juniors. At a bodyweight of 50.4kg, he squatted 182.5, benched 75 and deadlifted 92.5. The deadlift was always going to be his bête noire. The short limbs which gave him such good levers in the squat and bench, worked against him in the deadlift. Besides, his small hands made gripping the bar very difficult. Never the less, he easily won his class. Gerald also competed in this same competition. In less than a year since his Rhodesway exploits, his lifts had increased to a 230 squat, a 120 bench and an impressive 265 deadlift. At 16 years old, he was already outlifting his coach!

They continued their steady progress and this was rewarded in November, 1993 when they were both selected to represent Great Britain at the World Junior Championships. The team consisted of six lifters, and to have discovered and coached two of them was a huge feather in my cap. The event took place in Hamilton, Canada, which was a great free trip for them, but for me to accompany them would have meant paying for myself, so I was forced to give it a miss. They didn't let me down. Peter went 205kg, 95kg, and 110kg, for a 410kg total, his best to date. Gerald made his bid for glory via 272.5, 140, and 280 for a 692.5 total. Both of them were class winners and contributed to GB's high placing.

Their reward was to be again selected for the Junior squad the following year with another exotic trip, this time to Bali, Indonesia. They regaled me with many tales of their exploits, most of which are unrepeatable, but reminded me of my time in the Far East. It must be something they put in the water.

By 1995, Peter had graduated from the junior ranks and Gerald had the sole honour of representing the club at international level. This year's trip was to Delhi, yet another exotic destination for one so young. He had been lifting in the 125kg class, but for this competition, he reduced to the 110kg class as GB had another large lad in the form of Dean Bowring to fill this slot. In spite of the weight loss, Gerald did another impressive set of lifts via a 290squat, a 165 bench and a 310 deadlift for a 765 total and another win for his country.

Little Pete's finest hour probably came in September, 1996 when he was selected for the English senior squad in a match against Scotland. He was up against another very good 52kg lifter in the shape of John Maxwell. John had an extremely good deadlift, and it was important for Pete to get a substantial lead in the first two disciplines. This he did by way of a 235 squat and a 102.5 bench, both PB's. He crowned this by doing a PB deadlift of 115. As anticipated, Pete established a handy lead at the sub total stage, but John now started to reel-in this lead. It all came down to the final lift, and John called for the weight he needed to win. We watched with bated breath as it cleared the floor and began to inch up his legs. We could see the title slipping away, when at the critical moment, the bar stopped and did an almost imperceptible downwards movement. To his credit, John recovered and finished the lift, but had the referees noticed the slightest of double movements? We needn't have worried. John got three reds and the victory was Little Pete's.

Although he continued to compete for two or three years after this, Pete never achieved the same heights again. He seemed to lose his enthusiasm, and even missed one or two critical matches. His main purpose seemed to be to find himself a life partner, and he finally succeeded. After his marriage, he went the way of many a good lifter before him, and never competed again. I'm not necessarily blaming the wives for this. It could be that the lure of painting the kitchen ceiling is far greater than throwing lumps of iron about. OK, so I managed to combine the two, but I've already stated that my greatest regret was missing the children growing up.

Nowadays of course, Irene can't wait to throw me out so that she can watch her 'Lewd Women' in peace. Besides, it has one great advantage. It is a well known fact that weight training keeps you young, so Irene now has the toy boy she always wanted.

51

THE ODD COUPLE

The loss of Pete was considerably cushioned by the appearance of another superb lifter. Stevie Brown had been born blind, but he didn't let this apparent handicap hold him back. He had a full-time job as a machinist, and was an expert chess player. He had started going to the Richard Dunn Sports Centre to do some weight training, and the instructor there saw his potential and sent him along to me at Thornton Rec. I did my usual assessment by putting him through his paces on the three powerlifts and straight away, I could see I had another winner. I wasted no time in getting him signed up for the University squad, and, following my normal practice, had him competing as soon as possible. One of his early competitions was the West Ridings. With less than a year's training under his belt, he made a 155kg squat, a 75kg bench and a very impressive triple bodyweight 180kg deadlift.

As indicated, Steve is yet another small guy, weighing-in at a very compact 60kg. However, it isn't only in size that he and Gerald differ. In addition to his blindness, Steve is hard of hearing, requiring two deaf aids, and is also diabetic. In spite of this cruel hand that life has dealt him, Steve is one of the most placid people I have ever met, with never a bad word for anyone. Gerald, on the other hand, with his full health and his natural ability is pessimistic to the point of paranoia. In spite of this, the two of them hit it off, and we had many adventures together.

After three or four years of lifting, Steve was told by the British Blind Sport Association that a World Blind Powerlifting competition was about to be launched and was he interested? We didn't need to be asked twice, even when we found out that such an important and prestigious body as the BBSA received no Government funding whatsoever, and we would have to fund ourselves. They did send us a sponsorship pack to enable us to do our own fund raising, and so began another phase of my coaching duties. Over the years, I managed to build up quite a list of sponsors, varying from a few pounds to several hundreds. We also managed to raise a lot more through a variety of sponsored events, more of which later. However, one of my requests brought a very disappointing response. Over the previous several years, I had put many thousands of pounds into our Divisional coffers via my work as the courses coordinator. I wrote to our treasurer asking for a donation towards our trip to the World Blind's. He sent me a cheque for £25!

As it happened, this first competition was only in Arnhem, Holland, so the cost was not too great, and with other bits of sponsorship and our own money, we travelled over and had a terrific time lifting, meeting other lifters and officials, banqueting and sampling the local ale. In spite of his size, Stevie can knock a few back. Perhaps it's his diabeties requiring lots of sugar.

Our next trip to a World Blind Powerlifting meeting was to Ceske Budejovice in the Czech Republic, and once again, we set about fund raising. Gerald made a suggestion that could become a good money spinner, so we set about working out the details. His idea was for a sponsored waxing, with himself being the victim. The first job was to find a venue, so we approached Mary, the manageress of the students' bar. The Students Union had been a great supporter of our efforts in the past, and once again, came up trumps. It seemed that there would be a promotional event in the Mainline Bar, and Mary suggested we could follow this as the place was sure to be full. How right she was. The stuff they were promoting was called vodka jelly and, as you would expect, there were plenty of free samples of this potent concoction. I managed to miss this first part of the evening as I had to go home to collect the crucible, wax and papers. There was also another reason—I had been unable to find a beautician to do the actual waxing, and envisaged doing it myself. I thought therefore that I owed it to Gerald to be relatively sober.

As I returned to the bar, the promotion was drawing to a close and it was clear it had been a great success. I set up the table and plugged the crucible in, then got on the mike to explain the next part of the evening's entertainment. I introduced Steve to the crowd and told them of some of his achievements and why we needed the sponsorship. He got a hugh ovation. I next introduced Gerald, who, by this time had stripped down to a thong and looked very outstanding. A young lady approached me saying that she had been part of the vodka promotion team, but was also a trained beautician and did I need a hand? My luck was in once more, or to be more accurate, Gerald's luck. Instead of being manhandled by a rough sod like me, he had a lovely young lady to fondle him. I asked her where she would like to start, and she replied 'the bikini line.'

She took hold of Gerald's todger and held it firmly to one side whilst she exfoliated the inside of his thigh. She then pulled it over to the other side and repeated the process. I was more pleased than ever that she had saved me the embarrassment of that particular task. I asked her if that was a perk of the job.

"I suppose so," she replied, "although I have felt bigger ones."

Poor Gerald. Not only was he suffering for a good cause, he was having his manhood insulted as well.

After working her way down both legs, our savior told us she had to go. However, I had been watching carefully, and was now more confident I could manage. After a few successful strips, I had a bit of a brainwave. In addition to all of the sponsorship, Mary had also suggested that we could do a collection on the night, and so we had two of our lads circulating with collecting jars. I now suggested that if anyone wanted to do a strip, they would have to put some money in the jar. This idea was working well and the jars were filling up. Suddenly, a young guy rather the worse for drink stepped forward and said "I want to do an armpit." Gerald had been told that the easiest way to wax is to trim the hairs as short as possible beforehand in order to get the hot wax into the follicles and make the extraction easier. This, Gerald had done, with the exception of his armpits, which were still long and flowing.

Envisioning the problem, I told our drunken friend that the armpits were off-limits. However, he persisted with his demand, and in an effort to shut him up, Gerald said "OK. If you put a fiver in the jar, you can do one."

This he did and the results were as anticipated. The operation took forever, and Gerald was clearly in great pain. Eventually, it was all over and I thought we could get back to the normal waxing. At that moment, a demure young lady stepped forward from the crowd. She had a sweet smile, an angelic face, and was waving a fiver.

"I want to do the other armpit," she said.

Shortly after this the bar staff called final orders. The students began drifting in the direction of the disco and I began packing away the equipment. Gerald protested that he wasn't finished as his back still looked like a wool rug. I told him that he had sacrificed enough, but suspected that he was becoming addicted to the pain. This was confirmed the following day when he went to a beauty salon and paid for them to finish him off. Anyway, all this hard work was worth it. When we totalled up the sum of all the sponsorship monies and the collection jars, it came to over £500—a magnificent effort.

The trip to the Czech Republic was a memorable one. The town of Ceske Budejovice is medieval and its heart still lies unspoilt within its encompassing moat. However, there was one more thing that made the trip even more memorable. This is the HQ of the Budwieser brewery, they were sponsoring the event, and their products were freely available at every opportunity. For example, Steve duly won his class by a large margin, and as so often happens, he was called upon to do a drugs test. Usually, after a competition, lifters are dehydrated and require fluid before they can perform. To this end, water bottles are provided in the testing room. In this case, the room was filled with bottles of Bud. As his guide, I had naturally accompanied him and we both got stuck into a few. After about three or four, Stevie said "I think I can manage to pee now." "Well," I replied, "cross your legs and let's have a few more."

We were all taken to a nearby castle for the closing ceremony, and of course, the Bud was flowing. The ceremony itself was interesting to say the least, with the entertainment ranging from operatic arias to a guy doing a passable imitation of Freddie Mercury. There were prizes for everything, and Steve came away with two carrier bags full.

Meanwhile, Gerald was also continuing with his own impressive improvements. After a couple more trips to exotic locations, he bid farewell to the junior ranks, and within a short space of time, he was invited onto the senior squad. His first match was to represent Great Britain in the European Union Cup. As this was being held in

Birmingham, it meant that I could finally get to watch him on an international stage. In fact, the GB coach asked if I would like to prepare Gerald for the lifting. This was probably a wise move on his part as Gerald can be a bit of a prima donna at times as we were to find out.

We had finally settled on Gerald's optimum weight being in the 125kg class, but GB already had a good lifter in this category, and Gerald was asked to go up to the 145kg class. At the weigh-in he was a hefty 127.3, but was still the lightest man in the group. In addition, powerlifters don't mature until well into their 40's, and so Gerald was also the youngest. In spite of this, he set off to put some great lifts together. His third squat with 325 was a PB, as was his third bench of 212.5. At the sub-total stage, he was well placed with the leaders, and he still had his favourite deadlift to come. We retired to the warm-up room to prepare for the final discipline. The bars in there were brand new and the knurling was savage. As Gerald performed his final warm-up, he gave an anguished cry and dropped the bar. We rushed over to see what the matter was and he showed us his bleeding hands where the bar had ripped all his calluses off. We cleaned him up as best we could and made our way back to the main hall. I had posted 310kg for his opener, and, as this was the heaviest lift of the round, we had to wait for the rest of the group to perform. Finally it was his turn. He made a half-hearted attempt, uttered another strangled cry and dropped the bar. He came off and was surrounded by sympathetic team mates as he showed them his sore hands. I held my council. The second round started, and although we had elected to take the 310 again, this was still the heaviest lift of the round. At last it was time for him to go, and as I pulled him into his suit, I let him have both barrels. "If you think I've come all this way to watch you wimp out, you're mistaken," I said. "Now, go out there and lift that bloody bar or I'll kick your bloody arse all round this bloody hall."

I have never lost my temper with Gerald before and I could see the hurt in his eyes, but it worked. Not only did he pull the weight, he made it look easy. So much so that I put 325 down for his third and final lift, but I also kept a close eye on proceedings. As the third round opened up, the lesser lifters did their own thing, no doubt happy with their performance. As we got into the stronger guys, some of them called for a weight that would give them a title shot, but most of them failed. The penultimate lifter asked for the weight that would give him the slenderest of leads, and was successful, but I was prepared. I had positioned myself next to the MC's table and as soon as he announced 'good lift,' I asked for Gerald's final lift to be dropped to 312.5. The rules permit this as long as two criteria are met. Firstly the weight nominated must be greater than the lift just completed and secondly, you have to ask before the MC can announce your original weight. We had managed to satisfy both of these requirements. Although Gerald was now fired-up again and could probably have lifted the 325, we had decided that prudence was the order of the day, and merely take enough to win the class. Gerald duly pulled the 312.5 which made him tie on total with the Dane, but beat him by virtue of his lighter bodyweight.

Once all the euphoria had died down, Gerald asked me if I had really meant what I said earlier. I told him that, of course I meant it. Well, I may have to use that tactic again in the future.

This should have been the beginning of a rewarding career with the BAWLA senior squad, but due to a set of extenuating circumstances, it turned out to be one of Gerald's final competitions with the association, but more on that later.

Meanwhile, what was I up to? With World—class lifters to coach, my own lifting took a bit of a back seat. I was still doing the odd competition, but I had passed my peak, and had started the slow but inevitable slide. My interest began to perk up as I approached my 60th birthday. This meant a move into the Masters 3 category and a whole new set of records to look at. Indeed, at my first comp as an M3, I saw all my 9 lifts and all 3 totals become Divisional records. My GP at this time was actually encouraging me to continue my lifting, acknowledging the fact that it was helping to keep the arthritis at bay. Although this was true, it couldn't stop the insidious spread completely. My right shoulder continued to be the main problem. Not only was it painful to bench press, the increasing lack of mobility made it difficult to grasp the bar in the squat position. I reluctantly decided that I would have to quit, but I determined to go out with a bang. My final competition with BAWLA was the 2000 YNE Masters. I had got my bodyweight down to below 90kg, and after a token 145kg squat and a 105kg bench, I worked my way up to a 223kg deadlift, the extra half kilo being put on to break my final Divisional record.

I thought that was it for my lifting career. How wrong could I be?

52

AND THEN THERE WAS ONE

Round about this time, the University gym was having its second major addition in the form of a machine hall. The machines of choice were Nautilus, which turned out to be a wise decision. Arthur Jones, their inventor, was a very knowledgable man who thoroughly researched his machines, and then patented his findings. This meant that the many firms who followed his lead had to settle for second best.

This development had a double significance for me. As I reached my 65th birthday, my consultancy job with Bradford Council came to an end, and a number of my part-time jobs had finished as previously recorded. I was in need of a new challenge. Nautilus had arranged for a two day course for selected members of staff who were earmarked to work in the fitness suite, and I asked to go on this course. At the very least, it would add to my knowledge of all things physiological, but it may also lead to a job. I let it be known that I was available to help out, and was given a part-time job as an instructor. This was only supposed to help them over the initial rush of new members, but in practice, it continued for a number of years.

The other plus was that I was able to augment my training routine by utilizing the machines. A number of my free weight exercises had become increasingly difficult because of my joint problems, but I could manage several of the machine substitutes. Indeed, when Arthur Jones first began his project, it was to aid people with physical disorders, and it was only later that he saw the larger application.

Just one other small thing to sort out. I had been given free membership of the old gym, but would this be extended to include the new fitness suite? I was assured it would.

So what was Gerald up to at this time? His superior lifting had not gone down too well in all quarters. There was a lot of ill-feeling in many clubs that a drug-free lifter could beat their drugged-up super-stars. The Leeds club had tried to poach Gerald many years previously, and when he turned them down, their coach, Barry Nelson, allowed his resentment to fester. The Sunderland coach, Micky Finn was another who was particularly vitriolic in his snide remarks. Whenever he happened to be MC'ing one of Gerald's lifts, he would always refer to him as Gerald Pillock, and all his acolytes would snigger.

This pair of nasties had travelled down to Birmingham with the express purpose of putting Gerald off as he made his senior debut in the EU Cup. They sat on the front row directly in front of him, making strange noises and pulling faces. They were beginning to get through to him, but I had hopefully learnt something during my years of coaching. I told him to channel all of his anger into the bar, and that the biggest put-down for them would be his victory. He achieved this as previously recorded, but the damage had been done. How could he continue to lift for an Association when officials from your own Division play idiotic tricks like that?

Shortly after this incident, he gave up competitive lifting.

Although I continued to get a steady trickle of new guys into the gym, I was now left with only one top lifter. However, Steve more than made up for his sole responsibility. We learnt that the next World Blinds was going to be something special. They had been holding the World Blind Games on a four year cycle for some time now, but at the next one, powerlifting was to be included for the first time. In view of this, we were asked to try and find some more lifters as Steve had been GB's only competitor to date. We did in fact know of one other, Ralph Sample from Gateshead. Ralph hadn't been born blind, but was gradually losing his sight, and definitely qualified. Although from Gateshead, he was not one of the Geordie Mafia, and hated the drugs culture as much as we did. He needed a guide and Gerald was happy to fill the breech, and so our little party became four.

In spite of the prestige of the event, there was still no financial aid forthcoming from the Government, although sports like athletics, swimming and judo got support from their own National bodies. As recorded, although our own National body had money in the bank, it wasn't prepared to let any of it go. It was looking like we would have to mount a massive sponsorship campaign when the BBSA told us the good news. They had managed to obtain the full cost for the four of us with Barclay's Bank being our benefactor.

We had a trip down to Birmingham to pick up our National uniforms, and meet with the other competitors and officials, and before long, we were on our way.

The venue was Laval University in Quebec, Canada. We stayed in one of the halls of residence at one end of a hugh campus. Opposite was a large building housing among other things, a canteen which served bounteous meals three times a day. Also within this building was the students' bar, and although all four of us were mature adults, the UK management team had asked us to avoid it as they didn't want us setting a bad example to the younger competitors. Anyway, our first priority was to get some serious lifting done.

Fortunately, they had scheduled the powerlifting for the first two days. First up was Stevie and he duly won GB a gold medal. The following day was Ralph's turn and he obliged with another. The management team were ecstatic. Knowing nothing of our sport, they had no idea what to expect, although I had told them that both of our guys were British champions, lifting against sighted opponents.

From my point of view, our job was over, and we still had eight days to enjoy ourselves. We filled our days by watching the other competitors, going for walks in the large wood that formed part of the campus or taking a bus ride into the nearby City to explore. We found the place where General Wolfe routed the French many years previously, and for which, many of the locals still havn't forgiven us. Among other sleights, many of them refuse to use any other language except French. Strange behaviour indeed for an English speaking country, based on some distant historical event, but then again, if it wasn't for wierdos like this, the rest of us wouldn't be able to feel superior.

The real challenge became what to do with the evenings. Ralph had let it be known that, like us he enjoyed his beer. Indeed, one of his other hobbies was brewing his own, but with the student bar being off limits, it became a route march to find a bar. Once settled inside we found there was another problem. Firstly, they refused to serve you at the bar, claiming it was waitress service only. Secondly, not only did the waitresses want tips, they literally demanded them. This sort of behaviour did not go down too well with us Brits. Why not pay the staff a decent wage in the first place and price the beer accordingly. That way, everyone would know where they stood.

We got into the habit of telling the waitress we would give her a big tip at the end of the evening, and then when she was busy, we would do a runner. This was all very well, but we couldn't use the same bar twice, and our nightly excursions were getting longer and longer. On our penultimate night, we found ourselves in yet another bar and resolved to do our usual move. I don't know if the jungle drums had been busy, but this time they were waiting or us. As we approached the door on our way out, two bouncers appeared and demanded that we leave a tip. They were big blokes, but Gerald was even bigger. "Move out of the way," he said to the first one "or I'll move you. Then I'll start on your boyfriend," he said, pointing to the second one. They meekly stood aside, but our moment of triumph was short-lived. Outside the door stood two Mounties with their guns drawn. I had Steve on one arm and Ralph on the other so that Gerald could be ready for trouble. They stood aside to let us pass but closed ranks again on Gerald and told him that if he didn't leave a tip, he would be locked up. Gerald sensibly coughed-up. After all, a Mountie always gets his money.

The following night was to be our last, and ban or no ban, we resolved to spend it in the students' bar. As we walked in, we saw the place was heaving. Not only was the entire UK Management Team there, but also most of the competitors. In fact, one of them told us they had been going in ever since the first night.

How I hate hypocrisy. To make matters worse, the beer in there was much cheaper, and there was no expectation of a tip.

Gerald decided to take Ralph on at a drinking contest. Having heard of Ralph's reputation, I declined. The accepted method of buying beer over there is to buy jugs, or pitchers as they are known, holding approximately four pints. Gerald and Ralph had a round to themselves, and Steve and I had another at a much more sedate pace. After several jugs, I could see that Gerald was feeling the effects. He was making his way back from the bar once more but in a very unsteady fashion. I went to help him, and just as we met, he collapsed in a heap. I managed to catch the jug without spilling a drop, and carried it back to our table for Ralph to consume on his own. Gerald remained asleep in the centre of the floor for some time. Eventually he woke-up and challenged one of the blind athletes to a game of pool. Gerald almost beat him.

Meanwhile, Ralph had carried on drinking, and at the end of the evening, his head was down on the table. By this time, Gerald had sobered up sufficiently, and carried Ralph back to his bed. I declared the contest an honourable draw.

Shortly after this, Steve passed his 40th birthday and moved into the ranks of the masters. His initial win at the British went unnoticed but when he repeated this the following year, he got an invite onto the Masters' squad. The one slight drawback to this was BAWLA's policy of financing overseas trips. It went something like this:-

The Junior squad are skint, and will require financing.

The Senior squad carry prestige and will require financing.

The Masters' squad are all extremely rich and can pay for themselves.

By this time, we were getting quite good at raising money, although of course, we had to raise twice as much as everyone else. The big event this year was an abseil down the face of a dam. With many of the club members joining in, plus Dominic and Gabrielle, we raised just short of £900, once again, a magnificent effort.

The first call on Steve for international duty was the European Masters Championships. We found ourselves back in the Czech Republic, this time at a place called Ostrava, near the Polish border. As this was an industrial town, off the usual tourist routes, the price of beer was even cheaper. I recorded in my diary at the time that a pint of strong ale cost the equivalent of 35p. However, drinking had to wait 'til the serious business of lifting was out of the way. Once again, the advantage of being in one of the lighter classes meant that happened fairly quickly.

The remainder of the British team had taken Steve to their hearts, particularly the ladies, and I became virtually redundant in the warm up room. Steve scored a creditable 2nd place in the competition, and, as such, earned himself an invite to the World Masters later that year. As these were to be in India, the pressure was on our fund-raising skills once more.

Nearer the departure date, we found out exactly how much we would need. The trip would last for ten days, and we would be staying in a luxury 5 star hotel. The cost of all this high living was to be £1100 per head. We couldn't go to our usual supporters so soon after our last fund raiser, but where else could we try? I had a bit of a brainwave, but would it work? It occurred to me that with all the Indian Restaurants in Bradford, this could be a fruitful source of sponsorship. I mentioned this idea to one of our fellow trainees, Zaf, and he said leave it with him. A few days later, he told us the tremendous news. Apparently, he was very friendly with the management of one of our local restaurants, Mumtaz, and they would sponsor Steve for the full amount. As usual, we put all the sponsorship money into one pot and split it down the middle. Still, it was a tremendous start, and with one or two other bits from our regular sources, the final cost to us was much more manageable.

The competition was in the city of Udaipur in central India. The British team were met at the airport, given garlands, and driven to our hotel, the Fatah Prakash Palace. I have stayed in many hotels with the name 'Palace' in their title, but, with the possible exception of one in Romania, this was the only genuine article. Built on a hill next to a lake, the walled complex housed in fact, four palaces. The original one was many centuries old and is now a museum. Two later additions now formed the hotel, whilst the newest part houses The Maharajah of Rajasthan and his retinue.

The rooms were huge and full of antique furniture which reflected the faded glory of the Raj. Everywhere there were quaint reminders of this. I remember a sign in the bathroom over one of the taps. It read "Please wait a moment or two for the arrival of the hot water" There was a large dinning hall hung with portraits of former maharajahs and scenes of epic battles. However, whenever the weather was nice, which was most of the time, we ate at one or other of the two outdoor dining areas. One overlooked the lake and was known as 'The Sundown Terrace,' and the other one was by the swimming pool. Built on islands in the lake were two further palaces, and on a hilltop in the distance was yet another, known as 'The Monsoon Palace.' All of these featured heavily in the Bond movie 'Octopussy' with one of the lake palaces being Octopussy's lair and the Monsoon palace being the location of the final fight scene.

The venue itself was a local college, and we were taken there on our first full day for the opening ceremony. Back home, the banner above the door might have read 'Welcome to the World Masters.' However, I felt that their version was much more appropriate. It read 'Welcome to the Masters of the World.' We were once again treated to a very varied opening ceremony. There were many ethnic acts as one would expect, but the strangest of them all was a bodybuilding show where all the contestants were fully dressed.

The following day, the lifting got under way. In view of the heat, this only took place in the evening, which accounted for the exceptionally long time for the meet, but there were no complaints on our part. First it was ladies day and we went along to give them a shout. Our girls got us off to a flying start, winning four gold medals between them. The following day was the turn of the smaller guys, including Steve. The 60kg class was large, but looking down the list of openers, I could see it was going to be a threeway battle for the medals between a Pakistani lifter, a Russian lifter and Steve. The three referees for this group were introduced to the crowd—a Pakistani, a Russian and an Indian! In my long lifting career, I have always found referees to be basically honest, so thought no more about it, but in this instance, I was wrong. Following normal procedure, I had asked Steve to open with an easy [for him] 170kg, and he got three white lights. For his second, we upped it to 180, once again, well within his capabilities. However, by now two of the referees must have seen the danger he posed to their lifters and gave him a red light. The rules state that all three referees must display at the same time in order to be unbiased. However, the Indian referee was clearly unsure of himself, and waited to see what the others did before following them. Three red lights for a perfectly good squat! We had planned to go 185 or even 190 for our third, but common sense dictated that we had to take the 180 again. This time, Steve sank so low, his bum almost touched the floor. Once again—three red lights. I was so incensed, I went to see the jury. Their chairman told me I was quite right, and that both of his 'failed' squats had been well down. However, he said that the jury could only intervene in the case of two reds and one white. In our instance of three reds, they were powerless. We carried on with a good 90kg bench and an excellent 210kg deadlift, the best in the class. However, we were unable to pull back the 10 or 15 kg we had been cheated out of and had to settle for a bronze medal.

On the positive side, Stevie made many new friends that day including the local newspapermen. His photograph and a good write-up were all over the following day's papers.

Powerlifting, along with all sport is a very visual thing, and must be hard work for someone like Steve. He does however love exploring, although I'm not always sure about my powers of description. Although we watched some of the other lifting, we also decided to 'see' the sights. Our first trip was relatively straight forward. We explored the museum part of our hotel, and took a boat ride over to one of the lake palaces for some high class tiffin.

Everywhere we went, we were treated with the utmost curtesy and I made a note in my diary that Steve can open doors. For example, one evening when we got to the poolside dining area, it was full and the waiter asked if we would mind waiting in the bar for a table. Well, OK if you twist my arm! As we made our way up the broad flight of stairs towards the bar, we passed a seated Indian gentleman playing the sittah. He invited us to sit on the carpet next to him, and he allowed Steve to run his fingers over the instrument whilst he explained how it worked. He then played us a couple of tunes and finally, gave Steve a cassette of his music.

For our next trip, we decided to explore the town. When we exited the main gates of the complex, we were met by a bewildering cluster of buildings, streets and alleyways. As I stood there wondering how to proceed, a young Indian boy rode up on his bike. In perfect English, he told us he had seen Steve's photo in the paper, and could he be of any help. I explained that we wanted to do a bit of exploring, but were uncertain how to procede. He offered to be our guide if we would allow him to practice his English on us. I thought that his English was probably better than mine, but told him we would be pleased to accept his offer. He abandoned his bike at the side of the road and we plunged into the maze of alleyways. He showed us so many sights it would be impossible to list them all. One I do remember was a small temple dedicated to monkeys. When I asked him where the monkeys were, he replied that they had gone to the forest but returned every evening. Sure enough, that evening as we stood on the battlements of our hotel, we saw them running across the rooftops in the direction of their temple home.

Eventually, he asked us if we required a drink, and told us there was a cafe nearby. We were parched and readily agreed. The waiter came for our order and we asked for a couple of beers and a fruit juice for our friend. The waiter was most apologetic but told us that he didn't sell beer so we settled for a fruit juice as well. Our young guide then told us that his brother had a shop nearby and would be happy to meet us. We found ourselves in a shop selling nothing but rolls of cloth being introduced to his older brother. He in turn introduced us to his girl friend, a lovely young Indian lady dressed in the full regalia. "I'm very pleased to meet you," I said with the exaggerated slowness one tends to use when addressing foreigners. "Nah then, boys," she replied. "Ow's it going?"

She was an Essex Girl, born and bred. She had been travelling the World, had reached Udaipur and decided to stay for a while.

Meanwhile, our young guide was upset that we had been unable to buy any beer and he had volunteered to go and fetch some. He seemed to be gone a long time, and I asked his brother if everything was OK. He replied that that part of Udaipur was known as 'the Holy City' and beer sales were forbidden. His brother had to travel a considerable distance to find a shop selling any. I felt embarassed to be so ignorant of local customs, and this feeling was compounded when our young friend finally returned. I had given him the money for four bottles, expecting him and his brother to join Steve and I. We found out that they were strict Hindus and didn't touch alcohol. Steve and I had to force two down each while they kept us company with cups of tea.

As it was getting near to mealtime, we said our farewells but arranged to meet up with our young guide the following day to do some more exploring. We hired one of their quaint threewheeler taxis for the day and were taken everywhere including the Monsoon Palace. On the 'plane back to the UK, we regaled our companions with our adventures, and they all expressed regret that they hadn't done more themselves. There's a lot to be said for having an inquisitive companion.

So what was Gerald up to during all this time? Although his self-imposed exile from BAWLA prevented him from competing, he was still coming along to the gym and training regularly. However, he was missing the buzz of participation, and one day he told us he was joining a local amateur rugby league club. The thought of acquiring 20 stones of solid muscle must have been very exciting for Victoria Rangers, but, knowing Gerald as we did, his clubmates were rather more cautious. After his first game, Gerald walked into the gym with a huge bruise on his arm; after his second, he showed up with an even bigger one on his thigh. After his third game, he appeared in the doorway with his arm in a sling. He had broken his collar bone! [Did I mention he was accident prone?] That, of course was the end of his career as a rugby star, but it didn't really matter as other exciting events were about to happen.

53

PASTURES NEW

Gerald found out via the internet that a relatively new powerlifting association had come into being. It appeared that many others were fed up with the sham of drugs testing that went on within BAWLA and had decided to do something about it. In fact, it turned out that this skulduggery was not confined solely to Britain, but was World-wide. So much so that the World Drugs Free Powerlifting Association had been formed with most of the World's leading powerlifting nations becoming involved. The relevant one for us was the British Drugs Free Powerlifting Association, and they ran competitions at Divisional and National level. Gerald joined at the beginning of 2004 and prepared to make his debut.

Our Division was so under-represented at that time that we shared the Divisional Championships with our neighbours from the North West. That is how, one day in February we found ourselves in the pleasant little town of Bentham preparing to watch Gerald's big comeback. However, we found out the existence of a rule that states a lifter must be a member for at least four months before they can start breaking records. With this in mind, Gerald only did his openers. Even so, his total would still have been enough to give him the 'best lifter' trophy, but once again, the four month rule applied.

To add insult to injury, he was chosen yet again for a drugs test. They were quite nice about it though, and explained that anyone coming over from BAWLA was automatically tested. Can't say I blame them.

I had three other guys from the club lifting that day, and they all did well, reflecting the advantages of a level playing field. I also learnt a lot about BDFPA that would be of great benefit to me in particular and the club in general. When I had started lifting many years previously, the kit had been very basic. A 'T' shirt and a leotard for the body and a variety of footwear depending upon the lift being attempted. Weightlifting boots with their solid soles and slightly raised heel are the preferred option for the squat. These can also be used for benching although most lifters prefer trainers. For the deadlift, it is advantageous to have your feet as close to the ground as possible, and deadlifting slippers have become the norm based on ballet shoes. Over a period of time, the leotard gradually evolved with the material becoming thicker and less pliable. It also became the practice to buy one that was extremely tight in the upper thighs and buttocks, the theory being that, once down in the low squat position, the elasticity in the suit would help you stand up again. These so-called super suits became so tight that it required the assistance of a mate or two to pull you into the damn thing. They definitely gave the wearer an advantage, and so there was no alternative but to wear one. I acquired a second-hand one, and although tight, I could still pull it on by myself. What's more, it didn't leave a nasty ring of broken blood vessels around my upper thigh when I took it off.

The next innovation had been the bench-suit. This was made of the same thick material as the super-suits but the so-called advantage was in the positioning of the sleeves. Instead of at the side as per normal, these are placed on the front so that the wearers walk around like zombies. The idea once again is that, as the bar is lowered to the chest, the panel between the sleeves will stretch. This stored elasticity can then be used to push up ever heavier amounts of weight. Once again, it takes two people a lot of effort to pull the wearer in and out of these shirts, and once again a tell-tale ring of broken blood vessels remains, this time around the upper arm.

Luckily, by the time these appeared, I was in the twilight of my lifting career, so I never bothered with one, but both Gerald and Steve had the not inconsiderable expense of buying a bench shirt. Why did BAWLA tolerate them when it clearly opened up the sport to such ridicule? Well, the American manufacturer had been very crafty and was donating sums of money to the various governing bodies throughout the lifting world, the implication being that this sponsorship would cease if the suits were banned. However, since none of this sponsorship money found its way into the WDFPA coffers, they didn't feel constrained to promote them. What it did in fact, rather cleverly, was to run two competitions, one for lovers of bondage known as 'Equipped' lifting and one for the more traditional exponents known as 'Unequipped' competition. No prizes for guessing which one I encourage all my new lifters to adopt. Let's face it—if powerlifting does ever become an Olympic sport (and that is a big 'if' in spite of it being one of the largest minority sports), I would hazard a guess that they will insist on it being the unequipped version.

A second innovation that WDFPA introduced was the concept of 'single' competition. The idea here was that, although all three lifts are to be contested, each one will count as a separate competition. Lifters can of course enter for all three lifts, but it is also possible to enter only one or two. This has advantages for people that like to specialize in one or another of the lifts, or, more importantly, for people like me who can only do one lift. As previously mentioned, the pain in my arthritic shoulder prevented any meaningful benchpress, but it also prevented me from getting my arm far enough back to grasp the bar for the squat. I was continuing to train my legs on the leg press machine as an assistance exercise for my deadlifting, which I still continued to do, although I never expected to be doing it again in competition. Fate moves in mysterious ways.

There was yet another innovation, and once again, it could have been introduced especially for me. This one stated that age related classes should go up in five year increments rather than the ten years that BAWLA used. This is a much more sensible arrangement as my research has shown that from the age of about fifty, strength begins its steady decline. It is inconceivable therefore that a 59 year old should be trying to compete on an equal footing with a 50 year old.

Their drugs testing policy is also very open. Rules state that 10% of lifters will be tested at every competition. In theory, these 10% can be random, but experience has shown that a more targeted approach is preferable. For example, all lifters coming over from BAWLA are tested as Gerald found out. In addition, anyone making rapid progress or showing exceptional strength can be nominated. On the other hand, there is no point in testing the same lifters over and over again as BAWLA had done. The tests cost £200 per sample, a considerable amount of money for a self-financing organization, and the aim was to actually catch the cheats, not protect them as BAWLA did. The results of all these tests are openly published in our newsletter, and I am happy to say that a positive result is a very rare happening indeed.

As if all this wasn't exciting enough, there was more to come. The sequence of events is, to a point, similar to that of BAWLA. At the lowest level, clubs themselves can organize competitions. This is basically to blood newcomers in familiar surroundings. The next step up the ladder is the Divisionals, and these are open to all standards of lifters within your particular Division. Indeed, it is particularly important that experienced lifters should compete alongside the beginners. Firstly, it eliminates all prima donna attitudes (although these are very rare in our sport), and secondly, it gives the beginners a chance to see the super stars in action. There are minimum standards to achieve at these Divisionals in order to proceed to the next level, the Nationals. However, these standards are not too onerous, and I can usually get a beginner to the required level in a relatively short time. It is the next stage that really begins to get exciting. The winner of each class at the Nationals gets an automatic invite to the Europeans and the Worlds. In practice however, this invite is usually extended to the first three. With so many age and bodyweight classes competing, it would be an unlucky person indeed who does not qualify to represent his Country. As a fledgling organization, it is important that we send as large a squad as possible in order to boost the home country's efforts. However, being self financing, cost is also a huge consideration, and some exotic destinations may have to be declined.

During Gerald's inaugural year with BDFPA we took this accepted route. Having qualified at Bentham, the next step was the National Full Power which was being held at Grangemouth, near Edinburgh. The longish drive was made tolerable by the pleasant scenery en-route and the relatively traffic-free roads. Lifting in the 125kg equipped class, this time Gerald deigned to do two attempts at each lift. Even so, he easily won his class, giving him a first British title with the new association, and also his first British record with them.

As a result, he was invited firstly to the Europeans, which were being held in Pescara, Italy. He was up against a very good Frenchman, and at the subtotal stage, he was actually 15kg behind. However, his superior deadlifting saw him through, breaking three more British records and his first European record. The second big trip that year was to Atlanta, Georgia, and the World Championships.

We flew out in good time in order to acclimatise and also have time to do some sightseeing. The lifting venue was the Airport Hilton, which was also the place at which we stayed, so all very convenient. There was a regular shuttle bus from the hotel to the airport and a monorail to central Atlanta, making our trips both quick and cheap. We found the monorails remarkably quiet from a conversation point of view, but once the locals caught our 'quaint' accents, they became quite animated. Most wanted to know what we were doing there, and once we had explained about the World Championship, they inevitably said they would come along to support us. A nice gesture but I doubted if any of them made it. The tiredness in their eyes suggested they would spend their weekend resting. The American Dream comes at a price!

Another snippet from my diary at that time refers to their lack of any culinary skills. The entry reads "How can you ruin a chicken salad? Answer—Cut the chicken into small pieces and deep- fry them in fat. Next, cover the salad in some goo called 'mayo'" Another first was the fact that I was charged to watch my own lifter perform. The land of opportunity indeed.

Gerald's big day dawned and his first hurdle was to make the weight after all the American rubbish he had scoffed. At the second attempt, he managed to just squeeze under and it was time to have a look at the opposition. Looking down the list of posted openers, one opponent stood out, the Russian Maxim Tikhimov. This was to be the first of many clashes that Gerald had with this particular opponent. Max took the lead after the squats, they were pretty well matched on the bench, but his deadlift once again saw Gerald home. More records, a World title and a successful conclusion to his first year with a new Association.

Whilst all this was going on, I was busy training up for my own big comeback after five years in the wilderness. This finally took place at the 2005 Divisionals, once again being held at Bentham. I had bought myself a new leotard for the occasion so that I could lift under the unequipped banner. It should be noted here that because of the relatively small entry at the Divisionals, the Full Power, Singles, equipped and unequipped were all contested at the same meeting. I was now 67 years old which meant, under the BAWLA rules, I would have been a M3. However, under the sensible BDFPA rules, I was a much more impressive M6. Weighing-in at a relatively light 91.3kg, I deadlifted 180, 190 and a final 200kg. I felt there was more there but the same four month rule applied to me as it had for Gerald, and I didn't want to show my hand too early.

I had easily qualified for the British Single lifts which that year were being held at the end of March, but the date clashed with a skiing holiday I had already booked with Anne and the grandchildren. I wrote to the BDFPA secretary explaining the situation and was given dispensation to lift at the Europeans and the Worlds. The European Singles were being held in Naples at the end of May and I was looking forward to some big lifts. I had got my bodyweight up to 94.5kg and my training cycle had gone well. My opener with 180kg gave me my first European record. I upped this to 192.5kg for my second which felt OK so I asked for 205kg for my third, which would have been a World record. However, on the day it wouldn't budge. I put this down to a combination of the oppressive heat and a lack of sleep due to Gerald's snoring.

Still, there was the World Singles Championships to look forward to, which were being held at Witney in Oxfordshire. It's nice of course to travel to all the different foreign parts, some of which you would never consider if not for the competition, but it is also nice, once in a while to perform on home soil. There was still the question of driving down the M1, which can be very traumatic and energy sapping. Irene had accompanied me to my matches in the early days, but after 27 years, her interest had waned. However, I persuaded her to come to this one and do the driving whilst I got my head down.

On the appointed day I weighed-in at 97.3kg, very close to my heaviest ever. They were using two platforms which was an innovation to me and meant that your class came round much quicker than normal. I went into the warm-up room in what I thought was plenty of time, and I did my rather elaborate stretching routine. I then started on my warm-ups, intending to do four. I completed the first three and was loading the bar for my final warm-up when I heard the MC announce over the tannoy "The bar is loaded and the next lifter is Eddie Bennett."

After this announcement the lifter has one minute in which to make his attempt. I rushed onto the platform, grabbed the bar, did the quickest mental rehearsal ever and then easily pulled my opener of 190kg. There were a total of eight lifters in the 100kg class, so I now had time to recover my breath and prepare for my next attempt. I had posted 205kg again as I was determine to claim my first World record. When my turn came, I was fully prepared yet composed and confident. I could hear Irene shouting encouragement as the bar slid up my legs and I stood erect to receive three white lights. My first World record at the age of 67, and I still had one lift to go, but what was I to put on?

Well, there was no contest really. Gerald's best bench to date was 212.5kg, and it was only a matter of time before he got 215. Similarly, Steve's best deadlift was 212.5, and he had had a number of attempts at 215. I was really the unknown quantity, not having lifted for so long. However, in order to spice our lifting up, the three of us made a pact that, whoever was first to the magic 215, the other two would give him a fiver. This was it then without question. I went for the money. It was hard going but I managed to keep it moving and locked it out. I don't know what was more satisfying, establishing a very creditable World record or taking a fiver of those two buggers. Incidentally, Gerald got his own 215 five months later and Steve also eventually got his although it took another two years.

As the only Masters 6 in the 100kg class, I automatically became the World Champion. Equally satisfying was the fact that I came fourth overall out of the eight lifters in the 100kg class, in spite of the fact that I was by far the oldest competitor. It seems that all those years in BAWLA battling the cheats had paid off.

Speaking of BAWLA, what was Steve up to whilst all this was going on? We had decided to stick with them as, up to that point they had been pleasant enough with him and he was also an established member of the Masters squad. We therefore started the year off in the normal fashion by travelling up to Gateshead for the Divisionals. Little did we realize all the animosity that had been directed at Gerald would now be focussed on Steve. There was no hint of the unpleasantness to come as we stood outside the weigh-in room awaiting our turn. Finally the door opened and Micky Finn stuck his head out. Looking at Steve he said "You can't lift. You haven't paid your entry fee."

"Yes we have," I protested. "I posted it to you along with a nice chatty letter."

"Yeah, I remember that letter. I chucked it in the bin, so your cheque must have gone with it. That means you haven't paid, so you can't lift."

"Come on Steve," I said. "Let's go home and you can join Gerald and myself with the drugs- free lot."

We made to depart but were stopped by the Divisional Secretary, Ian Hampson, who had been watching the whole procedure.

"Wait a minute," he said. "I'll sort everything out."

He disappeared into the weigh-in room and re-appeared a few minutes later saying it was all sorted and Steve could lift, but I would have to make out another cheque to replace the missing one. This I agreed to do whilst mentally resolving to keep a close eye on my next statement. But why had Ian intervened on our behalf? Although he had been a regular member of our club in the past, I never considered him to be particularly close. I was soon to find out. He took me to one side and explained that Gavin Walker, who you may remember had taken over from me as Courses Coordinator, had decided he had earned enough money for the Association and he had gone back into business for himself. In effect, Ian wanted to know if I was interested in taking my old job back. I must admit that I got some perverse pleasure in informing him that I was no longer a member of BAWLA and would be unable to accept his kind offer.

Although Steve lifted in that competition, his heart was no longer in it. He didn't even bother putting his supersuit or bench shirt on, preferring to lift in his leotard. He still comfortably won his class though, which meant an automatic invite to the Nationals. The ultimate irony from Gateshead was that he was nominated once again to do a drugs test. Why didn't the testers realize they were being manipulated? Didn't they ever consult their own records and see the same few names occurring time after time?

At the subsequent Nationals, he again went through the motions without any real conviction. His total was 17.5kg down on his previous best and he was even beaten into second place. By the rules of competition, this meant that his place on the British squad went to his opponent. This blow was softened somewhat by yet another trip to the Czech Republic to again lift in the World Blinds. Although this one wasn't sponsored by Budweiser, we still managed to get plenty down us as we celebrated his return to winning ways.

The following year, Steve signed up for BDFPA.

With all ties to BAWLA now severed, this enabled a number of changes to be made. The whole University club was affiliated to BDFPA, which ensured a steady stream of lifters. Some were shooting stars, destined to shine briefly, and then fade. Others were like myself for whom lifting had become a way of life and couldn't imagine not being involved in some way. This in turn meant that our own North East Division now had enough lifters to warrant its own Divisionals, and with the University being the largest club, it was also the logical place to hold them. For this relatively minor contest, we decided to hold it in our training room. It was a little cramped, but at least we didn't have to hump a load of iron about.

Emboldened by this success, we made a bid to stage the British Singles, but we would clearly need a bigger venue. The main sports hall itself was a candidate but was not really suitable. Firstly, it has a sprung floor, and although powerlifters don't normally drop weights, there was no point in taking risks. Secondly, the windowless construction was not conducive to our family friendly sport. I approached Jon Archbald, the bars and venue manager at the Students Union, with a suggestion and he agreed straight away. The idea was to hold the event in the students' communal building. The dance area on the lower ground floor was ideal—a solid floor; roomy enough for the largest of audiences; an adjacent area suitable for warm-ups; a cafe, shop and bar all within the building; and doors leading out into a grassy amphitheatre where children can play in safety. I did mention that we are family friendly, didn't I?

There were a couple of teething problems as one would expect when tackling an enterprise of this size for the first time, but all in all, everyone involved seemed well pleased. There was just one fly in the ointment from my point of view. I was due to lift in the deadlift on the Sunday. I opened with a safe 190kg and called for what should have been a comfortable 205 for my second. I gave it my best shot but it refused to move. I was completely devoid of energy and passed my third attempt having learnt a valuable lesson. You cannot spend two days humping lumps of iron about, looking after other lifters, keeping an eye on other organizational details and still manage to lift on top form.

Anyway, my 190 was more than enough to give me the M6 title and qualify me for both the Europeans and the Worlds, but events conspired to ensure that I did neither that year. The Europeans were once again being held in Italy, but they clashed with my La Santa timeshare weeks. The Worlds were held in Bendigo, Australia, but whether or not I would have travelled all that way is a moot point. In the event, the decision was made for me. I had been pestering my doctor for some time to see if they could restore some mobility to my shoulder, and he finally referred me to a consultant. He in turn, had some X-rays taken and found bits of bone and cartilage floating about in there. He agreed to remove these by keyhole surgery, and the date set for this coincided with the Worlds, but there was no question really of which one to go for. The chance of doing all three lifts again was too good to miss.

The first job was to have a pre-op and this was conducted by an amply proportioned nurse. After taking my height and bodyweight, she solemnly told me that I was obese. This of course was according to the totally useless bodymass index. This takes no notice whatever of a person's muscularity or bone density which are both affected by heavy weight training. In fact, I regularly have my bodyfat checked, and it usually hovers around a relatively healthy 15%. Anyway, I think that even our tubby little nurse realized that something was not quite right, because she said that I was perfectly fit enough to withstand the rigours of the operation. This passed off very smoothly the following week, but was it a success? Well, the consultant told me that he had certainly removed a number of foreign bodies, so it was just a case of waiting for the tiny incisions to heal. Within a fortnight I was back in the gym, testing out my 'new' shoulder. Perhaps my expectations had been too high. The range of movement had definitely improved, but still not enough to hold the bar in the squat position. In the benchpress, the pain had subsided and the horrible grinding noise had almost disappeared. The benchpress still forms part of my training routine, but I haven't had the confidence yet to perform it in competition. I suppose one day they will discover a cure for arthritis, especially if they give it the high profile of cancer, but I'm not holding my breath.

On the bright side, my two top lifters were re-united again under the same banner. Stevie had quickly settled into life within a different organization and made many new admirers with both his lifting and his courage. His finest performance in his inaugural year came in the European Full Championships in Rouen, France. His three lifts of 185kg; 100kg and 210kg gave him his best ever total of 495kg. Gerald had succeeded in getting back to his previous best, and was now pushing his lifts to new limits. After a good British followed by an equally good Europeans, he made a massive breakthrough at the World Full Power in Cork, Ireland.

The aim of every powerlifter is to put together all three of their best lifts in the same contest, but for various reasons, this seldom happens. On this occasion it did. His three lifts of 340kg; 220kg and 340.5kg were all PB's, and his total of 900kg was a massive 40kg up on his previous best. The icing on the cake was that extra 1/2kg on his deadlift which gave him his first World record. Remember, in the senior category (ie between the ages of 23 and 39) the competition is much more fierce and records are harder to come by.

2007 was to be a momentous year for two of us. First up was Steve. In February of that year he moved into the ranks of an M2, which meant a whole new range of records to shoot for. His first opportunity came at the British Full being held in Tamworth, and he didn't let me down, breaking two squat, one bench, two deadlift and two total World records. Not a bad day's work. At the Europeans a month later, he upped the squat, deadlift and total to give himself three more. Finally, at the Worlds he improved the deadlift yet again, incidentally hitting that elusive 215kg. (but the little bugger didn't get his fiver back!)

That same year, I was to move into the ranks of an M7, but my birthday didn't fall until October, by which time all the comps had finished. Instead, I decided to drop my bodyweight to the 90's and have a go at the records in this lower division. I needed to qualify at this new bodyweight at the Divisionals, and in doing so my three deadlifts of 170kg; 180kg and 190kg gave me three new British records. The final two were also in excess of the current World record, but remember that these cannot be broken at Divisional level. For the European Singles that year, we travelled to Zurich, where I found myself up against a Swiss opponent, Rene. I looked on the board to compare openers. I had posted 180kg to his 160kg, so I dismissed him from my calculations. I safely got my opener and confidently asked for 190kg for my second. It should have been a formality, but it wouldn't budge. I called for it for my third and spent the intervening time psyching myself up. All to no avail—a Zurich gnome must have stuck it to the floor. Meanwhile, what was Rene up to? He had successfully pulled his second with 170kg, followed by a third with 180kg. This meant that we were tied on total, but, following the rules of competition, the title went to him on lighter bodyweight. More controversially, the 180kg, as mentioned, had also been a World record and Rene was allowed to claim this. I had been at the Congress meeting when this piece of legislation was passed. I disagreed with it then and I still do. It's only logical that the first person to achieve a record should be able to claim it. After all, subsequent lifters have the option of putting on a further 1/2kg to retake the record.

What had gone wrong? I could put it down to lack of sleep again due to Gerald's excessive snoring, but there was a more likely explanation. Our hotel was down in a valley, whereas the venue was on the top of a nearby Alp. I had been eating the plentiful meals the Swiss prepare and in order to keep my bodyweight below the 90kg limit, I had elected to walk to the venue every day rather than travel on the bus provided. It seemed as though I had simply run out of steam. I elected never to dismiss an opponent again. Whatever they say about old dogs, this one was willing to learn.

Anyway, these setbacks ensured that my next training cycle would be productive. The British Singles were again being held at Bradford Uni. Because of the need to hold them in the summer holidays, the usual sequence of events had gone slightly awry. This suited my chances of returning to winning ways as it cut out all the tiring travel. I also resolved not to get too involved in the running of it. The club was thriving with bodies and the University itself was prepared to help out. That was the intention, but in reality, I couldn't stand back completely. At least, the boys ensured that I didn't do anything too heavy. It must have worked because my opener with 182.5kg reclaimed my World record. I pushed it higher with my second of 190kg, but my third with 195kg wouldn't budge. Of course, the drop in bodyweight could account for some loss in power, as could my advancing years, but I had dropped 25kg in just two years. Was the dreaded arthritis gaining ground quicker than I had hoped?

Later that year saw us back in Pescara, Italy, for the World Singles and a chance to renew battle with my friend, Rene. This time I was determined to lift with my head and not my heart. I saw that he had posted 170 for his opener, so I went 172.5. He called for 175 for a second so I did 177.5. He jumped to 182.5 for his third and I followed with 185. No flashy attempts at a record, just be content with becoming the World Champion.

Five days later, I reached the milestone of becoming an M7. Irene asked what I wanted for my 70th and I asked for a new weightlifting belt. I had had my old one for 30 years and it was beginning to look a little frayed at the edges, much like myself. I hope my new one lasts as long.

54

A FAMILY AFFAIR

I was looking forward to 2008. It was a big year for me of course as a new Masters 7, but I also had plans for Steve. However, not even I had imagined what a momentous year it would turn out to be.

In my own case, with my top weights now falling quite dramatically, I decided to share this year's competitions between two bodyweight categories in order to maximise my record setting potential. To this end, I qualified at the NE Divisionals at 90kg and a few weeks later, I qualified at the NW Divisionals as a 100kg lifter. All six of these lifts were British records and potential World records. I would now need to reproduce them on a National platform.

The plan for Steve was quite simple—get him to lift unequipped. This not only gave him a whole new range of records to aim for, it also meant less faffing about pulling supersuits and bench shirts on and off. There was also a less obvious bonus. Whilst it is acknowledged that a supersuit, for instance, can add as much as 40kg to a persons squat, this extra weight will also place additional stress on the lifters muscles and joints. I don't think I am being predjudiced when I say that equipped lifters seem to have more injuries than unequipped ones.

At the Divisionals, Steve only did one lift from each discipline, preferring to keep his full potential for a larger stage. This occurred at the British Full Power meeting which was being held at Tamworth. Our switch was justified when he broke 8 World records, the pick of them probably being his third deadlift with 200kg.

My own chance to shine came in May at the European Singles which were being held in Italy yet again. My usual travelling companion, Gerald, had got himself into some heavy courting and decided not to travel with me. I was quite prepared to go on my own when, out of the blue, grand-daughter Gabby offered to go with me. Well, of course I was glad to have her company, but I felt compelled to tell her that she would probably be bored out of her skull. In spite of this, she still wanted to come, and on the appointed day we set off. We boarded our 'plane at Leeds/Bradford Airport more or less on time and settled down, expecting a relatively short flight. It was at this point that the captain informed us of a strike at Milan Airport and told us that he couldn't leave until the strike was over. One hour later, he told us the strike was concluded and we could now leave. There was a muted cheer.

At Milan Airport, I asked at the help desk how to reach our intended destination and was told to catch the service bus into Milan and then catch a train onwards. After an hour's bus ride we reached Milan station which is reputed to be the largest in the World. Half an hour later I believed it. We were first directed up a long flight of stairs to the enquiry desk where a lady wrote a name and platform number on a piece of paper. We then made our way back down the long flight of stairs to the ticket office, and finally, back up the stairs once more to find that our platform was at the very end of this cavernous edifice. Our train was already there and we settled down thinking it wouldn't be long now. Half an hour later we set off. After about an hour we arrived at the station the lady in the enquiry office had written down and made our way outside to seek a taxi. After a long wait with no sign of one, I decided to ask if there was an alternative way of reaching our destination. Thankfully the chap I asked spoke perfect English and explained that our destination was still a considerable way off, but it would be much closer if we caught another train and went two stops back down the line. After another long wait, we eventually arrived at our new station and waited outside once again for a taxi. We were joined in the queue by two young ladies which was fairly encouraging. At least it meant the taxis must be operating. Eventually a people carrier pulled up bearing a taxi sign and discharged his passengers. We made to climb onboard but were stopped by the driver who said something in Italian that didn't sound too promising. One of the young girls translated for us. It appeared the driver already had another call booked. After some further dialogue, a compromise was reached—the driver agreed to take all three fares at once. We were too exhausted to argue and just flopped on board. He picked the other passenger up at a nearby hotel and told us via our young interpreter that he would have to drop him off first. We drove for miles through the now dark countryside 'til we reached his destination—the airport!

The young ladies told us, rather apologetically, that since we were roughly in the area they wanted to be, he would drop them off next. After his sat-nav managed to lose us in some roadworks, we finally discharged our translators and had the taxi to ourselves for the long journey back to our starting point. Our destination was only 4 or 5 miles further on. In the time we had been exploring the Italian countryside, we could have walked it.

By this time it was almost midnight and our hotel was in complete darkness. The taxi driver hammered on the door until an old harridan appeared and they proceeded to scream at each other in Italian. It appeared that she wasn't prepared to let us in, but I told the taxi driver to leave and we would sit on the step 'til she changed her mind. The old crone disappeared and came back with a younger woman who turned out to be her daughter, and was also the proprietor. She told us that she had been expecting us all day, and we replied we had been travelling all day. We tumbled into bed hungry and exhausted.

The following day, we found the venue OK and watched some of the lifting. There were a number of other Brits there including some female lifters, and they all made Gabby welcome. At lunchtime, I suggested that we might stroll into town for a bite to eat. There was food at the venue, but I thought it might be a good idea to get away for a while and perhaps relieve her boredom. The walk was a little longer than anticipated, the town centre wasn't much to write home about, and worst of all, all the restaurants were closed until the evening. We finally found a nice bar tucked away in a courtyard and settled for an ice cream and a drink. Later that day, we did finally manage to get a good meal inside us and walked back to the hotel, just managing to beat a torrential downpour. Did this mean our luck is changing at last, I wondered?

In view of our traumatic two days and the fact that I was lifting in the morning, we turned-in at 8.00 o'clock. The following day, we were up early and feasted on the strange concoctions that the continentals serve up for breakfast. I was lifting in the 100kg class for this particular competition, so I felt obliged to force some of it down. In the event, I weighed-in at a comfortable 94kg. I took Gabby into the warm-up room with me to help out. Her main job was to keep an eye on events on the platform so that I could time my warm-ups. This worked out well and I made an easy opener with 175kg. My second with 185 felt good so I asked for 195kg for my third. However, the curse of lifting abroad struck again and it refused to budge. I must definitely stop drinking the water.

Anyway, two more World records are not to be sneezed at, and it was time to go for a celebration. We made a foursome with two friends, Neil and Ann, a married couple who are both supurb lifters in their own right. Did I mention that it is a family oriented sport? We found a nice pizza restaurant and settled down for a meal and a few jars. The landlady brought our beers over in large stein-type glasses with thick glass bottoms. As we raised these to toast a successful weekend there was a loud crack and the bottom fell out of my glass, depositing its contents in my lap. The landlady was mortified. She whipped my tracky bottoms off and hung them on the pizza oven to dry. Next, she brought me a pair of hers from upstairs and helped me into them. Finally she pulled me another pint in a fresh glass and I only just managed to stop her stiring it with a metal rod. They have some strange habits on the continent.

Sometime later there was a strong cheesy smell drifting across the restaurant. At first we took this to be our pizzas gently simmering, but then I realized it was my tracky bottoms scorching on the oven. The landlady was very good about it though—she let me keep her old pair. Well, it saved buying Irene a pressy.

The following day it was back to Blighty, but with time to kill before our flight, we decided to have a look round Milan. We found a street full of fashion shops, and although I would normally stick pins in my eyes rather than enter one of these establishments, I felt I owed it to Gabby after all she had put up with. I even bought her a bit of something bearing a close resemblance to a dish-cloth.

We made it back to the 'plane without further incident and as we settled into our seats she turned to me and said "Grand-dad, can I ask you something?"

Here it comes, I thought.' Do you mind if I don't come anymore'. Well, I can't say that I blamed her. "Sure, go ahead," I replied.

"Do you think I could have a go at powerlifting?"

What!! That one came right out of the blue. As soon as I had recovered, I told her I would be more than happy to coach her.

We had our inaugural session at the Uni gym a few days later. Gabby had brought a friend, Jessica, with her as a training partner. Although I had spent all my life training alone, I would be the first to admit that it is advantageous to train with someone else, preferably someone of more or less equal ability and drive. This brings an element of competition into the training room and techniques are easier to learn when you watch others trying to master them. I did my usual beginners routine by introducing them to each of the lifts in turn and explaining the mechanics of each. No need to get too technical as this stage as there is plenty of time to expand at subsequent sessions. I let them have a go at each one and after a few very light ones to try the technique, I had them doing singles with a gradually increasing bar until they reached their current maximum. Remember that lifting requires both physical and psychological strength, and since beginners are normally short on both, there is no danger of any physical damage occurring by overloading. Once I had established this maximum, I then worked out the starting weights for their first training session proper. I usually set this at 80% of the 1rep max and find they can normally do 3 sets of 5 reps with this weight. Once this is achieved, the weight is increased by 2.5kg for the following session. In the early days, beginners usually find they are putting the weight up every week and in no time they are repping with the weight that was their one rep max. This is tremendous feedback, of course and spurs the beginner on to greater efforts.

This initial workout is also very useful to me. Long experience has taught me that a pupil's response to this early session is a very good indicator of their future potential. All participants in the sport will make tremendous gains, but some are destined to get there faster and achieve a higher peak. I was very pleased to note that Gabby in particular showed this early promise. Their squat poundages were relatively low, but I have come to expect this in all beginners. Although the thighs and buttocks are the most powerful muscles in the body, there is also a strong psychological force at work. The thought of a heavy weight driving you down into the ground and not being able to recover is a very potent one, and amply demonstrates why the mental aspects of lifting are so important. On the other hand, beginners make greater progress on this lift than the other two. Even at this early stage though, I was pleased to note that Gabby's technique was near perfect. Jess on the other hand had a self- imposed problem. Her other hobby was horse riding at which she had been competing for several years. The particular demands of this sport meant that her adductor muscles are much stronger than her abductors. In the low squat position, it is important to adopt a wide knee position in order to bring the body's centre of gravity over the feet. With a closer stance, the centre of gravity is further back and in order to compensate, the body is bent forward at the hip, thus placing a tremendous strain on the lower back. Although Jess started off in the correct stance, her strong adductors would invariably pull her out of position.

Both of the girls had good bench presses and both of them had excellent deadlifts. This is also what I have come to expect. The deadlift is the easiest to learn from a technique point of view, and if it is too heavy, it just refuses to budge as I had found out on numerous occasions. Jess also told me that she gets her strong back from heaving bales of hay about.

I started them off on a twice a week schedule reasoning that young girls would have plenty of other interest to occupy them. Besides, Stevie had always trained twice a week and look what he had achieved. Speaking of which, what was the little sod up to? His unequipped training had been going well and we were ready for our next challenge. This was to be the European Full Power which was being held in Ireland. We made our way to the beautiful town of Castle Blaney, and after the initial fright of being overweight at the first weigh-in, he put together another series of tremendous lifting, culminating with a further seven World records.

Meanwhile, the girls were improving so rapidly that I was keen to enter them into competition. The first job was to get them qualified. I spent a lot of time on the 'phone trying to find something suitable but to no avail, and I was finally obliged to put on a little comp myself. I called it the Northern Schools Championships for want of a name, advertised it on our website, paid for the relevant permit and notified all the relevant committees. On the day, only Jessie and Gabby turned up! OK, so it was devisive, but it was within the rules, and it is in everyones interest to get more bodies, particularly female ones, into the sport.

I let them compete as single event lifters as it wasn't a foregone conclusion they would qualify in all three disciplines. As a matter of fact, Gabby did manage to qualify in them all but Jess was in a higher age and bodyweight category, and her requirements were that much higher which meant she only qualified for the deadlift. Even so, after only two months training, this was extremely encouraging. The following week was the British Singles Championships, once again being held at Bradford University, and I entered them for it. Talk about cutting it fine.

A grandfather and grand-daughter competing at the same sporting event must be something of a rarity. Offhand I cannot think of many other sports where this would be possible. The Saturday was given over to the squats and the unequipped benchpress, which meant that Gabby would be up twice, but I would be free to look after her. She opened her squatting with a World record 55kg, but then disaster struck. In her second, she made a double movement, which is a technical fault, but still a reason for failure. She took the same weight for her third, but this time she lost her balance. Were nerves getting the better of her? I needn't have worried. When the benchpress came around, she proceeded serenely through her three lifts with 37.5kg; 40kg and 42.5kg. Indeed, so comfortable did these look that I asked for a fourth with 45.5kg. Once again, this extra half kilo was put on to break the World record. The rules governing fourth attempts are quite straightforward. Firstly, you must be successful with your third attempt, secondly, it must be a record—either National or international—and finally, the lift is not allowed to count towards the competition proper. Gabby was not concerned with these technicalities of course. All she had to do was to lift the damn thing, which she did quite comfortably. It had taken me 28 years to break my first World record and here was Gabby doing it after only ten weeks training. There ain't no justice! Of course, I don't mean that. In fact, it gives me greater pleasure to be part of Gabby's achievements than any of my own.

First up the following day was the equipped benchpress which gave us plenty of time to prepare for the deadlift which followed. With all three of us lifting, it could prove to be hectic, but in the event, there was no problem. As mentioned, we lift in flights which contain between 8 and 12 lifters, with each lifter in that flight completing a lift on the rising bar principal before the following round is commenced. This ensures firstly that lifters within the flight get adequate rest between attempts. Secondly, with flights arranged on a rising bodyweight principle, lifters can see precisely when they are due to perform and can plan their warm-ups accordingly. All the female lifters are placed inevitably in the first flight. The other girls made Jess and Gabby welcome and gave them plenty of encouragement. So much so that they both succeeded with all three lifts, in the process becoming British champions. Once again, Gabby asked for a fourth attempt with 113kg and secured her third World record of the weekend.

A few flights later it was my turn to shine, and I was determined not to be outdone by the girls. I had got my bodyweight down to the 90kg class, and my three lifts of 170kg; 180kg; 185kg were all Masters 7 World records. Later that day, Mark arrived on a flying visit from Lanzarote, so the evening's celebrations went down doubly well. My diary records it as a 'Diamond Day'

The girls had both qualified for the World Singles and were eager to get stuck into their training. However, Grand-dad knows best, and I insisted on them having a bit of time off. About this time, the Sports Centre was going through its third major make-over and we were moved to a temporary home in another part of the university. This was rather crowded but we coped, especially with the promise of a brand new gym to look forward to. In fact, I thought that I was to have an input into part of the new design. My friend Sue, who was the Sports Director, let it be known that the Project Architect was looking for sugestions from any interested parties. This certainly applied to me, but also, as a design engineer I knew my ideas were entirely feasible. I spent a considerable time with him showing how adjacent redundant areas could be incorporated. I also made the point that the room required a fire exit, being at the extremity of the building and at the foot of a flight of stairs. Sue told me that as soon as I left the office, he tore up all my drawings. Why go through this charade if he had no intention of listening? In fact, when we eventually got back, we found there was even worse news.

Our next training cycle in our temporary home proved to be very productive, and we travelled over to Antwerp for the World Singles with high hopes. Steve had decided to do the Singles that year instead of having the expense of travelling to America for the Full Power, so with daughter Anne and Jessie's parents also travelling, it promised to be a lively trip. This turned out to be truer than expected. The hotel was a dump and we all woke up covered in bites. Anyway, at least the venue was good, being an old army drill hall set in a pleasant park with deer wandering about. One potential problem—the entry was so high, they had decided to run the competition on two platforms.

Friday was squat day which meant that both Gabby and Steve would be in action. Gabby was up first and my hopes were high. She had started to overcome the psychological barrier that many beginners experience, but would her nerves hold out at such a prestigious event. I needn't have worried—she opened with a World record 57.5kg, increased it to 67.5kg for her second and then upped it again to 72.5kg for her third. Even this looked comfortable so we took a fourth with 77.5kg. Four World records in the opening session—not a bad morning's work. Soon it was Steve's turn to shine and he didn't let us down. He was lifting at a singles event for the first time and had a whole new set of records to aim for. His three lifts of 137.5; 147.5 and 152.5kg were all Masters 2, 60gk records.

Muted celebrations that night in view of the following day being the bench press event, with both Gabby and Steve once again due to lift. Her training cycle had suffered from that perennial benchers problem, rotator cuff soreness, so we had taken it easy. After a cautious start with 40kg, we upped the second to 46kg to marginally improve on her own record. Although this looked comfortable, her third with 47.5kg wouldn't budge. Steve was also suffering—he had a stomach bug—so I let him off with his opening 85kg.

The Sunday was our big day with all four of us lifting. After the formalities of weighing-in, I took a look at the running order for the day. Platform 1 was to be Flight 1 through to Flight 5 and platform 2 was to be Flight 6 throught to Flight 9. The girls were in Flight 1 as usual and I was in Flight 6! Not only that, but Steve was in Flight 2 which meant that he would be warming up whilst Flights 1 and 6 were lifting. Anyway, as mentioned, our sport is very friendly, and there was no problem finding other lifters to take care of Steve in the warm-up room. Anne was drafted in as a makeshift coach for the girls as the lifting got under way. I opened with a steady 175 then glanced across to see both girls open with a comfortable 95kg. For my second I took 187.5 to increase my own record, then again, watched the girls with 105kg.

The coach's job at competition is to give his charges a few words of encouragement, remind them of the rules and judge how easy or otherwise their current lift is and hence, assess how much weight to put on for their next attempt. I had managed to do this for the first two lifts, but for the third, both Gabby and I found ourselves on adjacent platforms at the same time. I had asked for an ambitious 195kg, but this fell foul of the dreaded overseas third lift bug. Meanwhile, Gabby was trying 115kg in order to push her own record a bit higher. Although she stood up with it, she failed it on a technicality. Would I have been able to prevent this if I had been able to watch? We shall never know, but the chances of such an occurance happening again are fairly remote.

It only remained for Steve to do his bit, and with the deadlift being his favourite, we were expecting big things. He didn't let us down, with his opening 190kg being yet another World record. He upped this further with his subsequent lifts of 200 and 210. The icing on the cake came when it was announced that he had won the trophy for the best overall deadlift. Little did I know at the time that this would be Steve's last competition.

55

FOOD FOR THOUGHT

I had always had a dodgy stomach for as long as I can remember. Usually, it was nothing worse than cramp, but occasionally I would get a pain that doubled me up. The first time this happened was at RAF Seletar. I got up in the middle of the night, 'phoned for an ambulance and was taken to the camp hospital. The following day when the MO made his rounds, I explained my symptoms. He confessed to not knowing the cause, gave me some stomach powder and discharged me.

Over the subsequent years, I occasionally had a bad attack, but thinking that doctors didn't know the cause, I never bothered to consult one again. I remember one night at home when I was having a particularly nasty one. I was aware I was keeping Irene awake with my moaning and groaning, so I went downstairs to lie on the couch. The next thing I remember was waking up on the floor. I had passed out.

After our Belgium trip, I had another doubling-up session. This time I thought that medical science must have moved on in the last 50 years so I went to see my doctor, who in turn referred me to a consultant. After the inevitable wait, I got to see the specialist. I explained my symptoms and he suggested I have an endoscopy. "In fact," he said "whilst we are at it, you may as well have a colonoscopy as well."

As someone who has trouble swallowing an asprin, I wasn't happy but what could I do.

"All right," I reluctantly agreed "but if you use the same camera, will you do the top end first," was the best I could manage. He didn't laugh either.

A date was set for the procedures at some months in the future. Whilst waiting, we paid one of our frequent visits to Skegness to visit Irene's sister Mary and our many nephews and nieces. I was explaining my trepidation about my forthcoming ordeal to them when niece Diana produced a book and suggested I read it. The book was by an American author, Doctor D'Adamo, in charge of research at a facility dedicated to eating disorders. It was called 'Eat Right For Your Type,' the type in the title referring to your blood group.

Upon returning home, I got stuck into the book and found it fascinating. It appears that all our ancestors living in what is now Africa had the same bloodgroup—type O. This bloodgroup has a particularly acidic stomach in order to cope with the hunter/gatherer type diet. As the herds became depleted, these people moved ever further afield, making their way into the middle east, the far east, and via a land bridge, into the Americas.One branch doubled back to occupy the area we now know as Europe. Early remains from all of these regions show that the blood group was still Type O. A move then began in the middle east towards domesticating animals and growing crops and peoples dietry habits began to change towards more grain and dairy products. Shortly after this other blood groups began to appear, firstly type A followed by type B. The theory states that these were mutations brought about by the changes in diet.

Having made this historic connection, the thrust of the book then goes on to explain that modern people should follow the diet that their bloodtype dictates, and recommends as a first step that everyone determines their own bloodtype. Although they must have this information on your notes, doctors seem very reluctant to divulge it. Perhaps they think that if everyone cured themselves, they will be out of a job. In fact, this information should be displayed on your donor card. Whatever, having donated blood in the past, I managed to find my old card and discovered I was a type O. Reading further into the book, it appears that we type O's find most grain and dairy produce hard to digest. Could this be the cause of all my stomach troubles over the years? Along with these two main food groups, there were others that had a detrimental effect. For instance, to we type O's, potatoes contain an indigestible lectin that wanders around the body and lodges in the joints, causing an arthritic—like condition. This was too much to hope for—surely it's not going to cure that as well. Potatoes in their many forms had been a staple part of my diet for as long as I can remember, so would it be a problem to give them up? As it happens, it wasn't too bad, particularly when I found out the potatoe was part of the deadly nightshade family. I also found that soya was a perfectly good alternative to dairy products in all of its forms. It was more difficult to find alternatives for grain products. For example, I have found only one breakfast cereal that doesn't contain gluten. With type O being the dominant blood group in the Western world, it seems that manufacturers are missing a trick here.

Within a very short time of starting the new eating plan, I began to notice a difference. I lost weight quite rapidly at first until it stabilized at about 5 or 6 kgs lower. The book explained that this would probably happen. Apparently the indigestible gluten lectins in grain also wander the body before lodging in the fatty tissue and contribute to bodyweight and nothing else. The second thing I noticed was that my joints did indeed become easier. I had got into the habit of walking sideway down the stairs one at a time, but now I could walk down them in a normal fashion. But what about the main reason for starting the diet? After more than a year, I have had no major stomach problems whatsoever, and the minor ones are very much reduced, usually following a lapse.

I contacted the consultant in the early days, as soon as it became clear the diet was working, and suggested we put the treatments on hold. He wasn't happy, but has accepted it. I told you doctors don't like people curing themselves, didn't I?

The big question is, what difference has it made to my training. The biggest difference is to my bench press. Although there is still some pain present in my shoulder, it is not so severe as it used to be. My poundages are up marginally, although not enough to warrent an excursion onto the platform. However, I have made myself a promise that if I can still manage the same poundages when I become an M8 next year, I will give it a go. Time will tell, but as I have emphazised throughout these ramblings, there is no harm in positive thinking.

56

MORE LOOSE ENDS

After about a year, the work on the Sports Centre was completed, and we moved back to the room that had been my second home for almost 40 years. What a disappointment! There was no doubt that the primary object of the new build had been achieved. The old undistinguished main entrance, which had been tucked away at the side of the building, was now replaced with a steel and glass edifice fronting onto the main road. The machine hall had been extended and now occupied two floors, also fronted with glass and steel and facing the main road. Training in there is like training in a shop window, which I suppose is what we are doing. In fact, you could say that the whole operation has been a window dressing exercise. Our poor little room, tucked away as it is at the rear of the building is completely devoid of any improvement. In fact, the situation had been made much worse. The already cramped space had been made considerably smaller by the inclusion of a large, noisy air conditioning unit. For a University that prides itself on being 'green', this is a decidedly eco-unfriendly move and all so unnecessary. Muscles work best when they are warm, and to constantly blow cold air on them is to invite injury. In addition, we have to suffer noise pollution in the form of the constant hum of machinery.

The news concerning Steve was even harder to bear. Upon returning from Antwerp, he developed a pain in his wrist. His doctor sent him to a specialist who, after a scan, informed him that one of the bones in his carpel tunnel had ceased to regenerate. He was at pains however to dispel any notion that this injury had been caused by lifting weights. Rather, he confirmed our belief that lifting heavy weights combats osteoporosis, and that his lifting had probably helped to delay the onset of the disease which he put down to a particularly virulent form of arthritis. The outcome was that Steve had to have that particular bone removed and replaced with a steel pin. This has resulted in a considerable loss of movement in his hand, and has caused him to give up his powerlifting. Yet another bodyblow dealt to him by the cruel hand of fate.

This only leaves Gerald to catch up on. He had continued to compete throughout the preceeding years with a considerable degree of success, and his totals were gradually improving. His best to date was an impressive 902.5kg, although if he managed to put his three best individual lifts together in the same competition, this total would increase to 915kg. He had often expressed the wish that his target was to total 1000kg. Now in his mid 30's, he had been lifting for about 20 years, and his progress had naturally slowed down. However, he still had at least ten more years to improve and he could have made his target merely by adding 2.5kg to each lift every year. Unfortunately, Gerald was in a hurry and couldn't wait that long. He dispensed with my services and found himself another coach with more radical ideas. I was perfectly happy with this arrangement, especially as Gerald had broken up with his latest girlfriend and was more morose than ever.

There was no animosity of course, just the usual banter, and I still used to spot for him. I had my reservations about one of his new training regimes, but kept my council as it appeared to be working. This involved the principle of overload, the theory being that if you handled a very heavy weight for a partial rep, then the weight you handled for a full rep would seem light by comparison. The theory is relatively sound, but the practice is fraught with danger.

In the squat, for instance, the trainee would perform a 'walk-out.' This involves loading the bar in excess of your best squat, lifting it out of the racks, walking back with it and adopting the starting position. The bar is then placed back in the racks without actually performing the lift. Although some muscular benefit may ensue, this is more a psychological benefit than a physiological one. We have already mentioned the negative thoughts that may develop during this walk out phase, and anything that can negate this feeling of negativity can only help. For the bench press, the move is more physical, and is known as the board press. This involves the two usual spotters plus a third team member who holds a thick board on the benchpresser's chest. This will effectively reduce the movement of the bar, thus enabling heavier weights to be used. Muscle growth will respond to these partial movements, although full range movements must also be incorporated in order to maintaim flexibility.

The partial deadlift is the easiest of the three to set up, but is also the one open to abuse. It can be accomplished in a number of ways, but our gym has a purpose-made piece of apparatus to accommodate the move. This consists of a cage-like stand with holes drilled at regular intervals up the legs. Pins are placed through these holes and the bar is placed across them enabling the bar to be raised to varying heights above the floor. On the fateful day, Gerald was performing with the pins placed very high which meant he was only lifting the bar an inch or so. The bar was loaded to 400kg which was 60kg in excess of Gerald's best deadlift. As mentioned, connective tissue will grow stronger as muscular strength increases, but it is a relatively slow process. In normal training, progress is normally slow enough to accommodate these changes, but any form of accelerated training is asking for trouble. This is one reason why drug users have so many injuries.

Sure enough, we all heard that sickening crack followed by an agonising scream. He had torn his bicep tendon at the elbow. He found himself back in hospital being treated for yet another injury. He would still come to the gym with his right arm in a sling and perform dumbbell exercises with his left arm, but then he dropped his bombshell. Due to the physical nature of his work, he was forced to take time off each time he was injured. This time, his bosses gave him an ultimatum. Any more time off due to self-imposed injury and he would be fired. Faced with this choice, he took the path of least resistance and gave up powerlifting.

What a year 2009 had turned out to be. I had lost my two top lifters and more was to come. Jess had found herself a boyfriend, and like many before her, had decided that courting was more important than lifting. Still, it could have been even worse. Gabby had also got a boyfriend, but rather than be intimidated by her strength, Wesley had decided to join her. Was this just a case of wanting to share her hobby, or was he genuinely interested in the sport? After almost a year of training, I believe the latter is the case. He has made excellent progress and has already won his first British title. As one door closes, another always seems to open.

We had been to an away competition and were faced with quite a long journey home. Gabby asked me how I got into powerlifting. "Well, love," I replied, "It's a long story. I better start at the beginning."

My earliest memories are of being evacuated to Filey. There were four of us at the time, all brothers, although eventually we would be joined by . . .

Powerlifting isn't only for men as Tim, Don, Andy and Joe observe

Little and Large give their coach a lift

One of Steve's many victories

The infamous four give our athletes some support in Quebec

The things a coach has to do

Celebrating the big Seven-Oh with brothers Mike, Chris Dave and
sister June

Grand-daughter and Grandfather—two world champions

One of the many beautiful locations Powerlifting takes you to,
this one is Malta